Fight or Die

Praise for the Pazman

"Vinny Paz—the Comeback Kid"

—John Saraceno, *USA Today*

"You have a fighter that may have the greatest comeback of all time. How many come back from a broken neck, which the doctors said he'd never do, and win a world title?"

—Teddy Atlas, ESPN boxing analyst

"Vinny has had a great career. I admire his guts and effort. He's a man with truly a champion's heart."

—Bill Parcells, NFL coaching great

"He's had a tremendous impact on boxing with his style of fighting. His journey was unlike any fighter that I have ever seen."

—Emanuel Steward, HBO boxing analyst

"Paz—A True Champ."

—Joe Frazier, Hall of Fame boxer

"After my two fights with Vinny Paz, I've grown to respect him both as a fighter and as a man."

—Roberto Duran, boxing legend

"You've done it all, Champ. You made people happy.... You entertained so many people. People love your style."

—Sugar Ray Leonard, Hall of Fame boxing champion

"As a fight fan I just want to thank Vinny for his years of determination. The energy and heart he always showed made it fun to go to the fights again."

—Pete Rose, MLB player and manager

"The most exciting boxer of this era. One of the good men in boxing. Nice guy and a great attraction."

—Bert Sugar, *Ring* magazine

FIGHT OR DIE

The Vinny Paz Story

TOMMY JON CADUTO

With a Foreword by
Bert Randolph Sugar

The Lyons Press
Guilford, Connecticut
An imprint of The Globe Pequot Press

The Lyons Press is an imprint of The Globe Pequot Press.

Photos provided by the Pazienza family

Project manager: Jessica Haberman
Text designer: Libby Kingsbury
Layout artist: Kim Burdick

Library of Congress Cataloging-in-Publication Data

Caduto, Tommy Jon.
  Fight or die : the Vinny Paz story / Tommy Jon Caduto.
    p. cm.
  ISBN 978-1-59921-556-3
  1. Paz, Vinny. 2. Boxers (Sports)—United States—Biography. I. Title.
  GV1132.P38C34 2009
  796.83092--dc22
  [B]

                                    2009002524

Printed in the United States of America

10 9 8 7 6 5 4 3 2 1

For my parents Michael and Kathleen Caduto and my little family, wife Jennifer and dog Moochie with whom I've shared my most joyous and memorable moments. A special thanks to my mother who has been so proud of my teaching and writing.

Contents

Acknowledgments

Thanks to Peter Conti for helping me find my literary voice and for the contributions he made to the writing of this book. Thanks also to Rick Pandolfini for his pragmatic and collaborative insight in both editing and developing this story.

Foreword

Watching Vinny Paz in the ring was akin to watching a ferret on a double cappuccino—a pretty good description considering that cappuccino was to Vinny what spinach was to Popeye. Truth be told, before each and every fight Vinny would dose himself with enough industrial-strength caffeine to walk on the Providence River. And its effects were evident, giving Vinny the look of someone who had just taken a four-way cold tablet and had to run three more ways to catch up with it.

Sometimes though its after-effects were just as evident, as they were in his non-performance against Roy Jones Jr. Explaining the absence of his usual fighting passion against Jones, Vinny told a sportswriter, "I was in the back drinking cappuccino at 8:00. By 9:30 I was jacked up; I was sweating; I was flying; I felt great. Then 10:30 came, then 11:30, then, at 12:30, we finally fought and I was crashing hard. And I couldn't come back from it. When you crash from caffeine, that's it. You're done!"

It was that feverish high-octane style, one that wouldn't bear the strictest form of investigation, that earned Vinny the nickname "The Pazmanian Devil," a takeoff on the name of the cartoon character in the Looney Tunes films, a nonstop whirling dervish. And like the Tazmanian Devil, Vinny was a whirlwind in the ring, throwing punches in a frenzied, wham-bam-thank-you-ma'am fashion from everywhere, sometimes from as far away as the third-row seats. Or so it seemed. Take the time he was knocked to one knee by Dana Rosenblatt. Even before the referee could start the count over the fallen Paz, Vinny leaped off the canvas and struck the startled Rosenblatt in the whiskers with a left that seemed to come off the floor.

But his frenetic, testosterone-fueled style was off-putting to boxing purists—those hardened-artery traditionalists who had been around since the time Adam first heard the rush of the apple salesman, back to the days of John L. Sullivan, and they viewed Paz as a lineal descendant of Jack the Ripper. Yet, that style won him the appreciation and affection of a growing army of fans, called "Pazmaniacs" in honor of their hero.

It was that style, coupled with his cockiness, his eye-catching coat-of-many-colors wardrobe, and his showmanship that made him one of the most colorful characters ever to come down the long pike of professional boxing. And it made him a favorite of TV suits who knew that an appearance by Vinny on their network guaranteed that there would be no dead air time. It was almost as if Vinny was a made-for-TV fighter, the cameras focusing on him so much that viewers came away with the impression that there was nobody in the ring but him.

From the day he saw the movie *Rocky* and determined to become a fighter, through his muscled adolescence when he won one hundred amateur bouts, Paz's path to the top of the mountain was almost preordained. To say he was destined for stardom would be the greatest understatement since a Crow scout told Colonel Custer there might be a little trouble along the shores of the Little Bighorn. And when he won his first 14 fights, 12 by knockout, his rise in fame became apparent not only to his fans throughout New England but also to the national press. *Boxing Illustrated* wrote, "This 21-year-old lightweight from Cranston,

Rhode Island, is destined for stardom. Pazienza is a lightweight to watch, especially next year when he begins to tangle with established 10-round fighters."

By 1986 Paz had moved up to the lightweight division's A-list, taking on, and beating, such bold-face names as former champion Harry Arroyo and ranking contender Roger Brown. Then, in just his 22nd professional fight, he faced IBF lightweight titlist Greg Haugen in front of his hometown fans at the Providence Civic Center and, despite stomach problems, a broken nose, and a bruised right hand, won a unanimous decision and the IBF belt.

Still, there were those critics who sniffed at Paz's enormous accomplishments, calling him a "showboat"—one writer even copping a line from Oakland pitcher Darold Knowles who had said of teammate Reggie Jackson, "There isn't enough mustard in the whole world to cover that hot dog." But to his legion of fans, Vinny was more than a Swiss movement to be watched. His pyrotechnics in the ring were, like garlic in a salad, enlivening, and his performances entertaining.

Vinny would lose the rematch and his title to Haugen, then move up to the 140-pound junior welterweight division to challenge Roger Mayweather for his WBC belt, losing a hard-fought battle that ended with his trainer, Lou Duva, wanting to "have a word" with Mayweather after the fight and getting decked for his efforts. Another try for the junior welterweight title against Hector Camacho came up short. Then, after winning the third fight in the "trilogy" against Haugen, a third attempt at the junior welterweight crown against Loreto Garza ended when Vinny—who had resorted to biting Garza and performing other crimes against the rules and the senses—was disqualified after he picked up Garza and threw him to the canvas.

But Vinny's biggest loss was not to come in the ring, but from outside. Just one month after losing to Garza, the governor of the state of Rhode Island shuttered forty-five banks and credit unions after the private fund that insured them went belly-up, and Vinny's folding money folded with his bank. Now, with everyone falling all over themselves telling him to "pack it in," and with his bank having bounced, Vinny found himself coping with the reversals of fortune, both figuratively and literally. However, with his remarkable resiliency, Vinny could no more be discouraged from soldiering on than ice welded or iron melted, and he determined to carry on, this time as a junior middleweight.

It was there, as a junior middleweight, that after three unsuccessful attempts at winning a second title to go with his lightweight title, Vinny finally succeeded, capturing his second gold ring (read: belt) by defeating Gilbert Dele for the WBA 154-pound crown—four years after beating Greg Haugen for the 135-pound lightweight title.

Against all odds Vinny had come back, silencing the naysayers and quieting the disparaging critics. And now, he held a contract calling for $250,000 for his first title defense, apparently stabilizing his finances and ensuring his future. But, rivaling the Biblical trials and tribulations of Job, more adversity lay ahead for Vinny.

The month after victory over Dele, Vinny was in a horrendous automobile accident and suffered serious injuries to his vertebrae. They were so serious, in fact, that Dr. Walter Cotter, the attending neurosurgeon at Kent County (Rhode Island) Hospital told him, "Sorry, son, you'll never fight again."

That was all Vinny had to hear. To him, adversity was the test of strong men, and in his mind's eye, no one was stronger in his determination and desire than he was. Vinny would not surrender to undeniable facts, but rather wanted to prove that if you're a professional, you can come back no matter what happens to you. Vinny, rather than going home and licking his wounds, embarked upon a grueling regimen of training even while wearing a halo-like neck brace that gave him the look of a visitor from outer space. And just thirteen months after the accident, he was back in the ring against Luis Santana and, miracle of miracles, won by unanimous decision.

It was the most amazing story of a New England boxer since the legendary Willie Pep had survived a near-fatal plane crash some forty years earlier. The featherweight champ's career, if not his ability to walk, was seemingly over. Or so it seemed. Then miraculously, six months later, without even waiting in line long enough to collect insurance on the injuries he had sustained in the crash, Pep was back in the ring again, not only walking, but winning.

Vinny, like Pep, would come back for 23 more fights, win 18 of them, and run his record to 50 wins against only 10 losses before finally, *finally* retiring in March of 2004.

We may think we know Vinny Paz just because we saw him in the ring. But his story is not just the story of a boxer who inspired a depth of affection in a generation of fans that has outlasted his career. The real story of Vinny Paz is inspirational, filled with hopes, dreams, desires, and disappointments. Like *Variety's* review of MGM's *That's Entertainment,* when they wrote, "Nobody can deny that it has been one hell of a past," nobody can deny that Vinny Paz has had one hell of a past.

So let me exit stage left so that you can read Vinny's no-holds-barred biography, one that will hold your attention without even the need for industrial-strength caffeine to keep you awake. It's that good.

—Bert Randolph Sugar

Prologue

Vinny Paz, age 45, formerly Vinny Pazienza, sits in his hotel suite at the Westin Hotel in Providence, Rhode Island. He is reading a treatment for a movie that is based on his life. Executives from a Hollywood production company are in the elevator making their way to Room 905 to see him. Over the course of his twenty-five year boxing career, Pazienza has grown from a 132-pound lightweight amateur to a 168-pound super-middleweight. In retirement, Vinny is now a comfortable and rugged albeit fit 5'7" 185 pounds, and the scale is no longer an issue in his life. The ring wars are worn on his face like medals of honor or a Purple Heart. He has scar tissue above both of his still piercing brown eyes and a nose that reveals his former trade. He is not your father's 45, as he still takes on the persona of a fighter or an entertainer.

The former boxing champion walks to the window and looks down on a city that has gone through a renaissance. New, high-end shopping malls have been built, and nuovo-style restaurants line the Providence River. A magical display of water-fires shoots into the sky. Water-fires are sparkling bonfires, set right within the river. The torch-lit vessels travel down the river, along Water-Place Park. Gondolas tread their way ever so slowly as lovers snuggle closely on this chilly September evening. The glimmer of the fire reflects in the tall glass windows of the modern buildings that have been erected over the last ten years, making this once old, tired, industrial city appealing to transients who once sped through on Interstate 95 heading north toward Boston or south toward New York City. Now those transients stop. They attend Brown University or Rhode Island School of Design. They dine at the Northeast's finest restaurants, like world-renowned Al-Forno and Capriccio. They work at G-Tech, an international conglomerate, and sell hedge funds from Morgan Stanley. Baby boomers, now empty nesters, have cashed out their suburban dream and have retaken to the city streets, living in stylish lofts and sprawling three-bedroom condominiums with concierge service and valet parking. A $4 grande latte at Starbucks, replacing their regular coffee at Dunkin' Donuts, is now the beverage of choice.

At one time Vinny Paz felt like he owned this city. He was once Providence's only professional sports "franchise." Yes, the city had the Red Sox, Bruins, Celtics, and Patriots, but they were not really Providence's teams—they belonged to Boston. That pulse truly beat 45 miles to the northeast. Vinny was Providence's own, the city's adopted son, the only time in recent memory the city had seen itself in a positive light on a national stage.

For once, Rhode Island was not making national headlines for a banking crisis, political scandal, or corruption like it did during Vincent "Buddy" Cianci's mayoral administration or Edward DiPrete's gubernatorial tenure, or the embarrassment of a New England crime boss conducting a ceremonial induction into the crime family, called *o'mearth,* [our life] on tape, under the surveillance of the FBI—the first real evidence to the world that there was a Mafia.

Vinny was what was right in the state when he fought, in the mid-1980s and 1990s. Prior to Providence's reformation, the desolate streets filled with people waiting on line to see Vinny fight. Locally Vinny was recession-proof. He filled the Providence

Civic Center from 1986 onward, through "Black Monday," when the Dow Jones dropped 22 percent in one day, and through an era with one of the highest unemployment rates in the state's history.

Thousands of fans would hustle by boarded-up department stores like Shepards and Gladdings on their way to the Providence Civic Center. For nearly twenty years he gave this city a pulse like Boston's, even if only for one night at a time. It was those nights that the city's restaurants filled, and its blue-collar people were willing to spend their hard-earned money on a good show, to be entertained.

He grew up before them on national television as a prestigious amateur, the captain of the 1982 national "Tour the World" United States Olympic team, and faded into the night as a celebrity and a five-time world champion, and for many people, an inspiration. But tonight along with each passing day, the memories of the crowd's once deafening roar becomes faint. The entourage is gone; only a few childhood friends remain. Gone are his confidants, managers, and trainers, along with those who once offered him guidance and security. Gone is his best friend and the man who once played all of those aforementioned roles. Vinny's father, Angelo Pazienza, passed away in 2003; his loving mother Louise just six months earlier.

Things have changed; the city and Vinny's career have been turned like an hourglass. Within the pages of that movie treatment, however, his story can be told and resurrected like the city that was once almost forgotten. He can move and inspire people again like he did in 1991, when he made the greatest comeback in sports history.

There is an echoing knock on the hotel door. Vinny drops the treatment on the Victorian dining-room table and checks himself one last time in the hotel's full-length mirror, patting the wrinkles from the sleeves of his designer shirt. He jogs to the foyer and opens the door.

The storytellers have arrived.

1　The Belt

"Seven, seven, hard three," Kevin Rooney barks at his fighter. "Move, Vinny, punch and get out, slip and make him pay. Hard seven again," he orders, his thick New York accent filling the Father and Son's Gym. To longtime boxing trainer Rooney, these numbers signify punch sequences. Seven: jab; two: straight right hand; one: left hook; four: right uppercut. To boxing champion Vinny Pazienza, they reflect one of many sparring sessions, yet another training camp, and, in this case, an opportunity to defend the World Boxing Association Middleweight Championship he had captured a month earlier.

On the other side of the gym, 71-year-old Angelo Pazienza watches acutely from the doorway, making sure his son is not disturbed and is receiving proper instruction from his trainer. Angelo is almost 6 feet tall, with mostly gray hair that creates its own style depending on Angelo's mood. Most days his hair parallels either the calm or the peril in his life, as his waves flow gently back from his forehead, impeccably neat, or it springs wildly from the sides or ascends from his scalp caught up in his adrenaline and activity.

And believe me: Most of Angelo's days, and nights for that matter, are active.

He checks in at the scale daily at roughly 202 pounds. If he goes up to 205, that means he's been drinking a little too much red wine. If he goes up to 208, he's been doubling up on his wife's biscotti; 211 pounds means too much of the aforementioned wine and biscotti, along with too much angel hair pasta.

Angelo wears glasses; sometimes they just rest on his chest, hanging by beaded holders. He puts them on mostly when he's bargaining, selling, hustling, or negotiating, and that's most of the time. And he's always impeccably dressed in the finest haberdashery: camel-hair or hounds-tooth Canali or Burberry jackets, Ermenegildo Zegna slacks, Bally or John Lobb shoes, and always a brilliant shirt that complements his pale blue eyes and square white teeth. On occasion he relaxes and wears sweatsuits that always match from head to toe and that are never understated. The sweatsuits, mostly velour, range from fire-engine red; to midnight black; to red, white, and green; to deep sky blue. They're mostly leftovers from Angelo working in Vinny's corner on fight night and his attempts to match Vinny's trunks.

"Don't hang inside Vinny, let's go, box and get out, box this guy." Vinny obeys his trainer's instruction and swiftly dances away from his 235-pound heavyweight sparring partner, Tommy "The Tank" Murphy. Tank tries to cut off the ring, attempting to corner the stout but elusive 175-pound middleweight to no avail. Pazienza is getting into a rhythm, bouncing on his toes, dotting under thunderous right hooks, flashing lightning-fast jabs to Tank's forehead. He bloodies Tank's nose, as he smoothly dances around the ring to the beat of the blaring boom box. Frustration is painted on the heavyweight's face. He has difficulty coping with the superior speed and boxing skills of the two-time champion of the world.

As the pace quickens, Rooney pushes the fighters harder. "Thirty seconds to the round, pick it up." Paz halts his dancing and the two confront each other in the center of the ring. They exchange heated flurries. Tank digs in his heavy legs, plotting thumping hooks to the champion's torso. "Step over and hook, Vinny," Rooney hollers. Right hooks and uppercuts are thrown with furious abandon. The bell rings and Vinny lands one last looping punch to the side of the head. "Enough! Enough! That's it, we're done," the trainer orders. About thirty onlookers and acquaintances gathered at Father and Son's Gym applaud the two fighters' work ethic. Vinny spits his mouthpiece to the canvas.

Vinny's heart thumps rapidly against the wall of his chest as he gasps for a long breath. He tears his headgear off and throws it to the floor, hoping he somehow might relieve the burning he feels in his muscles. He walks the ring in circles easing the intensity from his body. The beads of sweat pour into Vinny's eyes as he drapes himself in a towel, soothing the red welts on his midsection.

"Give me one more round, Tank! One more, Kevin?" Vinny asks. "No, that's it. Eight is good for today. Finish your floor routine. Eighteen more pounds, Vinny," Rooney exclaims. "You got four weeks. That's 4 1/2 pounds a week."

"Yeah I know. I lose 4 pounds a week; you gain 4 pounds a week. It's a push, right?"

"You fat bastard," Rooney laughs and retorts: "You chose this life."

It is a chosen life indeed, one of unending sacrifice. The body is physically abused; it was not built to sustain the consistent neurological distress that a boxer suffers when being hit. The trauma of broken hands, noses, and the building of scar tissue, which alters the appearance, is psychologically dispiriting to even the most devoted fighters. Emotionally, ten-week isolated training camps wear down the psyche. The rigors and seclusion, in many instances, encourage fighters to retire prematurely.

Today the scale is Vinny's friend: He's at 170 pounds, down by 2 pounds. By week's end, a possible 165. "Speed bag, Vinny, double the end bag, jump rope and five hundred situps," Rooney orders. Rat tat, tat, tat . . . tat, tat . . . the speed bag is put in blinding motion . . . the workout continues.

Vinny calls to me: "Tommy Jon, whatya think?" I'm a longtime childhood friend and Vinny's seeking affirmation regarding his sparring session. "Good work today, four weeks to go, you'll get sharper," I said.

Vinny and I met on a Pop Warner football field, playing for the Edgewood Eagles. Vinny was an 11-year-old kamikaze, a ball-hawking maniac tipping the scales at 95 pounds with rocks in his pocket while I was a 120-pound burly and bruising but green first-year 9-year-old fullback. While scrimmaging, Vinny got his licks in early and often, leaving me with red and blue bruises under my chin and chimes ringing in my ears. I was a battered and beaten fullback until I finally went to my 11-year-old cousin Tommy Mart (Martinelli) for help; he was also on the team. We, the two cousins bound together so closely by blood, conspired to take Vinny out, somehow, someway: chop blocks, clips, two-on-ones, whatever it took. We got close on a few occasions, but we never did take Vinny out. In fact, the more we fought and the harder we hit each other, the closer the three of us became. In time, the three of us were conspiring to take other guys out. Twenty years later, after Vinny had taken out hundreds of guys in the boxing ring throughout the world, amateur and pro, the three of us remained best friends.

Tommy Mart and I are first cousins on our mother's side, the entire family made of six sisters and two brothers. Since we spent just about every breathing moment together from the ages of 3 and 5, my middle name Jon forever followed my first name, Tommy, hence the name Tommy Jon. And Tommy's last name forever followed his first.

In our family we are the chosen ones in terms of height, which is always an issue to first- and second-generation Italian-American parents. Just two out of over fifty cousins made it over 5'11", making it ever so close to nirvana, or 6 feet. We're both broad shouldered with brown thick hair: My hair is a little straighter while Tommy Mart's is fuller and bushier, rising high always attempting to reach nirvana. It must be tamed, and he has cut his hair every two weeks since childhood. If Tommy goes past the two-week mark without his haircut, he does in fact become a 6-footer. We both hover around the 190- to 225-pound range depending on the severity of the New England winters. If the winters are longer than usual, it means a little more pasta and comfort food; pencil us in for 220. If spring comes early, our running gear is out and our abs are showing and we're looking closer to the 190-pound mark. We both have dark eyes and quiet demeanors. People often confuse us for one another. And we just usually reply the way we think the other one would, to avoid any more explanation than necessary. Around town we're known as the "two Tommys."

"It'll come, it'll come," I say. Vinny nods in agreement. I already know he's ready for top-ten contender Pat Lawlor, but there's no benefit in telling him. Contentment and self-satisfaction coupled are ingredients that can easily lead to an athlete's demise.

Nearby Angelo mops the sweat from the floor. Angelo always mops. It's a habit, more than anything, just one way to burn off his extra energy. "Tommy Jon," Angelo calls, "I got a treat for you tonight. I'm taking you to St. Anthony's for angel hair."

"Ange, I can't make it. I have to give Vinny a ride to—"

Angelo interrupts me. "Nope, I'll get Kurt to take Vinny to the post office and wherever the hell he's going. We're going for capellini. Vinny can't come with us; don't tell him we're going to eat. He's too heavy; he can't eat pasta." Kurt Reader, a friend and quasi-trainer, had offered to take Vinny to the post office following his workout.

The World Boxing Association (WBA) Championship belt Vinny won October 1 should have been returned to its rightful owner, Gilbert Dele. Vinny, in his euphoria following the fight, could not bear to relinquish his new prized possession. The champion always keeps his customized belt. The WBA then, in turn, authenticates a new belt for its new champion, in this case Vinny. On this day, Kurt picked Vinny up and drove him to Father and Son's Gym. Vinny planned on lifting weights at Gold's Gym in Warwick after his boxing workout. As a result, on this fateful day, he would need a ride.

By 2:30 p.m., the gym finally cleared out. Angelo and I remained behind. Onlookers and gym guests thank Angelo for the visit, as Vinny shrewdly slipped out of the back door with his hands wrapped in ice packs, too worn to socialize. But before he left he took a call from the *Boston Herald*'s boxing writer Ed Gray. Gray wanted a quote from Vinny regarding the recent bombshell Magic Johnson had dropped on the sporting nation. The basketball legend had announced that he was HIV-positive and that he was formally retiring from the NBA. Gray asked Vinny what he thought about the news. Vinny thought introspectively and looked around the room at his trophy case, then fixated on his aging father as he contemplated the question.

"Ya know, Ed, if you don't have your health, you don't have anything. You take it for granted and only miss it when it's gone. It's human nature I guess." Eerily he would learn that firsthand in just a few hours.

The energy that had previously filled the air throughout the workout session was expunged, and the gym was left in a state of quiet calm. The interior walls of the gym, a converted firehouse, are decorated with fight posters from boxing cards that Vinny headlined. Pazienza versus Frazier; Paz versus Haugen: Thunder and Lightning; Pazienza versus Camacho: Put Up or Shut Up. A quote from Vince Lombardi, "Our greatest glory is not in never failing, but is in rising every time we fall," serves as motivation in life and in the ring. Black-and-white photos from boxing yesteryear—Willie Pep, Carmen Basilio, Muhammad Ali, Rocky Marciano—hover atop the walls, boxing ghosts of the past integrated with contemporary greats Marvin Hagler, Ray Leonard, and Roberto Duran. Inspiration is drawn from these hallowed walls. Trophies fill a showcase: 1981 National Amateur Lightweight Champion; 1979 New England Golden Gloves Champion; 1987 International Boxing Federation Lightweight Champion of the World; 1990 WBA Middleweight Champion of the World. The Pazienza name is proudly represented as part of boxing history, appreciating the fact that Vinny, as a world champion, is in select company.

It's a bit early for dinner, so Angelo and I decide to re-watch the tape of Vinny's championship win over France's Gilbert Dele. The fight is only one month old and we can't help but savor the reminiscence of sweet victory. Angelo pops the tape in the VCR and we anxiously await Vinny's entrance into the ring. Viewing the fight on television, one gains a different perspective than at ringside, the intricacies of the fighters' slipping punches, the wincing of landed body punches, and the beauty of masterful footwork almost transformed into art. Each time we watch the fight, our anxieties re-emerge as if the outcome is unknown.

USA Network's Sean O'Grady begins his pre-fight commentary. "The champion Gilbert Dele is a nontraditional European boxer. He's athletic and clever, unlike most Europeans, who tend to be methodical, flat-footed, and predictable. Jab, right hand, left hook, two steps forward. Jab, right hand, left hook, two steps forward. Dele stands 5 feet 10 inches and enters the ring weighing 165 pounds, 11 pounds gained following yesterday's weigh-in. The films and scouting reports reveal that Dele is at his best when he presses the fight, cuts off the ring, and uses his athleticism to corner his opponent. What's more, he possesses devastating punching power; he's got the ability to hurt his opponents with either hand. He enters tonight's fight with an unblemished 29-0 record, with 24 coming by way of knockout. He's also a 3 to 1 favorite over tonight's opponent, Vinny Pazienza."

"Ahhh!" Angelo grumbles, "3 to 1 my ass. Those stupid bastards, they thought this guy was gonna come over here and bust my kid out. They'd never seen nobody like Vinny, with my kid's balls. He didn't know what to do when Vinny came out and—"

"Ange, you gotta say though, he was a tough guy," I chime in, playing devil's advocate.

"Yeah, he was a tough son of a bitch," Angelo acknowledges, lowering his tone, "but he ain't tougher than my kid."

"And now the end is near . . ." Frank Sinatra's voice radiates through the Providence Civic Center and its twelve thousand fans. "It's time, Vinny. Let's go . . . that's our cue," Kevin Rooney hollers out to Vinny in the dressing room. Throngs of people stand on their chairs awaiting Vinny's arrival, trying to get a first look at their hometown warrior. Electricity fills the air among the pro-Pazienza crowd, thousands of fans anticipating his arrival.

Vinny begins his march to the ring. As he makes his way through the tunnel, he becomes lost in the eight-man entourage. Rooney walks close behind, drilling last-minute instructions in Vinny's ear. "Use your speed, Vinny. You are too much for this guy, stick to our game plan. This is your night, champ." The words are lost in the moment. The frenzied crowd and the adrenaline from within seize Vinny's emotions and carry him into an elevated zone.

This is a zone that allows fighters to ignore pain, dissolve fears, and evoke instinctual human survival skills. Kill or be killed. Boxing is not a sport; it is survival. As Vinny enters the ring, his world shrinks to an area of 20 by 20 feet. For the next forty-eight minutes, he must do everything within his power to dominate every square inch of the area. Mentally, Vinny already knows there are no limitations in terms of meeting his desired end. Simply put, he is willing to pay the ultimate sacrifice—death, a notion which is very real in this game. What is unknown is how far his body will allow itself to be pushed before, physiologically, it decides to betray him. The body can make a coward out of the most hardened of men. Vinny makes his way up the stairs to the ring; nothing more is offered by his cornermen. Words are empty and irrelevant at this juncture. The fighter stands alone.

As the champion begins his walk into the ring, he seems to be unaffected by the hostile environment, 6,000 miles from home, a national television audience, and twelve thousand screaming fans. Gilbert Dele's body language exudes confidence, as the undefeated fighter enters the ring dancing, shadow-boxing, and smirking across the ring at Vinny. He is sure the former lightweight champion of the world will not be able to match his strength or resolve.

As the two meet in the center of the ring for the pre-fight instructions, neither man backs off. Both refuse to be intimidated and they repeatedly bang foreheads. Referee Luis Rivera steps between the two, tearing them apart.

"Ange, look at Dele; he's a cocky prick." I baited Angelo into a predictable but still hysterical response.

Seventy-one-year-old Angelo jumped from his recliner chair. "Tom Jon, this guy thinks Vinny's a sucka. He thinks he's a little guy. You stupid bastard!" He yells at the television as if Dele can hear his predictive words. "Watch what's going to happen to you now you dumb son of a bitch." Angelo, in his fire-engine red velour sweatsuit and matching red high-top Reeboks, excitedly began to throw a combination of punches. He hopped, he bounced on his toes, and he threw a flurry of jabs and uppercuts.

"Watch when Vinny comes out . . . he hits this bastard with a left hook right off the bat." He dramatically continued on in perfect rhythm, mimicking his son's fighting style while announcing excerpts of the fight. Angelo's white hair ascended wildly from his head as he quickened his furious pace. Amazing! *Seventy-one years old*, I thought.

What I was witnessing was the infusion of life pumped into a father by his son. It was because of Vinny that Angelo retained the same spirit and strength he held as a 40-year-old. Only his physical appearance revealed his advanced age. The idea of Vinny prepared to do battle at the highest level, doing what he loved the most, was Angelo's fountain of youth. Vinny was Angelo's Ponce de Leon.

By now USA's Sean O'Grady pitched his voice to exceed the frenzied noise pitch of the crowd. "For Vinny Pazienza to be successful, he must utilize his greatest strength, his speed. The former Lightweight Champion of the World may not be able to withstand the punching power of a true middleweight, so he needs to outspeed Dele and resist brawling with the bigger man. Remember, Pazienza is moving up 19 pounds in weight, chances are he will not be able to stand in there for too long, and he probably won't be able to hurt Dele. One more note, the only lightweight ever to move up successfully to middleweight," O'Grady pauses dramatically, ". . . the great Hands of Stone, Roberto Duran."

O'Grady reaffirms that Vinny is taking on a monumental task. Angelo cringes in his chair at the "expert" commentary. "Imagine this guy, he gives Vinny no shot. He can't hurt Dele?" Angelo asks rhetorically. "My kid can hurt anybody if he catches 'em right. How does this mayonnaise face," referring to O'Grady, "know how hard Vinny can punch? He never got hit by 'im."

"Vinny should whack O'Grady the next time he sees him," I add, and Angelo laughs heartily in agreement, taking me very seriously.

The bell sounds for round one. Vinny races out to the center of the ring; there is no feeling-out process, or touching of the gloves before rounds. The fight is on, another grudge match. All of them are. The magnitude of the fight is insignificant. Dele reaches out to Vinny, trying to "touch" his opponent. He wants to feel his speed, strength, and punching power. This tends to settle a fighter down, allows him to find a placid zone, and helps him reinforce the fact that his legs are steady beneath his trunk. Vinny rejects Dele's courting. "Seven, seven Vinny," Rooney calls from the corner. Vinny ignores the commands. He fires an unorthodox booming left hook. The champion is shaken immediately.

He follows up with a barrage of punches, some finding the mark, others missing, or blocked. Vinny's intent is clear, the message is sent. No words or actions pending. The round soon ends with Dele backed up against the ropes, Vinny banging his body with disdain. "That's it, champ!" Angelo calls to the television screen, gripping the arms of his recliner chair tightly. "He can't hurt you, champ!"

"Good round, good round." I broke in. "See, Ange, he's a lot stronger at this weight. Those goddamned Duvas. He should have moved up two years ago." Lou Duva and son Danny Duva were Vinny's manager and promoter, respectively. They chaired Main Events promotions, one of the three largest sports promotion companies in the world. Main Events had represented Vinny's boxing career since he turned pro in 1983.

"That fat bastard Lou had Vinny lose 25 or 30 pounds before fights, he didn't give a shit about my kid. When Vinny got sick starvin' himself, trying to make weight, that fat bastard ate everything in sight! Right?"

"When you're full no one else is hungry," I said, quoting my own father.

"You're right, Tommy Jon, I like that one."

In round two Vinny again raced from his corner. He locked his gloves beneath his opponent's shoulders and crashed his head under Dele's chin, walking him back to the same corner from which the fighter had just departed. Wild hooks, both right and left, uppercuts, and bolo punches were thrown from his knee, pinning Dele again to the ropes. Elbows and head butts were integrated into the combinations. Rhode Island's governor Bruce Sundlun and Providence mayor Buddy Cianci cheered just feet from the ring apron. The two led the crowd screaming encouragement to Vinny. Rivera moved in to take a closer look to see if Dele was seriously hurt. "TKO! TKO! TKO!" Kevin Rooney hollered from the corner, hoping for a stop to the fight.

However, yet again the champion was able to withstand Vinny's suffocating pressure. Just before the bell to end round two, Dele countered Vinny's attack with a crashing straight right hand sending his own message to Vinny. "I ain't going nowhere, kid, I ain't going nowhere," Dele spit his mouthpiece into his glove as he screamed in broken English to Vinny. The champion proudly walked to his corner.

Kevin Rooney met Vinny in the ring as he walked to the corner. "C'mon, Vinny, don't let this guy hit you like that. Give him angles, step to the side. Don't stand right in front of the fuck!"

"He can't hurt me, Kevin. He can't hurt me," Vinny interjected excitedly as he finally sat on his stool. "Use your jab, Vinny. I don't wanna hear that shit. I want you boxing this guy." Vinny appeased Kevin, accepting his instruction, but knew what he must do. With the first punch taken, he was confident Dele would not be able to hurt him.

As round three began Dele followed his corner's instructions. They knew he could only win this fight as the aggressor. Vinny obliges him. Tactically, the fight was changing; Vinny transformed himself from slugger to graceful boxer. He allowed Dele to move him. When Dele was set to punch, Vinny keenly slipped to the side, negating Dele's punching power. He flicked jabs at Dele's chest and midsection. When Dele reset to punch, Vinny bounced to the left or to the right.

Dele forged ahead through the middle rounds, never able to catch up to his opponent. His pressure was relentless, however, as he hoped he could at least break Vinny's will and spirit. Each instant Dele moved in on Vinny, he walked through a meat grinder, catching a combination of punches that began with punches buried deep into his kidneys and ended with heavy left hooks to his temple.

"My kid is outpunching this son of a bitch six to one," Angelo exclaimed.

As round six ended, Dele retreated to his corner visibly confused and looking to his trainers for answers. His legs were shaky, and his mind was numb from the exhaustion. He had entered a new territory, fighting an opponent with middleweight strength, coupled with the speed and stamina of a lightweight. Dele revealed the first chink in his armor, in an admission to his trainers that he was tiring. As he sprawled on his stool, Dele's arms dangled loosely by his side, his legs extended and spread apart. "He's too fast, I can't see the punches." Cut man Jose Motimbique pressed an en-swell firmly on Dele's swollen forehead, a metal tool kept iced that is used to alleviate swelling above fighter's eyes. "Keep pressing. He's getting tired. You've got him, keep pressing. Hit his body. He can't move his body. These rounds are yours. Show 'em who is champion." The corner exhorted their bewildered fighter.

In round seven, again Dele progressed ahead, knowing he must alter the fight in his favor. He leaned his fatigued body into Vinny, hoping to slow him down. He threw punches, not trying to be perfect, but just staying busy enough to keep himself in the fight. Vinny recognized a renewed spirit in his champion.

"What's keeping this fuck coming?" Vinny began to doubt himself, as Dele stepped up his assault on Vinny's body. "I can't keep this motherfucker off me. Fuck this, don't think like that, don't think like that. I'll die in here." For one split second Vinny's tired mind was beginning to take over his will. That one split second of resignation can manifest into a lifetime of quitting. In most instances, it separates those who never achieve, those who merely achieve, and those who achieve greatness. Vinny knew if he allowed his mind to be overtaken, his heart would soon follow, all of his past achievements lost, his opportunity for greatness unfulfilled. With that realization he regrouped, stepped back from Dele, and pounded his own stomach as he let out a primal scream, "Uuuuhhhhhhh!" heard above the twelve thousand fans.

It was at that moment that Dele had to know that he would not outwill his opponent. He looked into Vinny's eyes and saw a fierce determination that for the remainder of the fight he would not be able to match. Dele must have realized in this war of attrition he would be returning to Paris without his championship belt.

By round twelve, the fight was all but over. Dele trailed big on all three judges' scorecards. Vinny, still not completely satisfied with his performance, buzz-sawed his staggering opponent to the corner. He bounced his back from the rope using it as a springboard and hurled a left uppercut that immediately cracked Dele's cheekbone. The stricken fighter turned away from Vinny and pawed at his left eye and cheek with both gloves.

Vinny followed Dele and smashed his now fragile opponent with the final blow of the fight. Rivera leaped between the two, mercifully ending the contest.

"You ain't going nowhere, uh?" Angelo's voice echoed in the empty gym, remembering the words Dele spoke earlier. Angelo lifted himself from his chair. "I told him at the weigh-in Tommy Jon, he aiiiiinnn't—" accentuating the word— "seen nobody like my kid in his life. He didn't believe me. That stupid bastard thought I was bullshitting 'im. I'm not a bullshitter," he said gleefully, clicking the television off. "My kid is a champene because he's got balls like me. He didn't get his balls from his motha."

"That's a good thing, right?" I said.

"Ah, you're a smart-ass today, huh?" Angelo replied. "You better be careful or there'll be no capellini for you."

I became serious. "Angelo, Vinny and I have been friends since we were kids, eight or nine years old. I gotta tell ya, I'm really proud of him. Not because of all the television shit or celebrity shit, but because . . . I gotta be honest, watching him sacrifice so much, he inspired me to finish college, pay my dues, and . . . ."

"Tom Jon," Angelo said, as he gripped both hands on my shoulders, looked pleasantly into my eyes, and stepped a bit closer, "Vinny does it for you, you do for Vinny. You guys are like brothers. My kid loves you and your cousin Tommy like nobody else."

Angelo went on. "I tell Vinny too, those guys are your only friends; these other guys wanna be around him. Use 'im for broads, money, and whatever; that's all. I don't want anybody around my kid. His girl, she's another one, that fucking Nikki, that Fall River whore. You gotta talk to him about her. She's a busted suitcase, she's got a 9-year-old kid—"

"Ooohhh! Please don't start that, Ange, you turned a nice moment into a tirade now."

Vinny had met Nikki in 1987 while the two were appearing in a music video for a local rock band. Nikki was a background dancer and Vinny was appearing as himself—Vinny, the celebrity. Ethnically Nikki was a mix of Portuguese and French; she was dark skinned, her eyes dark brown and almond shaped. She wore her shiny black hair in a ponytail that accentuated her sharp cheekbones and her full red lips. Her teeth were pearly white and when she smiled she could take the kingdom from a prince.

But to her credit, Nikki supported herself, took little or no money from Vinny, and worked two jobs, one as a dental hygienist and the other as a waitress at Jimmy Birchfield's Classic restaurant. She was a hardworking girl from an old-school Portuguese family with a strong work ethic. To Angelo, however, Nikki or anyone else male or female who got too close to Vinny was a whore, hooker, freeloader, busted suitcase, con man, scam artist, etc.—except me and Tommy Mart.

"What? What? Come on, Tom Jon, he listens to you. My kid don't know I know about those French whores up there. She's gonna suck and fuck everything outta him. When she's all done with him, he'll be no good no more." He leaned over, grabbing his trench coat.

"Please, please stop," I said laughingly. "First of all, Vinny's 28. He's a big boy who can take care of himself, and secondly it's five o'clock. Can we go eat?"

"Okay, okay, you drive. I can't see at night." Angelo threw me the car keys as we made our way out of the gym and strolled to his white Chrysler New Yorker.

"Are there dockage fees for this boat?" I asked. "Smart-ass remark number two, yuppie. You're down to a half order now," Angelo kidded.

Angelo sometimes called me yuppie because I was taking grad courses at Rhode Island College, and his view of the world, for obvious reasons, was a bit different than mine. It didn't negate the fact one bit that I loved to hang out with the guy.

2   The Social Club

As Angelo and I made our way into St. Anthony's Social Club, the club owner, Mike the Cook, greeted us at the door. "Angelo, *come sta*. How you been?"

"How have I been? Last time I saw you, me and my kid wasn't champeen of the world."

"I know, I know, congratulations," Mike replied.

"You remember Vinny's friend Tom Jon, right?"

"Sure, Tommy, how ya doing?"

"Mike, I'm treating Tommy tonight to your angel hair. I been bragging about 'em."

"All right, come in, Ange." Mike put his arm in front of Angelo halting his entrance into the club. "Before you go in, I wanna warn you, that pain in my ass Louie Barone is in there playing pinochle."

"So what," Angelo replies.

"Well he's a ball breaker. Don't take him too seriously, that's all I'm telling ya." Barone was a small-time bookmaker who lived off his uncle's reputation of being an under-boss in New England's Patriarca crime family. This didn't mean shit to Angelo.

I knew Mike had a bad feeling; it was etched on his face and could be heard in his voice. There are two kinds of Italians, the first kind and the worst kind. The first kind embraces their cultural heritage by supporting those who emerge above. The worst kind are bitter about their personal plight and can't help but diminish those who succeed, to reconcile their individual underachievement. Louie Barone was the worst kind. Angelo always told Vinny that many Providence Italians cheered against Rocky Marciano, who was from Brockton, Massachusetts, twenty minutes from Providence. In fact, he fought 29 of his 49 fights at the old Rhode Island Auditorium. Imagine 49-0, a hometown guy, Heavyweight Champion of the World, and assholes like Louie Barone root for complete strangers.

"Me take something serious? Relax, I got no problem with none of these guys," Angelo assured Mike.

As Angelo finally broke through the doors and entered the club, a chorus of voices welcomed him. "Angelo!" Most put their cards or drinks down and walked toward the proud father and stuck out their hands. "Congratulations, where you been? How's the kid? Where's the champ? How's Vinny?" Questions surrounded Angelo from old friends and well-wishers. Meanwhile, Mike and I lagged behind. "Tommy, help me out here, huh? I know this fucking Louie Barone, he's an agitator. He knocks Vinny all over the joint. He never knows when to keep his fucking mouth shut. I don't want Angelo getting into it with him. Not here."

"Mike," I replied, "I'll try to keep Angelo away from him. Give us a table in the back."

Here I am, a 26-year-old guy, in an Italian social club where the average age is about 65, and he's getting agitated because he knew there was a real possibility Angelo might end up killing this guy, or at the very least giving him a beating. By the time we finished our capellini pomodoro and two bottles of pinot grigio, I was a bit more relaxed but still guarded because Louie Barone had made his way to the bar, just feet from our table.

Al Martino songs serenaded us as we sat reminiscing about the years gone by: craps games, Vegas junkets, and lost fortunes as a result of gambling. Guys like Buckles Baccari, Angelo's cousin Sal Pazienza, Charlie the Tuna, and even Mike the Cook shared tales about what could have been. The number-three dog that came up inches short at Lincoln Downs, the seven-card twenty-one the dealer pulled in Atlantic City's Trump Plaza to beat Baccari on a $3,000 double down. They laugh now, but they cursed when it happened.

Ultimately, Vinny became the topic of conversation. "*Cugi*," Angelo's cousin Sal asks, using the Italian word for cousin, "who's next for the champ?"

"A kid by the name of Pat Lawlor outta San Francisco; he's a tough white kid, but he's got no shot. Vinny sparred with him about six months ago and busted him out at the gym." Angelo laughs. "He's a nice kid too but—"

I interrupted, trying to change the subject, knowing Barone was listening in, trying to wedge himself into the conversation. In social club vernacular he was on Lake Erie (listening in). "Come on, Ange, let's go, it's almost six o'clock. I've got some errands to run."

"Where's the fight?" Charlie the Tuna asks, as if I never spoke.

"Trump Plaza, Atlantic City. For TV we've got HBO, but the best part, we're gonna make a killing, eight hundred large off this one," Angelo said. "Then we win, maybe we fight Ray Leonard or Roberto Duran for three, four, five million dollars!"

My eyes never left a now seething Barone, knowing those kinds of dollar figures were sure to elicit a response. He couldn't suppress his envy for another second. "When's your kid gonna fight? A real fighter, win a real title? That last guy was a real fucking stumblebum. Jesus Christ, nobody ever heard of these guys." Barone's statement brought an abrupt end to all conversation.

And he went on. "Angelo, no disrespect. You and Vinny have done great for yourselves, but I think me and my uncle Rudolph can help you guys out. We got a joint in New Haven. We'll get Vinny a name guy, Leonard, Duran. Of course we wet our beaks, you and Vinny get a piece."

Angelo shook his head and bit his bottom lip, "Get a piece? My kid's a two-time world champion; you're gonna take him to New Haven? That joint seats three thousand heads, tops! The mice get hunchback in that joint. What do you think this is, 1955? You're shootin' in to me, shaking down my kid?"

Louie shot back, knowing he had to save face. "Angelo, you know what? Fuck you and your kid, and get the fuck out of here. Your rights are hereby terminated at this club."

Angelo kicked back his chair loudly and hustled toward Barone, jabbing his finger into his throat upon arrival, his mouth just inches from Barone's face. "If my kid's name ever comes out of your mouth again, I'll stick you back in your mother's box." Angelo dug his finger deeper into Barone's throat as he pinned him to the bar, causing him to turn shades of blue and red. An espresso spilled into Barone's face. Angelo went on in his fury. "My kid is going to go down as the greatest fucking—"

"Angelo! Angelo!" Herbie the Bartender shouted. "Look at the television, something about Vinny!" Angelo relinquished his grip, shoving away Barone, and made his way to the television.

"Good evening, this is Cathy Rey with News Team 10. Breaking news out of Warwick tonight: Boxing champion Vinny Pazienza has been involved in a very serious auto accident." Angelo's knees buckled. "He was taken to Kent County Memorial Hospital where close friends and family have gathered waiting on word from doctors. He is believed to be in grave condition. At this time, neither the hospital nor the family has issued any statement and our information is a little sketchy. What we do know is apparently he was a passenger in a car, which lost control, veered across the highway median, and collided with a truck. There is no word on the driver of the vehicle in which Vinny Pazienza was a passenger, or any word on the driver of the truck. We will keep you updated as we learn more of the details." Before the news anchor could finish her statement, Angelo and I began our dreaded race to the hospital.

3 Tragedy

By chance, John Florio, Vinny's brother-in-law and a sales rep for Kearns Oil, received a phone call from Bill Thompson of Thrifty Car Rental, Post Road, Warwick, at approximately 4:00 p.m. "John, Billy from Thrifty."

"Billy boy, what can I do for ya?"

"I need a price on 400 gallons of Fram and about 260 gallons of Valvoline."

In the midst of giving Florio a work order, Thompson halted his conversation. "What the fuck . . . Johnny, Johnny hold on. It sounds like a fucking bomb exploded." Thompson ran outside about 30 yards to the site of the accident, where he saw that an older-model Lincoln Town Car had been hit head-on traveling southbound.

The other car, a gray Camaro occupied by Kurt Reader and Vinny, was headed northbound when Reader was cut off by a third vehicle. Reader, attempting to avoid the car, slammed on his car's brakes, losing control and sending the car into a wild tailspin. The Camaro veered dangerously above the highway median, barely missing a four-ton truck. *Fuuuuck, I'm never going to defend my title*, Vinny thought clutching the passenger door, holding on for his life as the two careened toward oncoming traffic. The car smashed the Lincoln, spun in the air, and landed broadside a quarter of the way up a telephone pole before it crashed to the ground. The Lincoln's once sturdy hood was folded in two; smoke billowed out of each front quarter. The nose of the car faced northward, while the rear end, almost removed from its axle, sat up on the curb facing oncoming traffic.

Billy Thompson's eyes followed the black skid marks as he looked through the dusty gray smoke rising above the accident scene. His eyes led him to the second car as the smell of burning rubber and gasoline filled the air. He heard the shattered glass that littered the streets beneath his feet as witnesses-turned-rescuers unsuccessfully tried to pry open the doors and free Kurt and Vinny from their car.

As Vinny released his grip from the door handles, he looked into his lap, his chin bent to his chest, before finally coming to. Vinny, instinctively, did not look to his left. "Kurt, you all right?" Vinny spoke, not knowing Kurt's fate. Reader's traumatized body shook and blood masked his eyes as his hands remained glued to the bent steering wheel. Kurt struggled to respond to Vinny's questions.

"Vinny Paz is in there," one voice called as the man tugged at the car's door handles. Thompson immediately turned and sprinted back to his phone. "Johnny, your brother-in-law is in the car, man. He's hurt bad."

"Billy, what are you talking about? Are you sure? What kind of car is it?"

"Some old Chevy piece a' shit, RI plated BR-38. People near the car are saying it's him." Florio knew the car; he knew the driver; he knew Kurt Reader.

Florio instantly called his wife, Vinny's sister, at home. "Doreen, I just got off the phone with Billy Thompson at Thrifty, your brother just got in a bad car accident up on Post Road. Get your mother and get to Kent County Hospital."

Vinny's 63-year-old mother, Louise, lived upstairs from Doreen. She heard her panicked daughter scream, "Mom, Mom, Vinny got into a bad car accident." Doreen then grabbed her jacket and keys, burst through the screen door, and raced to the hospital without her mother. Louise, unable to catch up with her hysterical daughter, or reach Angelo at the gym, called a close family friend, Tony Cipolla, for a ride to the hospital.

As emergency medical technicians arrived on the scene, they waited for Kurt and Vinny to be freed from the twisted wreckage by the jaws of life. As the car was split in two, EMTs were finally able to help. "Vinny, I'm going to move you very, very slowly," the assuring voice resonated in Vinny's ears. As the EMT approached Vinny, he slid his arms under Vinny's shoulders, reaching around from behind, and clenching his hands at Vinny's chest.

"My neck! My neck! Get off my neck!" A stinging hot pain shot up Vinny's spine, passing the base of his thick neck before settling at the back of his skull. The heat jettisoned throughout his body, numbing his arms and burning his back.

"Vinny, all right, all right, man." The EMT released Vinny back to the seat.

"I can't move my head," Vinny whispered.

Vinny was rushed to Kent County Hospital along with Kurt. They arrived with their clothes tattered and bloodied. Vinny was immediately treated as a spinal, vertebrae injury. He was put in traction, ensuring that ancillary movements would not cause further damage. When patients are put in spinal traction, parts of their spinal column are pulled in opposite directions in order to stabilize or change the position of damaged aspects of their spines. In Vinny's case, his head was placed between two blocks and attached to a weighted mechanized pulley apparatus that hung indiscreetly from the back of the black hospital table. Raw open bruises and shards of glass permeated his skull. Lacerations were opened along the hairline, as dried blood stained his brow and was spattered from his neckline to his ears.

Dr. Walter Cotter, 70, a neurosurgeon, began giving Vinny a variety of scenarios, which were at best speculative. Louise,

Doreen, John, and Tony circled the gurney. Vinny had already been taken for an MRI, brain scans, and x-rays.

"Is my son going to die?" Louise immediately asked Cotter.

"No. No, miss," the doctor replied. "He's stable, his vital signs are good, his blood pressure is okay. His lacerations are all superficial wounds; I mean no blood vessels or main arteries in his lungs or anywhere else have been punctured. We've given him a sedative and morphine for pain." The doctor continued. "Your son is strong, but there is spinal damage." Dr. Cotter turned to Vinny. "Vinny, you've broken your neck."

There are thirty-three bones in the spine called vertebrae. The cervical vertebrae are the seven vertebrae that form the upper part of the spine, between the skull and the chest. The cervical vertebrae are referred to medically as C1–C7. With a complete fracture, the bone breaks into several pieces; an incomplete fracture produces cracks or may be compressed into itself. A cervical fracture—a broken neck—often involves muscle sprain, dislocation of disks between the vertebrae, and damage to the spinal cord going both to the arms and the legs. The damage can be permanent and may lead to paralysis or even death if correct forms of treatment are not initiated immediately. Moreover, fracture-dislocation injuries are the most severe as they tend to result not only in multiple vertebrae being fractured but also complete detachment of a portion of the bone. The broken pieces can tear the membrane, called the dura, that protects the spinal cord. If the spinal cord is damaged, brain damage can result. With good reason, Dr. Cotter showed great caution.

"Doc, c'mon, cut through all the shit. Am I going to be able to fight again?"

Dr. Cotter, trying to clarify his prognosis, turned his attention to Vinny. He detailed each step of his grim medical opinion and its ramifications, both long and short term. "Son, we've got some problems here. You've broken your second [C2] and third [C3] vertebrae and you've dislocated your fifth [C5]," Cotter continued. "Right now, Vinny, because spinal injuries are unpredictable in their early stages and there is massive swelling around the injury, uncertainty is almost always the norm in primary vertebrae or spinal injuries."

"C'mon, can I fight again? Yes or no?"

The question caught Dr. Cotter off guard, as he felt Vinny didn't recognize the severity of his injuries. "We're dealing with much bigger issues here. Injuries that can change your day-to-day living abilities. No, Vinny," Dr. Cotter paused, shaking his head slightly. "You won't be able to fight."

Vinny's disillusioned eyes filled with tears, which streamed down his face atop raw red bruises. He yelled at Dr. Cotter: "You don't know me! You don't know what kind of a man I am!" His disappointment built into a frustrated anger. "You don't know me! You don't know what kind of a man I am!" he again hollered at the doctor. Vinny's body flexed and his face reddened as he struggled to move his inert body. "You hear me? Do you hear me?" He repeated again and again, "you don't know me," directing his rage toward Dr. Cotter.

"Okay, Vinny." Not wanting to risk further injury, Dr. Cotter pacified Vinny as nurses collectively tried to calm him. "Son, we'll see what we can do for you," Dr. Cotter promised.

Kent County was not an urban hospital. There were scattered visitors waiting for friends or loved ones. The emergency room itself could hold only about twenty people. The area began to fill slowly, but consistently. Vinny's friends entered cautiously, not knowing what to expect, or what to hear.

Word traveled quickly around the state of Rhode Island. By 5:30 p.m. the family's closest allies arrived. Part-time bodyguard and loyalist, the huge Henry Broccoli, longtime confidant Jimmy Birchfield, and attorney Everett Petronio gathered together. In the middle of his handball game at the Providence Y, Tommy Mart was told that Vinny had been in a bad car accident by fellow Y member Joe Mouro, who saw the accident firsthand from his rent-a-car business on Post Road. Tommy raced to Kent County Hospital in shorts and a sweaty T-shirt. He listened for clues as to what might have happened. They spoke quietly, sheepishly consoling one another. The news that was coming from intensive care was piecemeal; after all, family members did not know the extent of Vinny's injuries.

Louise and Doreen huddled with Vinny behind the triage doors. Faithful Louise held rosary beads to her lips, massaging the corded beads, weeping as if her own life was hanging in the balance, waiting for any sign of Angelo.

Angelo and I finally arrived at Kent County Hospital at roughly 6:20 p.m. I promised a very distraught Angelo that Vinny would be okay. I always felt that Vinny was in some ways invincible. He was the guy that always provided a sense of calm to others, and a sense that worry was needless. Alas, everything according to Vinny "was no big deal." He was the reassuring one in circumstances of doubt, proving time and time again, through his fighting, that anything could be achieved and anything could be overcome. Vinny always had been the eternal optimist. His optimism consistently insulated him from peripheral forces, because he consciously chose to diminish any existing dangers. Of course, I didn't have anything but a gut feeling and a sense of history to support his claims.

As Angelo entered the room, from behind the curtain, he heard the voice of his son.

"Dad? Dad?" Vinny could see his father walking toward him from the corners of his bruised eyes. When he heard his father's voice for the first time after the accident, Vinny could only imagine what he looked like immobilized and in traction. Vinny struggled to get a better view; barely able to move his head, he heard his father's deafening cries.

"No! No! No! Champ, champ, not you, champ." Angelo staggered toward Vinny, the green and white tiled floor seemingly jumping toward his face as he felt himself become light-headed, and indistinct blurry images caught his attention. "Vinny, champ, not you! Not you! Me, I should be there. Why couldn't this be me? I never saw you like this, champ," he openly wept. His body quivered; emotions had overtaken him, and he was sobbing profusely.

Angelo's eyes never left his son, as he moved about with inconsolable despair. The faster he tried to walk to Vinny, the more uncooperative Angelo's trembling body became. To see his strapping father emotionally debilitated weakened Vinny further. Vinny's voice cracked and his eyes welled with tears while he tried to convey some glimmer of hope to his father.

"Dad, I'm okay, I'm okay." He repeated again, "I'm okay. Call Danny Duva, tell him I need an extension on my title. Just tell him I got into an accident . . . I need an extension." Vinny tried to quell his own fears and his father's collectively. He knew his father could not withstand the pain he was enduring.

"No, no, Vinny," Angelo interrupted, unsuccessfully attempting to gather himself. "Champ, please," he cried, tears streaming down his paled cheeks, "forget about that now, forget boxing, you gotta get better," Angelo admonished. "I don't care about fighting." His aggrieved weeping persisted. Vinny did everything he could to mask his fears, to mask the numbness he felt throughout his wounded body. He refused to acknowledge the pain and uncertainty in which he now lived. Once these notions were accepted, they would then exist.

Dr. Cotter entered the triage asking everyone to clear out, father included. Angelo obliged, his voice continually cracking as his husky tone was coupled with tearful sighs. He looked back to his son. "Vinny, everything is gonna be okay, I won't allow anything to happen to us. All right, Vinny? All right, Vinny!" Angelo, for all practical purposes, was facing death himself. Introspection was unnecessary in this case. There was not life without Vinny, nor a need to take another breath if he could not witness his son living life the way he pleased.

"Please, sir." An intern ushered Angelo from his son's bedside; it was time for action. Dr. Cotter offered the family a brief explanation of the upcoming procedures, and told them he would first consult with his colleagues in neurology. Ultimately, he would offer them and Vinny few options.

Angelo came out of the intensive care unit to tell friends to go home. "There is nothing anyone can do," he told them. It was now close to 8:00 p.m. Most of the waiting room had cleared. Only the truest of friends remained: me, Birchfield, Petronio, Cipolla, and Martinelli. They predictably did not oblige Angelo's wishes.

"Ange, we're staying right here. Please!" Birchfield pleaded. Angelo sat down, putting his face in the palms of his hands, and then warily ran his fingers through his hair, feverishly scratching his skull. Each stroke became harder and coarser, revealing red scrapes through his thinning white hair.

By the time Dr. Cotter had finished consulting with the neurological team of specialists at Kent County Hospital, a concise consensus had been reached. Dr. Cotter would recommend to Vinny and his family that he be fitted for a halo vest. This would immobilize his neck and spine. In a best-case scenario, halo traction would allow the broken bones to fuse naturally without surgery. Surgery to fuse the bones would be a last resort. That procedure would definitely end Vinny's boxing career. His range of mobility could be reduced anywhere from 50 to 85 percent, a range that would not allow him to fight. Even if the halo was a short-term solution to the problem, at least further damage would be averted. The agonizing procedure would have to be done almost immediately. Once completed, specialists concluded that in roughly forty-eight to seventy-two hours the swelling would retreat from the damaged area.

Lou Duva sat in his Totowa, New Jersey, home watching ESPN's *SportsCenter* with his business partner and son Danny. At around 6:45 p.m., ESPN programming was interrupted and a statement similar to that read by Channel 10 in Rhode Island was given to a national audience. Again, Vinny's condition was reported as grave.

"Mr. Birchfield, there is a call for you." The receptionist in the waiting area handed the phone to Jimmy.

"Jimmy, it's Dan Duva. What the hell's happening? How's Vinny?" Danny's words raced from his mouth. "Danny?" Jimmy asked hesitantly. "Yeah, what's going on?"

"Danny, it ain't good. Vinny broke his neck in two or three places. He was in a bad car accident and we don't know much else."

"How's Angelo holding up?" Jimmy countered, and shook his head distraughtly as he stood quiet on the line. "He's a mess,"

Jimmy whispered, "We're all here for him though, me, Everett, Henry, and Tom Jon."

"Who's with Vinny?" Dan asked. "Just family and doctors now. I don't know what they're going to do next Danny." In the middle of their conversation, Lou picked up another phone line.

"Hey, Jimmy, what's going on? How is he?"

"I just told Danny, Lou, it's not good. He broke his neck and we're waiting to hear. Look, guys, I gotta go." Jimmy ended the call, now too nervous to be a messenger.

"Jimmy, call us when you hear something, huh? Tell Ange my father and I will catch a flight first thing in the morning. Send Vinny our love."

Meanwhile, Dr. Cotter approached Vinny with an optimistic smile. "Vinny, you are a great patient. Not one complaint all this time."

"What time is it, doc? Could I get some water?" a hoarse Vinny asked. "It's about 8:30 and of course you can have a drink. Nurse, could you please get Mr. Pazienza some water? Listen, Vinny," the doctor began as his family flanked the bed where Vinny lay motionless. "After consultation, our neurological team has concluded that our initial approach will be to fit you for a halo vest." He went on to explain the dynamics of how the vest would be outfitted and surgically prepared. Vinny and his family listened intently as the doctor spoke judiciously. "What we do is . . ."

After Vinny was given a local anesthetic, he was fit with a halo orthosis, also known as a halo vest. The device consists of a fiberglass body vest that is connected by vertical rods to a crown ring, which in turn is held in place by skull pins. The tips of the pins would penetrate the skin and embed in the skull bone. The halo would be attached to the skull by two posterior and two anterior pins, which would be inserted into the external bony table of the cranium. Dr. Cotter went on to explain that there were some risks involved regarding the halo ring and the penetration of the skull pins into Vinny's head.

First and foremost there was the risk of infection or intracranial abscess, which could prove to be deadly if the infection entered the bloodstream. Dr. Cotter stressed that meticulous care of the pin sites was essential to avoid this serious complication. The longer the halo was worn by Vinny, the greater the risk of infection. The skull pins had to be inspected and cleaned at least two times a day for the duration of time that Vinny would be wearing the halo vest. Pin loosening could also cause infection and pain to the front and back of the skull. During his time in the hospital the nurses would fully orient the Pazienza family with a teaching plan to show how to care for Vinny, and how Vinny could learn to care for himself.

Everyday tasks normally taken for granted such as brushing one's teeth, talking on the telephone, climbing stairs, sleeping, dressing and even eating hard foods would become arduous challenges for the two-time boxing world champion. To make matters worse, halo devices draw unwanted attention and are unsightly. The bulky vest and its superstructure can make the average person wearing it feel as if they are suspended in midair or even floating. Emotionally, a traumatic injury like a broken neck can lead to bouts of depression, self-loathing, and alcohol and drug addiction. Vinny not only had to face the greatest physical challenge of his life, but he also had to contend with the psychological implications of trauma to which no man is immune.

4 Where Did the Years Go?

A ngelo walked himself to the end of the corridor in the hospital waiting room. He pulled back the paisley-printed curtains and peeked through the blinds into the dimly lit parking lot. He gazed at the cars traveling by the hospital's main road, wondering if the passersby appreciated how fortunate they were not to be in his position. His mind searched for unanswerable questions: *What if I drove Vinny? Why Vinny? I should have gone home.* Before he knew it, Angelo had to confront the harsh reality of fate, which had crept into his life so swiftly.

"Ange, here, have a little drink." I held out my hand and offered him a cup of water. He shook his head stoically, finally grimacing.

"Tommy Jon, I remember when you guys were little kids. You were a fat little bastard, and Vinny was just a little shit, but you guys always had a good time and I always made sure I was there for my kid."

"Ayy! I wasn't fat, I told you a thousand times I was husky." I grinned and almost felt guilty, but for a brief moment we found room in our hearts to alleviate the despair. "Vinny knows he was lucky to have a great dad. Vinny knows," I confirmed before Angelo's eyes became glazed and his mind retreated to a time long past, before sports became a business, and before boxing defined his and Vinny's lives, before tonight.

Angelo rubbed his grizzled chin. "Where did the years go? Jesus Christ." Angelo shook his head and wondered aloud. "Sometimes I can't believe Vinny is 28. I can't believe I'm seventy-fucking-one years old."

Angelo Pazienza was born in 1919, a time that reflected the harsh realities of immigrant life in the United States. Cities and neighborhoods were divided among a multitude of ethnic groups: Russian, Polish, Italian, Jewish, and Irish, all divided despite their proximity.

Economic insecurity outweighed the risk of pursuing opportunity when Angelo's father, Domenic, died in 1919 at the age of 35 from influenza. With Angelo's mother, Angelina, unable to support herself and her child, she would have to forfeit her opportunity in the New World. The widow and her 2-year-old son Angelo left for Quacino, Italy, a small peasant town 100 miles south of Rome on December 20, 1921. It was here she and her mother would raise Angelo.

By 1936, however, at the age of 18, Angelo's desire to return to America became a reality. When his mother remarried in 1929, Angelo felt she betrayed the memory of his father and the patriarchal role he once held within the family. Moreover, Italy's fascist dictator Benito Mussolini had invaded Ethiopia and formed an alliance with Adolf Hitler's imperialist Nazi Germany. Out of growing contempt for both mother and country, and sensing a second European war was imminent, 17-year-old Angelo immigrated back to the United States.

Angelo returned to his birthplace of Providence, Rhode Island, in the winter of 1936, where he would live with his aunt Julianna, his mother's sister. Silver Lake was a close-knit Italian community in Rhode Island, not much different from South Philly, East Boston, Manhattan's Mulberry Street, or the Bronx's

Arthur Avenue. Italian immigrants settled uniformly in a common area where they were able to coexist comfortably within a much larger culture. The commonalities they shared within their community offered them solace while being so far from the old country. Familiar languages, dialects, religious values, music, and food helped to bridge the 6,000-mile gap from Providence tenements to the old *paese*. Many had settled and immigrated from different regions: Tuscany, Calabria, Napoli, etc. Each paese contributed to the neighborhood's cultural mores. Lighthearted arguments often arose regarding cooking, language, music, and singing. What is Italian? Each represented their paese proudly, claiming to be the only true Italians. Tomatoes versus no tomatoes on pasta, or pizza. "What music is more beautiful than Neapolitan?" the Neapolitans rhetorically asked. Genoans staked their claim on making the fruitiest vino, and on and on it went.

Small-time street hustlers, of which there were many, offered up ties, cardigan sweaters, and watches for a third of their value; even cloth was sold by the foot. "Caveat emptor"—buyer beware. It was this neighborhood that sculpted Angelo into the man he was, for better or worse.

By the time Angelo returned to the United States, he was 17 and had lost interest in school. His aunt had almost no control over the boy who was attracted to bookies and racket guys more than working guys. Working guys accepted the notion that a piece of the pie was better than no pie. Angelo simply figured if there was pie, it should be his. Beginning in 1939 and over the next twenty years, Angelo established himself as one of Providence's sharpest street guys. He proudly described a Providence guy as someone who would follow you into a revolving door and come out ahead. At the age of 20, he ran the biggest crap game in Silver Lake. Throughout the 1940s, Angelo took action on numbers, fights, and of course crap games. His once small book grew large enough that he was taking the edge off action from smaller bookies who couldn't tolerate big bets.

He and his cousin Sal also discovered they had a penchant for brokering stolen merchandise. Angelo figured, let the thieves take all the risks and he could buy, sell, and turn over the hot items at his discretion: gold, diamonds, furs, suits, dishes, cutlery, and even steaks. You name it, he had it. If there was a demand, he created a market. It was Adam Smith's invisible hand played out from the truck of a '48 Chrysler.

Ultimately, Angelo's fence became so large that it became his primary business, run out of his secondary business, Angelo's Barbershop. Angelo learned to cut hair in the mid-1950s and the barbershop he opened in Providence's Fox Point area allowed him to front his illegal fencing operation. Moreover, it provided a communal meeting place.

Over the next decade, Angelo banged around the big three of Providence's Italian neighborhoods: Silver Lake, Charles Street, and Federal Hill. He never aligned himself directly with any racket guys or crews. They were set up satellite-style in each district to ensure New England's Patriarca crime family, based in Federal Hill, could keep close tabs on all the local underworld action that they controlled. Why limit yourself as an earner by making rivalries with affiliations? He had more money than most of the guys he knew anyway. In fact, Angelo would grow to have a disdain for wiseguys. He figured they made themselves partners in money that they didn't earn: Whether it was booking, fencing, or protection, Providence's Patriarca family ultimately got a piece. Angelo, however, operated with a free pass because wiseguys always knew they could unload their merchandise, getting top dollar. Angelo always had a pocketful of money, at least five grand, C-notes always on the bottom, making sure to never show his poke. As a result, he could buy any stolen ticket—immediately C.O.D.

The large sums of money he made fencing hot goods between Monday and Friday was used as his bankroll for weekend gambling and cabareting sprees. Friday nights were craps games in The Hill's Decatur Square. Saturday nights usually meant *mangia bevé* [eating and drinking] and broads at the El Morocco supper club, barely home on time to get ready for Sunday morning's Silver Lake craps game. Most Monday mornings he would be close to broke, or have at least ten or fifteen thousand tucked away safely in his boot.

Soon his lifestyle would undergo some changes: Angelo met and married Louise Monte in 1952. He noticed the petite 27-year-old several days in a row at a bus stop waiting for the downtown connector to take her to her job as a seamstress at Shepards Department store. Angelo glided by in his Chrysler, made small talk, and courted her from across his bench seat for about a week every day like clockwork. Louise finally accepted his overtures. It was a story repeated countless times: neighborhood guy meets neighborhood girl, and they start to look for a house in the suburbs.

In fall of 1955, the first of his two children was born, a daughter, Doreen. Seven years later, in 1962, Louise gave birth to a son, Vinny. Due to growing family obligations and concerns, one would figure Angelo would have to grow more conservative in his laissez- faire lifestyle, right? Wrong. In fact, Angelo felt a greater pressure to earn as much money as possible to support his family while supplementing and maintaining his lifestyle outside the home. He always took great pride in providing for his family and his marriage to Louise, which was what a lot of Italian marriages were in those days, an extension of motherly care. Cooking, domestic chores, raising kids, etc. There was love, but almost in some kind of medieval king of the cave manner. When once asked by Vinny as a little boy if his father loved the woman he married in 1952, Angelo responded to Vinny's question. "What are ya kidding? Your mother was the catch of the neighborhood. She could always clean top to bottom."

5 This Thing of Ours

In the years to follow, Angelo's world changed. The center of his world became a humble two-story tenement in Cranston, a suburb of Providence. Three doors down the hall on the left was a short-ceilinged, 4 1/2-foot by 8 1/2-foot hovel Vinny called his greatest impediment—his bedroom. He always told his father if he had had a bigger bedroom when he was a kid, he would have gone on to be heavyweight champ of the world. He had no choice but to stop growing at 5' 7".

The most important day of the week for Angelo was Sunday. Sunday morning meant watching Vinny play football, Sunday afternoon was rigatoni, and taking action while watching the New York Giants.

To Vinny, Sunday was game day. The Edgewood Eagles were Rhode Island pre-teen champs four consecutive years. Vinny was captain for two years, and the team was unscored upon for two years. Angelo looked on intently as Vinny organized his team into rows for pregame warm-ups. It was here Vinny found a comfort zone, in an arena ready to do battle with other 13- and

14-year-olds. He barked orders at both the organized and disorganized teammates.

"Helmets on! Helmets on! Let's go! Buckle your chinstraps! Let's go!" There was no need for any of the five coaches to interfere; one 13-year-old had already begun the pregame drills, "Get in line, lateral stretch, 1, 2, 3, 1, 2, 3 . . . 1, 2, 3 . . ." He walked the rows like a drill sergeant, slapping helmets and punching the shoulder pads of his teammates, "We're gonna kick ass today," Vinny barked.

The day started with Angelo escorting Vinny proudly to the Cranston Stadium. It was here Vinny would demonstrate his coming of manhood to his father and himself. Even in this venue, at this young age, there is a hierarchy of command. It is based solely on strength, both physical and mental.

Angelo knew then what other fathers did not: His son was different from the other kids. He saw it in his eyes, and he was not reluctant to tell the other fathers his kid was different. Oftentimes, Angelo made claims like a prophet about his son who had barely reached puberty.

"My kid has balls, you see, he's got balls. Vinny ain't afraid of nobody." He cupped his hands in parenthesis. "Vinny is gonna be a pro because he's got balls." The other fathers often felt Angelo was too brash and outspoken. But Angelo wasn't diminishing the abilities of the other boys. He liked all the kids and rooted for all the kids. He was just pro-son—pro-Vinny.

Angelo knew what all the boys who played knew—me and Tommy Mart included—but could not tell their fathers: Vinny was different. His eyes were piercing behind the mask. The boys told their dads he was "good." How could they tell their fathers the 13-year-old, 95-pound kid unmasked their truth?

They didn't like pain; they were tough, but there were limits. Vinny was a truth machine; his eyes revealed that, and his play and his athletic demeanor demonstrated that truth would be told between the lines. Who would be more determined? Who would take the first step back? Whose character would bend if not break? His piercing eyes never wavered, never blinked. Angelo knew,

Vinny knew, the other kids knew. Only the other fathers behind the fence did not know.

Angelo realized he was also different from the fathers behind the fence. He was from another time, another place. He had Vinny later than most, 42. He was a bit older, in his mid-50s. Most of the fathers were in their 30s. He was gray, spoke broken English in a rough gravelly tone, and was very animated when telling stories or talking to the kids or coaches. As far as Angelo was concerned, these children were no longer boys: They were young men who already had begun to establish characteristics that would carry them to success or lead them to failure. He did not let the fact that he was obviously older than every father alienate him from his son's childhood. In fact, he established with his outgoing, over-the-top personality that he belonged, because he brought a lifetime of experience and a wealth of knowledge to any environment he chose to enter.

Vinny's first friend was his father; after all his father assured him time and time again that "no one could ever protect him" like his old man. "If any son of a bitch ever bothers my kid," raising his hand, clenching a fist with great intensity looking to his son, "I'll kill the bastards. Ya hear, I don't care who they are or where they come from. You tell your old man." If Angelo indulged himself in his homemade vino, his intensity would become greater, louder, and more threatening to hypothetical foes.

Louise understood early on: Her son was first—the son of Angelo. Doreen realized that she too would have to take a backseat to her younger brother: not in the eyes of Louise, who cared and catered to both children equally, but in the eyes of her father who saw his boy as his legacy.

6 Rocky! Rocky!

"Cut me, Mick, cut me. I can't see nothin," Vinny begged from his Park Ave cinema seat. Rocky was doing everything he could to win the heavyweight championship of the world from Apollo Creed, leaving his blood and guts on his stool. It's 1976 and Vinny was watching *Rocky* for the first time from the aging neighborhood theater. Rocky implored his trainer to slit open his swollen eyelids so he could continue to battle.

Vinny called to the screen, encouraging Rocky to keep throwing punches, "The body, Rock, the body!" He bounced in his seat unable to control himself.

"He doesn't like it to the body!" Vinny yelled. Murmurs grew to a chorus of chants throughout our frenzied section, Vinny leading the way: "Roc-ky! Roc-ky!"

"If you don't quiet down, you're out! Last warning." The balding usher at the Park Cinema threatened to kick Vinny out of the theater. As fate would have it, the usher didn't throw him out, and Vinny didn't miss the song, the fight, or "Adrian! Adrian!" If he had, Vinny might have missed his destiny.

I met up with Vinny by chance after the movie, standing in front of the bright black and white marquee.

"I'm going home, Tommy."

"What do ya mean, kid, veal parm? Eggplant parm? We've got practice tomorrow night, fill up."

Vinny shook his head. "I'm not going, I'm gonna work out on my own."

"Vin, we got football practice. What are you talking about? Plus your father will kick your ass if you don't go."

"Yeah, yeah, my father, I'll talk to you tomorrow."

"No, you won't. Your jaw's gonna be wired. Your dad'll kill you if you don't go to practice."

Vinny held out a flyer he pulled from the telephone pole that read OCEAN STATE BOXING. "I'm not going to practice, and I'm going to do this with my father."

"What about football? Vinny? What about ball, man?" He started shadow-boxing around me, throwing punches, backpedaling toward home.

Vinny turned his back and jogged into the dark throwing punches like Rocky Balboa, humming the tune of Bill Conti's "Gonna Fly Now." By the time he reached Watermen Avenue, he was in full-fledged song, huffing and puffing and running down the street.

The next morning Louise and Angelo woke up to find Vinny's empty bed. "Louise, Louise, where's Vinny? He's got school in half an hour and he's not in his room, all his shit is gone."

"Angelo, here he comes, running." She noticed her son come racing down the street as she shook out her mop from her second-story window. *What'd this little bastard do now?* Angelo thought. As Vinny made his way to the top of the stairs, Angelo barked at him like a drill sergeant.

"Let's go, you're gonna be late. You got ten minutes to get to class."

"I'm not going. Listen, Pop, I'm going to training." Vinny took a deep breath. "I wanna box, I'm training to box."

"Oranges? Or what? Box what, Vinny? Are you damp or what,

kid? Box? Why, 'cause you saw some Walt Disney movie down the street? Forget boxing! This is reality, pal," Angelo laughed heartily. "Louise, your kid wants to be like Rocky Graziano, walking backwards. You remember Georgie Arraujo, Vinny?" Angelo sarcastically asked.

Arraujo was a Providence lightweight who once fought and beat the great Sandy Sadler and was considered by many the greatest fighter to ever come out of Rhode Island.

"He comes in the barbershop. Some days he knows my name, some days he doesn't. Some days he tries to pay me twice. I cut hair good, but not that good. Forget about fighting. Play football with your friends. Plus, you already did the boxing thing at CLCF [Cranston League for Cranston's Future], or did you forget?"

"I was 7 years old. I'm 14 now, and I know what I want to do. I wanna box. I ran 3 miles this morning. Listen to what I'm saying, I wanna do this."

"You wanna box?" Angelo's tone turned serious as he shook his finger at Vinny.

"First you play football, because you don't quit—I don't make quitters. You don't quit on people or yourself. You're gonna finish what you start and that goes for boxing too. If you're gonna do this, you're gonna do it right. We're gonna get you a trainer, the right equipment, the right clothes. We're gonna look like the pros. If not, we don't do it. All right, Vinny? Now go get dressed for school."

Vinny knew if he got the consent of his father they would be in for the long haul. There would be no turning back. The point of return would only come as a result of a lack of talent. The end would not come by lack of persistence, nor would it come because an impetuous teen grew bored. Vinny knew this. To his credit, he did not hesitate.

"All right, all right, like the pros." He was in. The only way out would have to come at the pounding hands of another.

As Angelo awaited the novelty of boxing to wear thin, Vinny immersed himself further in his training, his sparring sessions, and the lifestyle of a fighter, from sunup training regimens to drinking eggs for breakfast.

Just like that, Vinny was gone to me and to his friends. We were like most 13-, 14-, and 15-year-olds in the world, undecided, agonizing about whether we should eat Corn Flakes or Cap'n Crunch for breakfast, and Vinny had set his career in motion. He woke up at 5:00 a.m. before school, ran 3 or 4 miles, got to class, earned decent grades, studied after school, and got to Ocean State Boxing in Providence faithfully by 6:00 p.m. He trained two hours a night, come hell or high water. For Vinny and his friends there was no more Park Cinema, no more Edgewood Eagles, and worst of all for me, no more Big Cheese Pizza: in short, no more best friend. In some selfish, demented way, I wanted him to lose—not to be beaten, mind you, just lose so we could go back to the way things were, attending CYO dances, playing street hockey, and trying to feel up the two prettiest Irish girls in the neighborhood, Kate Brown and Kathy Quinn.

But, we knew Vinny best. We knew that he would not lose. There was no history of losing. Vinny was going to pierce his eyes at his opponent through his boxing headgear the same way he pierced through the face mask of his football helmet—with disdain, contempt, and ultimately with utter dominance.

After months of training, Vinny's first amateur fight took place at Cardines Field in Newport in the spring of 1977, six months after seeing *Rocky*, in front of former featherweight champ and boxing legend Willie Pep. Pep had fought over 250 fights and lost but 12. He was truly a fighter who revolutionized the sport, making it a true art form rather than a sport of brute thuggery. "Will-o the Wisp" as he was known actually often won rounds without throwing a single punch. His defense and tactical counter-movements often made opponents look as if they were fighting the invisible man. His career bridged three decades from 1940 to 1966 and he fought the likes of the great Sandy Sadler and the unbreakable Chalky Wright. Pep was a local Connecticut guy who often came to Providence to roll the dice in Angelo's crap game. When Pep found out Vinny would be making his amateur debut, he offered Angelo his support.

To his and my surprise, Vinny would lose; his nose was

bloodied and his eye was blackened. He climbed through the ropes and made his way down the ring stairs, too embarrassed to face his father, Pep, or his buddies.

"Vinny, Vinny, come here," Angelo hollered, cupping his hands to his mouth. "Come here." As Vinny finally arrived with his blood-spattered muscle shirt, Angelo embraced him with a glowing hug.

"All right, Vinny, good job, good job, next time we get 'em, uh." He wiped the sweat from his boy's shoulders with the bloody towel from the trainer's bucket.

"Willie, what'd I tell you about my kid. He's got big-time balls. Look at 'im, he looks like the Rocky movie now. Next time he gets that kid he'll take him. What the hell, the kid had 18 fights, he's 21 for Christ's sake. We'll get em." Angelo offered words of encouragement and immense support. He wasn't about to kick his kid when he was down. He knew the world would do that.

After Vinny's loss, the guys weren't happy like we thought we would be. Tommy Mart and I had come to terms with spending less time with our best friend. And that night we were really proud of him, fighting in front of complete strangers, not being afraid or embarrassed to lose in front of a crowd, risking getting knocked out or having his ass kicked in front of his friends and guys from the neighborhood. That alone took courage. Plus, his friends knew he wasn't going to just quit. He was going to go back to the gym and make himself faster, stronger, and better. And if he lost again, he would go back again, and keep going back until he won, until he won so often he would forget the feeling of losing, making sure he did not have to feel the embarrassment of walking out of the ring, around the ring apron a dejected loser. Having to face his father, friends, and Willie Pep, looking across the ring at another guy, being embraced by trainers, family, and the crowd—that sight to Vinny was intolerable.

7   The Amateurs

By the fall of 1977, Vinny had started to show some great technical improvement in his sparring. His trainer, Freddie LaFazia, who was an Ocean State house trainer, saw the same attributes in Vinny that Angelo recognized early on.

"Vinny had great hand speed and great wheels. He was undersized in terms of height, about 5'5", but had good reflexes and great athletic ability. Vinny was a good student, followed directions real good. Vinny had an intangible you couldn't teach," LaFazia would recall.

"He had the ability to dominate opponents with his sheer will. You can't teach will or determination in this game." In fact, Freddie felt Vinny was coming along so well in the gym, he encouraged him to enter the Junior Olympics in New York, although he was still too young to apply for amateur status (qualifying age was 16). Vinny could not yet enter the Southern New England Golden Gloves.

"Freddie, is my kid ready? The last guy he fought had 18 fights, don't want this kid in there gettin' hurt, ya hear?" Angelo warned.

"Vinny's coming along faster than any kids in this gym; I've seen kids come and go for twenty years; he's way ahead of the curve. No shittin', Vinny could make some noise at the games," Freddie promised.

LaFazia's prediction rang true as Vinny not only made noise as an unseeded fighter, but nearly won the tournament, knocking down the 120-pound favorite twice in the second round. The decision did not go his way, but after only six months of organized boxing, being able to walk away with a silver medal in the national Junior Olympic games was quite an achievement.

"Ange, Paul Morrisette, the promoter who runs the New England Golden Gloves, saw Vinny fight at the show, he was shocked to find out he's a novice, a beginner. Vinny impressed the fuck out of him. Paulie's brought along guys like Marvin Hagler and his kid brother Robbie Sims and other top amateurs, he knows his shit," LaFazia told Angelo excitedly as trainer, father, and fighter boarded the Amtrak 119 at New York's Penn Station to return to Providence. Moreover, Freddie was proud of the work he had done with Vinny.

"Freddie, let me tell ya something, before we go any further, my kid beat that guy, easy. We're not happy, we didn't come over here to come in second or to impress the Frenchmen."

"Ange, that's not the point—" Angelo interrupted Freddie. "My kid is like his old man." Angelo raised his voice, confronting the trainer as a subordinate, poking his finger into his chest. "You're happy with second, we're not. Next time I'm gonna bang out one of those motherfucking judges. You didn't put up no squawk. What the fuck, Freddie, you with us or what?"

Freddie knew at that moment he was an outsider looking in, but he wasn't going to walk away regardless of Angelo's badgering. He knew Vinny had real potential. He was hoping to catch lightning in a bottle with Vinny, thinking he had enough skill to win the nationals and maybe even a chance to earn a spot on the prestigious U.S. Olympic Team.

Over the next two years, 1979 and 1980, Vinny's skills became more refined and he was more determined than ever to redeem his loss at the Junior Nationals. He registered at RIJC (Rhode Island Junior College), majored in business, made honors, but never considered a four-year college. Boxing would be his business. He won a slew of Golden Glove tournaments in Lowell, Massachusetts, and throughout New England, becoming a local golden boy and a big drawing card for promoter Paul Morrisette. Vinny's fighting style was schizophrenic and teetered from ballerina to wild bull, from a graceful boxer, dancing around his opponents in concerto, to a buzz saw, clearing anything in his path. Some nights two or three thousand people would crowd into Lincoln Park to see Vinny fight. Angelo brought guys from all over Providence, Boston, and Fall River. He promoted his kid at daytime craps games, on Atlantic City junkets, during weekend partying sprees, and in every social club around town.

Vinny became the 1981 New England Lightweight Champion and accepted a bid to the National Sports Festival in Syracuse, New York. He would be pitted against the very best amateurs in the country, all Olympic hopefuls, representing every region of the United States.

Vinny would make the transformation from a local up-and-comer to a national boxing prodigy, as he won his three qualifying matches and advanced to the gold medal round of the tournament. The gold medal winner would receive an invitation to the Olympic Training Complex in Colorado Springs and a place on the 1982 U.S. Olympic Team.

All that was left between Vinny and Colorado was the No. 1 ranked lightweight in America, 6'1" Timmy "The Mountain" Raban. The bout was televised nationally on ABC's *Wide World of Sports.*

Raban, who hailed from New Orleans, dominated the first three rounds of the gold medal round with his superior reach; he used his jab to bloody Vinny's face to a crimson red. He stood tall from his back leg, throwing rocketlike crosses, keeping Vinny frustrated and at bay. Vinny trailed the fight badly on all three judges' scorecards. Becoming desperate he abandoned all the boxing technique Freddie had taught him and threw punches frantically from all angles, hitting Raban's forearms, kidneys, even thighs. Each time Vinny crouched to fire, Raban stung his face with his whiplike jab, spilling blood from his nose, unsuccessfully attempting to discourage Vinny's advances by letting him taste his own blood, which ran down his lips. The faster Vinny came forward, the more stinging the punches became.

"Twenty seconds, twenty seconds," the corner hollered to its bloodied but unrelenting fighter. "Vinny, goddammit, put your hands up," Angelo hollered from the corner as he became less concerned with victory and more with Vinny's well-being.

A punch rang through Vinny's ears as he peeked through his headgear at his father with an assuring nod. Vinny saw an opening through his swollen eyes. As Raban threw out a listless jab, Vinny stepped to his right and fired a looping right hand that crushed against the side of Raban's temple, causing his legs to tremble; his torso folded in two, as his eyes disappeared into his forehead as the back of his skull crashed against the canvas.

"Raban is down, Raban is down, 4, 5, 6 . . ." ABC's Chris Schenkel's voice and body rose concomitantly from his ringside chair, his yellow blazer speckled with Vinny's blood.

"Raban's not getting up, the fight is over, out of nowhere the fight is over, Raban won't make the count, Vinny Pazienza has just scored an improbable last-second knockout, à la Raging Bull," Schenkel proclaimed, "and has just become the No. 1 ranked lightweight in the United States. Pazienza has just set himself up—" in dramatic fashion Schenkel's voice rose— "to compete for Olympic gold."

In a flash, with one lightning right hand, Vinny's future became boundless. Boxing architects would now get the chance to sculpt and mold him. If those eight seconds had run their course, he would have been driving back home to Rhode Island with Angelo, back to Ocean State Boxing, back to Paul Morrisette's now seemingly obscure circuit. Instead, he would be boarding a plane headed to Colorado Springs, Colorado, home of the United States Olympic Training Facility, where he would begin his training to take on the world.

In Vinny's mind, the world could wait because he had an order of personal business to take care of in the city. His business there didn't have a particular name or address, but she was 5'10" with long legs, mocha skin, full red lips, and perfect round tits with hard nipples that stared Vinny directly in the eyes.

"Worked the same street for over a year," she told Vinny proudly like she was adding to her resume.

"Skull or trim?" she asked. Vinny didn't know hooker/pimp lingo.

"Blow job or pussy, white boy? Twenty for head, fifty for the pussy." He wanted it all; he deserved it all. This was his reward. So he gave her the fifty. The ebony goddess broke his cherry while Vinny wore his gold medal from the festival around his neck. Finally, at 18, Vinny could go off to war.

Vinny would admit later on that his vision may have been distorted by those eighteen years of anticipation. In retrospect, she probably wasn't 5'10", her skin was a couple of shades darker than mocha, and her lips weren't so full. As for being an ebony goddess . . . well. She was big and boxy, wore a tight fade, lisped when she spoke, and had a large gap in her teeth. In truth, she resembled heavyweight champion Larry Holmes.

Back home, the Pazienzas were invited to Jimmy Birchfield's Classic to celebrate their Sports Festival victory. Jimmy was Rhode Island's answer to New York's famous restaurateur–saloon keeper Toots Shor. He was a great schmoozer and often sponsored athletes and performers who were broke, but who were climbing their way to the top—free dinner, free party, and guests of honor. It was rumored that Birchfield had a piece of welterweight champion Sugar Ray Leonard, and now he was courting Vinny.

While Jimmy Birchfield was courting Vinny to be maybe his next investment opportunity, Tommy Mart and I were courting him to be our next strong safety in our weekly sandlot neighborhood football game. On the Sunday morning following Birchfield's bash, our neighborhood, Federal Hill, was playing its rival neighborhood to the north, Messer Street, also known as the Wrecking Crew. The Wrecking Crew was not made up of guys from the other side of the tracks, because where these animals were from, tracks never got laid. They were all much older, in their mid-20s and beyond, and most of them had a long rap sheet that started with misdemeanor beefs and ended in hard felonies. They even had a taxi squad from which the JV hoodlums-in-waiting were called up to the team in case one of the regulars was locked up for not paying child support or for a bar fight. Their lives revolved around solidifying their reputations as badasses long after adolescence and long after the real world cared who they were. But within those 24 blocks that started from Providence's downtown and rolled westward through old ungentrified Victorian homes, worn-out tenements, and carnivorous streets into the heart of Messer Street onward toward Olneyville, the Wrecking Crew were stars. They were made up of neighborhood legend and mythology, most of them too unorganized to play organized sports.

There was Howie Smith, a 6'3" rangy wide receiver with golden blond hair and a body a pro athlete would envy. His workout regiment consisted of four 40-ounce Budweisers a day, two dime bags, and any pill he could get his tongue on. Then there was Mingo and his brother Moochie. Mingo was a half-white, half-black nationalist who always wore red, black, and green clothes and a matching skullcap, paying homage to the African flag. He was a militant ten years past his time. While most Americans in the country were attempting to come together, Mingo was still talking about the race riots he participated in at Central High School in 1972 and the need to galvanize his people under a postmodern version of the Black Panthers.

Moochie, his kid brother, wasn't as political but was a far better athlete. Moochie had a better disposition, but wouldn't dare talk to anybody from our team when his older brother was around. He gained his rep on the basketball courts of Wiggins Village Housing Project. He aspired to be the East Coast Slick Watts (a point guard for the Seattle Supersonics in the late 1970s). He also wore throwback jerseys twenty-five years before they became fashionable and was the fastest guy on their team without even trying. He just glided to his spots. And there was Todd Harris, the legitimate Division I football prospect with a great game and bad grades. Harris couldn't get into a four-year school regardless of his abilities, forcing him to attend junior college. He soon flunked out of school, losing his scholarship at Dean College in Franklin, Massachusetts, only to come home to top the depth chart at running back for his neighborhood team.

Kevin Stenson was his brooding bodyguard and lead blocker. Stenson, a future professional heavyweight fighter who appeared on Vinny's undercards years later, didn't have too much time left on this earth. "Bam Bam," as he was called, became a leg-breaker for a shylock for an upstart racket guy when he wasn't fighting. Evidently, Bam Bam put too much fear into one of the collectee's bones, as he was found shot in the head in an alley in the south side of Providence. He remained in a coma for years before he finally died.

The first game against the Wrecking Crew a month earlier had ended in a 6–6 tie when a brawl broke out in the second quarter and the game had to be stopped on account of blood. It was the closest Messer Street had come to losing a game in years, as they staked claim to an undefeated record that went back to forever. Not surprisingly, there are no records confirming the achievements of the Wrecking Crew in the archives of the Brown University Library.

When we asked Vinny the night before at the party to be our "monster back," meaning he could rove the field on the defensive side of the ball taking out whomever he liked at his discretion, he wasn't exactly moved. But when we went on to tell him of the free-for-all fight that resulted in three knockouts, fourteen lost teeth, two broken jaws, and a beating handed out with the heel of an onlooker's Giorgio Brutini shoe, Vinny got excited.

"Why don't you just come and say you need a ringer. You wanna use me to bang out a couple guys."

"No, that ain't it, Vin." I appealed to Vinny as a friend first and as an athlete second. "What the fuck, kid, you're never around, we never see you anymore. Plus, you haven't played ball since high school. Remember the Rogers game and when you picked off that pass with eight seconds left?" Vinny's face lit up.

I knew I had him, no need to go on. "Ten o'clock tomorrow morning, be ready."

Our team was made up of younger guys between the ages of 17 and 21 who still hoped to have a life beyond the sandlot gridiron. Ray J, 19 years old, had a 4-inch scar down the right side of his face, from eye to mouth, but no one ever dared call him Scarface. A good athlete, 6 feet 185 pounds, Catholic school–educated, Ray J was de facto caretaker of his three younger siblings and mother. Ray J's father abandoned the family when he was only 11, so Raymond saw to it that his kid sisters and brother always had food on the table and attended the same parochial schools he attended. How he did it I never really knew or never really asked. For instance, one morning I got a call about 4:00 a.m. and I awoke from a groggy sleep to hear Ray J's voice on the other end. "Tommy, wake up, c'mon, wake up . . . you know that black and red Puma sweatsuit top you've been wearing of mine . . . get up and burn it." I assume Raymond wasn't on his way to a day of trading stock.

Ray J was our quarterback and middle linebacker. Raymond was a sweet kid who loved his family and friends more than anything else. He still called his grandmother "nonna" as in, "when the game's over or after the riot squad comes to break up the game against these fucking criminals and gangbangers, I'm going to my nonna's for macaroni." He was a 12-year-old kid stuck in a growing man's body.

Billy French was the safety and tight end. He was called "Billy French" because the sandwiches he made for you at his father's grocery store were always finished off with French's mustard. He ran the corner store at Depasquale Avenue and Europe Street in the neighborhood. He was always such a generous guy; he'd never allow you to pay for the 8-inch pickles that marinated in his big wooden barrel or the cheese sandwiches that he made for you personally. Billy French would split a whole loaf of Italian bread down the middle, layer it with a half a pound of American cheese, and top it off with French's yellow mustard. Billy started shaving at about the age of 11 and driving to Lincoln Greyhound Park about a year before that. As a 20-year-old Billy loved to bet on the dogs and pro football. On Sunday after the neighborhood game, win, lose, or draw, he'd rent a suite at the Biltmore Hotel downtown, go to Stop and Shop Market, and buy $200 worth of food. He'd gamble and eat until the Monday Night Football game ended the following evening. He watched the pro games alone and ate to calm his nerves; and who could blame him, as he bet one hundred times on each game, or $500, then wheeled them into parlays, teasers, and if-reverses. One night he was down so much money and gorging himself in his hotel room to the point that he watched Monday Night Football from the perch of the porcelain toilet, shitting and eating a bowl of Cocoa Puffs at the same time.

Then there was Stevie CeCe, all-state wrestler, football player at the University of Rhode Island. Stevie often missed practice at URI because he was too busy keeping tabs on his girlfriend, a grad student from Long Island named Anna who lived in Coddington Hall on the other side of campus. When she'd go out at night, Stevie would go buy himself newspapers and a box of cigars and sit in front of her dorm until she got home safely at night without any guests. He'd sit in his father's station wagon, light up a stogie at the end of the campus quad, and smoke and read, read and smoke, for hours on end, until Anna finally got home and he tucked her in with his eyes as he looked through the sliding glass doors into the room until the lights went out. He was so exhausted from his stakeouts he'd oversleep most of the time and miss football practice. Stevie never missed a game against the Wrecking Crew though. No matter what time Anna got in, Stevie would make his way back to the city from the North Kingston campus. And lastly there were the Fazios. They were a family of unending brothers who made up the rest of the team. They ranged from age 16 to 21 and they seemed to come in duplicates, some 5'4" and stocky, others 6 feet tall and lanky. It was genetics gone awry. And then there was Tommy Mart and me, and the ringer, Vinny.

This time, the game made it to halftime and the score was deadlocked, both teams' defenses holding the other offense scoreless. But Messer Street was driving down the field and their former star running back, 220-pound Todd Harris, began picking up yardage in big chunks, leaving our defense on its heels. "Let's go," Stevie "CeCe" hollered in the huddle. "We gotta stop 'em on this play. On my mother's soul, we gotta stop 'em, God bless that woman, she's a saint. She's a diabetic. Her sugar was 400 this mornin'." My eyes and Tommy Mart's met in agreement as if to say, "Wow, this guy's a fucking lunatic." *Good defensive call*, I thought sarcastically. How Stevie Calise's mother's bout with diabetes was related to stopping Todd Harris from running wild, I had no idea. Angelo Ballacone, our 155-pound nose tackle and not exactly a Rhodes Scholar candidate, missed the point completely. "Stevie, your mother's a diabetic, she ain't old, is she? My mother's got congestive heart failure. She on insulin?" Ballacone went on more about CeCe's mother.

"Oh, what the fuck, is this Our Lady of Fatima Hospital?" Ray J interrupted, clapping his hands together in a praying motion, shaking, looking up to the sky for answers. "With all due respect to your mother, Stevie, I'm sorry she's gotta suffer but that doesn't mean I gotta too with these stories."

Billy French stepped in quickly before the huddle broke and gave the definitive pep talk. His body led his head to the center of the huddle below everyone else's, his 1970s Billy Kilmer No. 17 Washington Redskins burgundy and gold jersey torn at the shoulder; he looked up through the top of his eyes, looking from left to right, and spoke. "None of us in this huddle are stool pigeons, none of us are rats, like these Messer Street guys in that huddle. Howie Smith, father and his uncle, both rats. Sean Chase's father's a half a cop and Todd Harris ratted on Billy Noto for stealing a fucking Thunderbird. All rats. They'll all be in witness protection in twenty years living in some fucking trailer park in Arizona wearing rugs and hustling encyclopedias." Not exactly Knute Rockne's "win one for the Gipper" speech, but for where we were from, it worked.

As Todd Harris broke through the line, he cut back against the grain, leaving defenders on his right hip as he cut left. Vinny stayed home and held his position as Harris lifted his head and switched the ball to his left hand ready to make his move to the edge, when out of the dusty cloud of dirt rising above the fray Vinny unloaded his right open forearm through Harris's neck, clotheslining him, lifting his feet above his head, and sending the back of his neck slamming to the ground, followed by the rest of his body. At that very moment Angelo's roaring Chrysler came to a sliding dirt halt on the field, just feet from Harris's outstretched body. Angelo summoned Vinny to his dusty car. "What anyone got a beef with my kid. 'Cause if you do we'll handle it right now." He confronted the Wrecking Crew's top thug, Mingo. Angelo reached into his back pocket for his hankerchief and blew his nose. "You're lucky I showed up now before Vinny busted you guys out." He tucked his handkerchief back into his pants and walked to his car accompanied by Tommy and me. "What's the matter with you two and my kid? The three of you got farts in your head? Vinny's going to the Olympics and you two got 'im playin' sandlot ball." With that Angelo sped off for 15 yards and stopped short again, causing another ball of dust to rise above the field. He rolled down his window and called to me and Tommy. "Vinny's mother's making spaghettine and squash flowers today at two, come over."

8   Russia and the Soviets

I f war is an extension of politics, then sports in the Cold War era was an extension of war. The United States, led by President Jimmy Carter, boycotted the 1980 Summer Olympic Games in protest of the Soviet Union's 1979 invasion and occupation of Afghanistan. The summer games, which were held in Moscow, went on without American presence. Political tensions between the two superpowers had escalated with the hostilities playing themselves out in various sports arenas, the 1972 Soviet basketball team stealing the gold and handing the American team their first defeat in Olympic competition, and the U.S. 1980 gold medal hockey team upsetting the great Soviets in Lake Placid. It was Soviet-allied Communist country, Cuba, whose amateur, undefeated fighter, Teofilo Stevenson, was the greatest heavyweight in the world—not American Muhammad Ali, according to the Reds.

Individually they were each great athletes; collectively, they were each countries' symbol of nationalism and political propaganda. Boxing represented this rivalry in its purest sense.

Boxing had both athletic and geopolitical implications. It was more than sports: It was socialism versus capitalism, communism versus democracy, Karl Marx pitted against Adam Smith. It was serious business and held serious ramifications.

When Vinny arrived at the Olympic Training Camp (OTC) in the late summer of 1981, he had mixed emotions. He knew he was among boxing's prestigious elite, as he wore the same USA jersey that Cassius Clay, George Foreman, Joe Frazier and other boxing icons had worn. The dominance of the last competing team, which won six gold medals at the 1976 Montreal Games, left not only a great legacy, but also heightened expectations for future teams. Ray Leonard, Aaron Pryor, Aaron Davis, Michael Spinks, all future professionals, some world champions, and some Hall of Fame members: These were the footsteps and shadows that the 1984 team had to follow. The 1980 team never competed because of the boycott.

Vinny appreciated the sense of history. He knew that if he could win a gold medal in Los Angeles, he could write his own ticket to the pros with a big fat contract, and a big name that meant big fat endorsement deals. "Vinny Paz eats Wheaties while winning gold," along with, "Baseball, apple pie, Chevrolet, and Vinny Paz"?

He could dream of the future, but he lived in the present. Dorm life was like being institutionalized, doing time for a crime he didn't commit. Moreover, if you're a self-admitted *mamone* [momma's boy], who was going to clean your room, iron your shirts, and make you meatballs with raisins? After all, Vinny wasn't even allowed to sleep over at friends' houses when he was a kid. He just wasn't the co-op type. The first couple of days of orientation were like boot camp. The athletes ate when coaches said to eat and slept when they were told to sleep.

Olympic coach Pat Napi was all business: 6:00 a.m. wakeups, jog the hills 5 or 6 miles, and gym work in the afternoon. Most of the kids at the Olympic Training Camp needed the discipline, the regimen, but Vinny did all this stuff on his own anyway. This meant that the training "was no big deal." Work ethic, discipline, and desire were Vinny's built-in characteristics.

Coach Pat Napi was preparing this team to tour the world in 1982. His team would consist of one fighter representing each weight class from 105 pounds to super-heavyweight. Each fighter would have to win his own box-off, in his own weight division, to earn a seat on the team. The tour was touted as USA versus The World. There would be competitions in Ireland, Scandinavia, Yugoslavia, Hungary, the Soviet Union, and Cuba.

The American coaches knew many of the fighters in the Communist and Eastern Bloc nations would be great pros, never mind great amateurs. Because athletes could not turn pro in Communist countries, most retained amateur status to earn a living. As a result, most members of Communist and Eastern Bloc nations' teams were men, not teenagers, had international experience, and most had won medals in previous Olympic competitions. Finally, it was their job and they were dependent on their government to support their families. In short, they couldn't afford to lose their fights. Napi could only take standouts on this tour.

Vinny made friends with most of the fighters at the OTC, although almost all were from backgrounds very different from his: Hispanic kids, like 125-pounder Dino Ramirez from La Puenta, California; black kids from the inner cities like Mike Tyson of Brooklyn; Evander Holyfield of Atlanta; and Meldrick Taylor of Philadelphia. Vinny was a white kid from the suburbs, a white kid who now had a 139-pound black roommate from St. Louis, Vincent Webb. The odd thing was, to the black kids, Vinny wasn't white at all, he was "I-talian." In time, he would be referred to by his teammates as the crazy "I-talian" because of his "colorful" fighting style, meaning that he fought like a black kid, a fighting style fashioned after his boyhood idol Muhammad Ali. It seemed incongruous with the fictional gladiator he worshipped, Rocky Balboa, and his last-man-standing mentality.

Vinny knew, ultimately, he would have to break bones to make his own bones in the ring. And that wouldn't be easy, because before any sparring session took place, Vinny saw raw boxing talent in the gym like he had never seen before.

All of the guys he befriended—Holyfield, Biggs, Whitaker, Taylor, Tyson, Bowe, Hill, Barkley, and many more—were blue-chip studs. If Vinny had any chance of making this team, he would have to have tunnel vision and intensity.

Soon sparring with Vinny became a chore to guys like Pernell Whitaker and Meldrick Taylor, or anyone else close to the 132-pound weight class. He was the No. 1 ranked 132-pound lightweight in the United States, but was still awed by the talent around him. These guys knew the "crazy I-talian" was going to bring it, day in and day out. His training habits were relentless and his sparring was not sparring at all. Instead, they were all-out, balls-to-the-wall fights. He threw, punched, elbowed, delivered body shots, and caused mayhem whenever or for whomever he sparred. Three minutes, three rounds, bell to bell, day in, day out. On one occasion, after slick southpaw Whitaker was knocked to the canvas with a torrid body shot, he complained to both Napi and Vinny. It wasn't Vinny's intent to hurt or embarrass Whitaker; he was just going at the only speed he knew how, furiously. Moreover, Vinny knew these guys were so talented he couldn't digress, period.

Meanwhile Tyson walked the strip malls, exhibiting dual personalities on his days off. One moment he'd be relaxed and joking with his buddies, and the next moment he'd begin intimidating women for "dates," often berating them if the women refused his advances: "Whatsa matter, you don't like me because I'm a nigger? I'll make you my nigger, you fucking white bitch." Often Vinny, who liked the "relaxed" Tyson, would talk him down and convince him to move on. "Mike, just let's go, we'll go see a movie."

Back at camp Vinny called home. "Dad." Vinny called his father for the first time in almost a week.

"Vinny, goddammit, I haven't heard from you in five days, what's going on?"

"Ahh, what's going on, I'm sucking weight again. I gotta stay around 132. I dropped this kid today, Pernell Whitaker from Virgina. He's a slick lefty brother, tough, tough to fight, but I banged his body."

"Good! Good!" Angelo's spirits lifted. "What Napi say? I told him you'd bust those guys out. What kinda name is Pernell anyway? Pernell, Tyrell, Getwell, Jesus Christ." Angelo amused himself.

"Those people don't like it to the body, keep doin' that, Vinny, nobody'll touch ya. You'll bang out all those guys."

"Yeah, Dad, I'll bust everybody out. It's easy right, 'cause I'm out here doin' it. You know how good these guys are." He became irritated with his father. "I watch Dino trying to make weight, 125, starving himself, sitting in saunas, wearing plastics, taking Ex-Lax. Then go out and fight against the best fighters in the country. I hate making weight. I hate dieting."

"I know it ain't easy, Vinny, you wanted this, you wanted to be a fighter. There's always a chair open for you at the barbershop." Angelo knew Vinny would rather take the electric chair than stand behind a barber's chair. And with that said, it was time to say goodbye.

"Love you, Vinny."

"Love you, Pop. Tell Mom I miss her." He wouldn't call home until the next "good" day.

The next good day came sooner rather than later, when Vinny won his first intramural box-offs. The North American Boxing Championships would be his first international competition, held in L.A. In 1981, Vinny started the tournament off with two wins before beating the Canadian lightweight champion in the semifinals, which allowed him to qualify for the finals against two-time Cuban gold medalist Angel Herrera. Herrera won a close split decision, but never seemed to gain control of the fight. Napi was satisfied with Vinny's performance and planned to take him to Cuba six months later to try and avenge his defeat.

In the interim, Napi, so impressed with Vinny's spirit and work ethic, named him Team USA Captain. He would have the honor of carrying the American flag into the ring and at pre- and post-fight ceremonies.

When Vinny entered the ring in the Havana Dome, he was faced with five thousand hostile, whistling Cubans, a military dictator in army fatigues named Fidel Castro, and Angel Herrera. Vinny had two choices: allow the situation to overwhelm him, or he could, with mental toughness, control his surroundings and come out fighting. He chose the latter, as the well-muscled Herrera retreated and tried to counterpunch Vinny, avoiding and countering Vinny's tenacious charges. From ringside, it appeared as if a 28-year-old man was being pestered by a 19-year-old boy who hadn't fully reached puberty. Just when Castro looked to the Cuban coaches with a pleased nod, Vinny unleashed a crushing left hook that sent shock waves through his opponent's skull, down his vertebrae, his legs first buckling, then trembling.

Oh my God, I hurt this motherfucka. Two-time Olympic gold medalist, in front of Fidel Castro, I gotta knock him out. Vinny moved toward him attempting to finish off Herrera. Herrera grabbed Vinny and held his torso and arms, which rested on his waist so tight Vinny felt like he was in a vise. The more Vinny struggled to get out, the tighter the vise became. Herrera would regroup and survive the rest of the fight. When the decision was read at the end of the third round, Vinny's heart was telling him he had won, but his intellect was telling him that he had lost. There's no way he would get a decision in Havana in front of Fidel Castro. To win, he'd have to knock out Herrera. Twice.

The next major stop on the tour would be the USSR: three venues, three competitions broadcast live throughout the Soviet Union. One competition would be held in Moscow, one in Leningrad, and one in the Ukraine. Vinny, although frustrated by his defeat in Havana and bewildered by the amateur international scoring methods, felt confident that he could beat anyone in the world. And like Angelo, Vinny felt he could make money anywhere in the world. Before he left for Russia, Vinny packed all the blue jeans he could find and stuffed them into two hot Louis Vuitton suitcases, which Angelo had brought home from the "barbershop."

Vinny had his pulse on international commodities and knew blue jeans could be sold underground in Russia for at least a hundred dollars a pair, or traded for Russian goods. New Yorker

Pat Napi saw Vinny as an East Coast city slicker, and he too packed Vinny's bag with American "commodities." Vinny was far more slippery in the ring than out of it. As he hustled his wares on the streets of Moscow, he was promptly arrested and jailed for selling unlicensed goods. Coach Napi, who should have been charged as an accessory, picked Vinny up from the Moscow police station. Two hours later, Vinny was arrested again, this time with a red, white, and blue USA gym bag full of Beluga caviar, fur hats, and rubles. Again he was released to Napi, this time with a warning. One more incident would lead to prosecution. Hoping to avoid an international diplomatic blunder, and probably the loss of his job, Napi shadowed Vinny for the rest of the trip.

This time Vinny would leave the Soviet Union dissatisfied. He fought in two of three competitions, in Moscow and Donetsk. He lost split decisions in both Soviet cities. Again, Vinny was left utterly frustrated by a loss in a fight he thought that he had clearly won. Coach Napi kept Vinny from fighting in Leningrad, and gave Vinny's alternate, Charlie Brown, an opportunity to try his luck. Brown did not fare much better.

The rematch of the superpower boxing teams would take place a few months later at War Memorial Coliseum, Syracuse, New York, in the good old U.S. of A. Home cooking, nonhostile judges, and a wildly supportive crowd was just the recipe a now disillusioned Vinny needed. Angel Herrera was the past, and so were Donetsk and Moscow.

Sure, his opponent Victor Domyenko was the 1980 Soviet Union gold medal winner, and sure he was the iron of the Soviet team. Vinny was at home, he had a national following, and he revved up the crowd just like he did back home at Lincoln Park. He was never so sure of himself, never so ready to show Lou Duva and Shelley Finkel, of Main Events, who made the trip up from New Jersey and New York City respectively, that he was the best amateur lightweight fighter in the world, bar none. Shelley Finkel, a New York City rock concert promoter and the moneyman behind Main Events, had seen Vinny fight at the National Sports

Festival two years earlier and had had people whispering in his ear about Vinny ever since.

Domyenko was a stocky left-hander. On paper he presented Vinny many problems. He was cock-strong, awkward, and he was a crisp counter-puncher, with loads of experience and reserves of strength. In the ring, however, Vinny easily solved his style and simply beat him with a combination of power and speed. Domyenko was outboxed and outpunched from bell to bell. He bled from the nose like a stuck pig, breathing heavily from his snout. The blood covered the white CCCP letters blended into his red team shirt, fading his identity. Vinny was brilliant. His feet barely touched the canvas as he dazzled the War Memorial crowd with amazing double and triple jabs followed by hard right hands, which rippled against the head of Victor Domyenko. In the third round, the iron man, Domyenko, met the canvas from one of the many right hands he received from Vinny. But he would endure the beating like the champion he was and finish the fight on his feet.

Finkel and Duva didn't just see a great performance; they heard dollar signs cachinging in their heads. They saw the crowd and how Vinny played to them, almost as if the crowd and Vinny had a symbiotic relationship, almost as if they were one. They saw him race and jump to the turnbuckle as the final bell rung, Vinny's hands raised in victory, the railing crowd with their arms open ready to catch him. It was Vinny at his finest: four parts fighter, three parts warrior, and three parts entertainer.

Shelley and Lou saw not only a white kid, but a white Italian-American, a legacy of Marciano, Pep, LaMotta, and Graziano, a legacy that pulled at the heartstrings, purse strings, and could lead to big draws in heavily populated Italian-American markets: New York, Philadelphia, Chicago, and Boston, big markets and a marketable prospect, a fusion of the old and new. In name and stature, he resembled an era gone by, the golden years of boxing, fighters who were willing to pay the tariff, pain for glory, their heart willing and their minds wanting, like Trojan warriors defending their city in Homer's *Iliad*.

Pat Napi pulled Vinny down from the turnbuckles and harshly reminded him this was amateur competition, where "you don't show up your opponents." As Coach Napi continued to lecture Vinny about the virtues of sportsmanship and gentlemanly behavior, the decision of the fight was read to the crowd. It was barely audible to Vinny, and he thought he heard, "the winner in the blue corner." He flashed his head back, checking the color of his corner, the red corner. What he saw across the ring told him all that he needed to know. Domyenko's hands were raised above his head while the Soviet cornerman patched up his open wounds. To Vinny, the scene played itself out in slow motion, almost like he had no part in the production, but instead was a spectator in the audience of a Broadway play that had gone bad for the lead character.

Two Soviet judges scored the fight for guess whom? Domyenko. Vinny carried the lone American judge; it was a split decision loss for the American.

Angelo chastised Napi before he could work his way down to the ring apron. "Wouldn't it have just been easier to take a head count of the judges. Fuck the fighting! We're wasting our time here. What the fuck, Pat, why does my kid get two Russian judges?" Angelo was doing what he did, what Napi and Freddie LaFazia didn't do, protect Vinny. The crowd booed ferociously. They threw bottles, chairs, fight programs, popcorn, and even folding chairs into the ring.

Lou Duva and Shelley Finkel cared little about the rogue decision. They knew all too well about the politics and larceny of the boxing business. Tonight Vinny Pazienza's heartache couldn't have worked out better for Main Events. This gave Lou Duva more leverage in convincing his prize recruit to turn pro.

Immediately following the fight, Duva and Finkel met with Angelo and Vinny. First they congratulated them on a great fight, but quickly offered the two a dose of reality. Shelley Finkel was refined and distinguished looking. He wore tortoise-shell glasses and a glen plaid Hickey Freeman suit. Shelley took a genuine liking to Vinny.

"Vinny, your style is not geared toward amateur boxing." He offered his opinion, first speaking carefully, calculating each word. "Those judges don't like any flamboyancy whatsoever. Your coaches don't like your bolo punches, or your dancing around the ring. They like mechanical fighters, amateur fighting is about scoring points, not knocking guys out or entertainment."

Lou Duva was short and stout with a jowled and droopy lovable bulldog face. He was a "foist and thoird" Jersey guy who had been knocked around the sport of boxing for forty years. First he boxed, then he trained and managed fighters for years in relative anonymity until he met up with Finkel. Finkel became Duva's partner in the early 1980s when he became Main Events financier and oversaw the promotion for Sugar Ray Leonard versus Tommy Hearns I, one of the first pay-per-view box office bonanzas. As a result, Duva became a boxing big shot in his 50s through his 60s. Duva was a guy Angelo could relate to, a Damon Runyon character who could have been from Silver Lake.

"Vinny, come down to my camp, do some sparring with some of my guys. Shelley's right, you know, the amateur game is wrong for you. You'll never get the decision in a big fight, your style is all wrong."

Meanwhile, back home, Vito Fiore, a fringe wiseguy, who managed and trained local fighters and was in other ways "connected" to the New England pro boxing racket, kept close tabs on Vinny. He promoted small shows at small venues, like Rocky Point and Lincoln Park. At the same time Vinny was being wooed by prestigious Main Events, Vito Fiore offered Angelo five thousand dollars for Vinny's contractual rights over coffee at his Piccolo Roma Bakery.

Angelo stood up and pushed his espresso cup and *sfogiatell* plate across the table. He grinned and reached down into his Florsheim bank and pulled out ten large. He straightened up with a laughing smile, wiping Fiore's shirt clean of powdered sugar.

"With all due respect, Vito, you think my kid needs your 5 Gs? My kid's going big-time. We're going with the Jew from New York and the fat man [which was how he referred to Duva]."

Vinny never knew about the offer until years later; Angelo simply warned him at the time, "street guys or college guys, everybody's out to make a buck." That was the common thread. In Angelo's grand plan, there would be no wiseguys riding Vinny's coattails.

You didn't have to be a Madison Avenue executive to see what Fiore saw when he watched Vinny on ABC's *Wide World of Sports* the year before in the North American Games from Biloxi, Mississippi. Another crowd captivated by Vinny, attaching themselves to Vinny's urgent fighting style, another announcer singing his praises, this time legendary announcer Keith Jackson in his famous Georgian Southern drawl after Vinny pounded out a win against Ireland's Patsy Ormand:

"Vince Pazienza comes into the ring with his big white cowboy hat and . . . his big grin and you just can't help but take a likin' to him." Of course there was really no cowboy hat, but there was a *High Noon*, save-the-day atmosphere that made Vinny seem like Gary Cooper. The fights were followed by great post-fight interviews, something rarely done with amateur fighters . . . except Vinny.

A few weeks after Syracuse, Angelo and Vinny drove down to Totowa, New Jersey, home base of Main Events, to spar with future world champions, featherweight Rocky Lockridge and lightweight Livingstone Bramble. This was Duva's final test and Vinny passed it with flying colors, as he not only held his own, but dominated two of Lou's best protégés.

Vinny's amateur career was history. The 1984 Summer Olympics was now a faded dream, his 112-10 amateur record tabula rasa. One week later, he was 0-0, and Vinny and Angelo officially signed a pro contract with Main Events. The contract included four years guaranteed, with no money up front for exclusive rights to train, manage, and promote Vinny. The first year Main Events agreed to pay Team Pazienza $250 a week, the second year $500, the third year $750, and the fourth year $900. The terms of each fight would be ancillary and supplemental.

This was chump change to Angelo, but not bad for a 20-year-old in 1983. Vinny was excited to become Main Events' main attraction, and of course, Angelo would always help supplement Vinny's lifestyle if he needed more.

Business-wise, Angelo liked the dynamics of Main Events, a Jewish-Italian partnership. Finkel, the moneyman, was shrewd and had a long history of successful business ventures, first with promoting rock concerts, and now boxing.

Duva, the Italian loyalist, could be trusted, because after all, Angelo thought he was a *paisan*.

Angelo wasn't a student of Renaissance literature, because if he were, he might have seen the Machiavelli in Duva. Lou ran his family like the Medicis of sixteenth-century Florence. Dan was his eldest boy, beneficiary of primogeniture, the Princeton-bred lawyer, his top advisor and confidant. Dino, the youngest, was a devoted soldier mentored by Lou the prince, who sat atop his boxing kingdom, his stable of fighters vassals to a feudal lord.

Angelo knew business and knew The Prince was going to take care of his house first. He was going to make his end from Vinny's sweat and toil, which was fine. How generous the prince would be could only be proven in time.

As for Vinny, he was barely 20, and he had blind faith in his Italian connection Lou Duva. He was flattered to be part of the Main Events stable, which included No. 1 middleweight contender Tony Ayala, a world-ranked Bobby Czyz, and Vinny's sparring partners Rocky Lockridge and Livingstone Bramble.

Main Events quickly arranged a hometown press conference to announce the signing of the contract. Rhode Island's premier paper, the *Providence Journal*, and local network affiliates NBC 10, ABC 6, and CBS 12 all attended. Rhode Island didn't have a professional sports franchise, only a Providence College basketball program, which was a decade beyond its glory years of Ernie DiGregorio and Marvin Barnes. As a result, a decorated amateur athlete signing on with a prestigious national boxing promoting team warranted top billing.

Angelo set the venue, Cranston's Antonio's restaurant. Vinny no longer had to be suffocated by his amateur status. Authoritarianism and collectivism, the characteristics of a team, were replaced by crass commercialism, self-promotion, and individu-alism. Vinny wore a white suit with a white cowboy hat, while Angelo echoed behind the scenes that his kid was the second coming of Willie Pep. Vinny promised Lou Duva and the Rhode Island press that he would be their next world champion and that he would make up for the loss of Tony Ayala. Ayala, Main Events' No. 1 prospect, was convicted and sentenced to fifteen to twenty years in prison for the sexual assault and rape of a New Jersey woman the very same day Vinny signed on with Main Events.

The local press played up the local boy does good story and predicted Vinny would singlehandedly save Main Events.

9 Vinny the Pro

With the Olympic training team in his rearview mirror, Vinny debuted in Atlantic City at the Sands Hotel on May 26, 1983, against an overmatched tough plumber from Puerto Rico named Alfredo "Chino" Rivera. Plumber isn't boxing slang for hard worker or comer; he was really a plumber. In fact, Rivera, who was brought in as an "opponent," probably made more money replacing a sink valve in San Juan than he earned that night in Atlantic City. Vinny didn't fare too much better; he netted only twenty-four dollars, which he quickly lost at a Sands blackjack table.

While Angelo played craps on one side of the casino, Vinny snuck down to the tables just before checkout. If Rivera couldn't satisfy Vinny's need for action, perhaps a blackjack dealer could. Plus, only twenty-four dollars after a long training camp and a pro debut? He wasn't trying to break the bank, but he deserved at least a few hundred after all was said and done. Meanwhile, on the other side of the casino, Angelo lost $24,000 on the craps table. In the ring, Vinny had been his usual pugnacious self, a whirling dervish who seemed to be in five places at once, throwing punches in bunches with relentless energy.

This was the cost for forfeiting Olympic exposure. It was almost like being back with Paul Morrisette at the Newport Casino or Lincoln Park, starting all over again from the bottom up: short money purses, no endorsement deals, no pictures on the Wheaties box, no national television cameras. Keith Jackson and the *Wide World of Sports* were absent: Only a local telecast, grainy as the Zapruder film, showed Vinny pummel Rivera into submission in round four—not to mention a five-hour car ride back to Rhode Island.

As Angelo, Vinny, myself, and Nikki made our way up the Garden State Parkway, Angelo wasn't fretting about the $24,000 he had dropped at the blackjack table. He was thinking about Vinny's win and celebrating his way. He was thinking of all things Jersey tomatoes, more specifically tomatoes oreganata, consisting of olive oil, sliced tomatoes, garlic, and fresh oregano, a perfect Italian summertime salad. As Angelo exited the Parkway, he followed signs that led him to a creamery/burger joint. As Vinny, Nikki, and I looked up and down the oversize menu made up mostly of potato skins and ice cream sundaes, a wide-eyed teenage waitress approached the table.

"May I offer you something to dri—?" Angelo interrupted in mid-sentence and growled. "I want tomatoes oreganata."

"Excuse me, sir, I don't think we have that. I've never heard—" Angelo interrupted again.

"I said I want tomatoes oreganata, what do you mean you never heard of it. Go get the chef." Two minutes later, the 17-year-old, very white, very American waitress led Angelo to the kitchen where he put a white apron over his beige Canali sportjacket and began showing the 18-year-old Puerto Rican fry cook how to cut garlic ever so thinly and lectured him on the importance of extra-virgin olive oil and fresh oregano. The gastronomic lesson continued, "Never use dry spices. They got no flavor."

Vinny, Nikki, and I shook our heads at one another. "It's his world, the rest of us are just along for the ride," Vinny reminded his friends.

Mike Ratte, a friend of Vinny's and a reporter from Cox Cable Rhode Island, did a feature following the win and figured every great story, great fighter, and even not so great fighter needs a nickname. There was, of course, "The Greatest" Ali, "Sugar Ray [I and II]," Rocky "The Rock" Marciano, Roberto "Hands of Stone" Duran, Tommy "Hit Man" Hearns, Mitch "Blood" Green, and the infamous Frank "The Animal" Fletcher. Ratte branded him Vinny "The Pazmanian Devil" Pazienza. The moniker epitomized his personality and fit him like a boxing glove.

In the twelve months forthcoming, Vinny would be challenged more and more by a grueling schedule and less by the quality of his opponents. Lou planned to have him fight eleven times throughout his rookie season, four four-rounders, four six-rounders, and three eight-rounders. There was constant sparring, a constant battle to make the 135-pound weight limit, and constant travel. From May 26 to December 14, 1983, Vinny fought 11 fights and came out professionally unscathed and physically unblemished, recording 11 knockouts. He fought eleven guys, some flying under the boxing radar screen with unfamiliar names like Dangerfield, Zelinski, and Carberry, guys brought in to build his confidence more than challenge him. Six of those fights took place in Atlantic City, now his second hometown, one in Las Vegas, two in Lou's headquarters of Totowa, and one in Beaumont, Texas, on a Rocky Lockridge undercard.

Most of the time Vinny stayed at one of the Duvas' training camps in Great Gorge, New Jersey, or Houston, Texas, or traveled with Lou to various places as chief sparring partner for either Rocky Lockridge or Livingstone Bramble. Both were well- seasoned pros and upcoming world champions. The regimen remained the same for one year. Duva was killing two birds with one stone: free sparring for contenders, earning real paydays, and the rookie learned his craft and fine-tuned his skills with experienced pros. While the bottom line worked out for Lou, the reality was a green 20-year-old workhorse taking a beating every day, regardless of how well or poorly he performed in the sparring sessions. Tough-as-nails, talented fighters shoot their load every day in the gym, becoming used up and burned out professional sparring partners and nothing more. Vinny lived boxing in the present tense. Each day he laced his gloves and strapped his headgear for sparring, saving nothing for tomorrow, achieving only for today. Win each sparring session. Win each round, with each minute within that round. Win each heated exchange. Win the one-minute break between rounds. Stand first and race to the center of the ring at the bell. Competition would challenge his character and will, like those autumn football mornings in Edgewood when he barked orders at teammates, ready to expose the truths within each opponent. He thought of Vince Lombardi, and his gym back home: "Winning isn't a sometime thing, it's an all the time thing."

Rocky Lockridge had already fought for a world title and had thirty fights under his belt. Before Vinny threw one professional punch, he spent one month in San Remo, Italy, getting Lockridge ready for his April 24th date with five-year reigning WBA featherweight king Eusebio Pedroza. The sparring was especially brutal; Rocky was locked in, trying to avenge his first defeat to Pedroza, a fifteen-round loss, three years earlier back in the U.S. As for Vinny, he was trying to impress upon Lou that he belonged in the big time.

If Vinny couldn't make it back home, Angelo brought Rhode Island to both Vinny and his camp. Tommy Brooks, Kenny Weldon, and Georgie Benton were the house trainers for Main Events. While Weldon was based mostly in Houston, Brooks and Benton spent the most time with Vinny. Brooks loved Vinny's speed and footwork. Weldon, a good 'ol Texas boy, loved Vinny because he was white, and Georgie loved Vinny because of Louise's artichokes.

The only reprieve Vinny got during the year was a return home on December 2nd to fight Emilio Diaz at the West Warwick Civic Center. Vinny was 11 and 0, and couldn't wait to get back to Louise, her raisin meatballs, and his hovel of a bedroom.

Seven years into his boxing career, Louise still had never seen Vinny fight, live or on television. She would not be in attendance in West Warwick either. Twenty years later, she would be able to make the same claim. But, she came a long way from the mother in 1976 who at first refused to let her baby fight. Before Angelo consented, she petitioned to him fervently that she didn't want Vinny boxing. The image of punch-drunk Rocky Graziano on his 1960s TV show, theatrically slurring his words, and Georgie Arraujo slowly sauntering into Angelo's barbershop, carefully placing one foot in front of the other, head down to keep his balance, stuck in Louise's brain.

Now on the Vinny bandwagon, part of Team Pazienza, Louise held two posts. The first was as a self-appointed conduit to St. Jude and the Baby Jesus, to ensure her family's safety and well-being in a makeshift kitchen shrine next to Angelo's biscotti and wine biscuits. It would be here that she would spend every fight night for the rest of Vinny's career, candles lit, rosary beads in hand, awaiting Angelo's post-fight phone call. The second was to be an ace VCR operator for newscasts, appearances, talk shows, and fight highlights. Anywhere Vinny's mug appeared, Louise's VCR was taping and editing. Friends later called her hallway closet, a career's worth of tapes in chronological order that were noted and alphabetized, the "Pazedential" library.

The Diaz homecoming fight was anticlimactic and somewhat disappointing. Angelo and Jimmy Birchfield humped the fight around town and ticket sales were good, but not great. It was a Friday night, during Christmas season, a tough sell because money around that time of year is usually short. The venue itself stank; the building was cold, all concrete with bench seats and dim lighting. West Warwick is in an old mill town about 15 miles southwest of Providence, with no trendy restaurants, strip clubs, or casinos, and no pre- or post-fight entertainment, period. About 2,500 quiet loyalists watched Vinny outwork Emilio Diaz. The first two rounds, Vinny looked tight, and he was pressing himself more than Diaz, trying to look perfect, do too much, and finish too fast in front of the hometown crowd. When finally Vinny dropped Diaz in the third with a wicked left hook to the body, the fight ended in a TKO. Diaz made it to his feet, beating the ten count, but wound up breaking his left wrist when trying to break his fall. Vinny gained his ninth victory, but walked away feeling he had cheated the people who paid their hard-earned money to see a great performance. Brooks told Vinny that a win was a win, and to be happy. To Vinny, that was bullshit. A win is a win if people walk out of the auditorium excited, not indifferent. Following West Warwick, it was on the road again.

Vinny's next two fights were against Philly guys. Boxing aficionados, or anyone who knows anything about boxing, knows about the legend of Philadelphia fighters. The reputation of being gutsy, brawny, rugged, and enduring precedes them. Joe Frazier, Joey Giardello, Marvin Hagler, and fictional Rocky Balboa were all comers, no-quit Philly fighters, all guys who made their reps in the gym before ever being able to get on a fight card. Duva planned the last two eight-rounders against Mike Golden and Richie McCain to see whether or not Vinny was able to make the jump to being a full-time ten-round fighter. Golden or McCain were never going to be world champions, or top ten guys for that matter, but they were hardened by the Philly streets and dozens of gym wars. Both were iron jawed, and both would last the eight rounds. Both would lose decisions to Vinny. Richie McCain would take the worst beating of the two, lasting eight rounds, with a jaw swollen the size of a grapefruit. Both were rugged tests; both were good wins. Vinny became a full-time ten-round fighter.

On August 30, one day after the McCain fight, Vinny checked himself into Rhode Island Hospital and went under the care of his father's doctor, Dr. Catanzaro. Vinny had not passed the physical leading up to the fight, but promised Dr. Dogget, who diagnosed Vinny with a double hernia, that he had no pain whatsoever and that he would have it taken care of right after the fight. Dr. Catanzaro did the same operation on Angelo years earlier. In reality, the pain was excruciating. Every time Vinny dug his toes into the canvas and set to punch and to roll his hips, the hernia ripped through his groin, taking away his breath for a second before he was able to refocus and reset himself in his boxing stance. He would be out of action for six weeks with a chance to recover at home before heading back to Italy.

To Main Events, who was orchestrating Vinny's career, there were no real distractions between the April 15th Michael Golden fight and the August 29th Richie McCain fight. But to Vinny, there was one big distraction—the 1984 Olympics in Los Angeles. Vinny watched from his Cranston parlor as his former sparring mates Pernell Whitaker and Meldrick Taylor boxed themselves into Olympic history and the hearts of stars and stripes flag wavers, corporate America, and Main Events: Both won gold medals. Whitaker outshined Luis Ortiz of Peru, and Meldrick Taylor outclassed Nigerian Peter Konwegwachie. They now held the same vaunted status as Leonard, Foreman, Ali, and other American Olympic gold medal winners, and now they were big-time breadwinners.

Moreover, Lou was in Los Angeles leading a Main Events coup in the boxing world. Main Events' rivals, the bombastic Don King and erudite Bob Arum, sat idly by as Main Events raided the U.S. boxing team, signing five of its thirteen medal-winning fighters: lightweights Meldrick Taylor and Pernell Whitaker; welterweight Mark Breland; and heavyweight Tyrell Biggs. All won gold medals. Light-heavyweight Evander Holyfield would have been a gold medalist, but he was disqualified for hitting his opponent after the bell in his semifinal match, knocking him out cold. He wound up with a disappointing bronze medal.

Angelo knew that Vinny didn't give a shit about the business side of it. He knew Vinny's heart was aching watching Whitaker. Angelo sat with his legs up in his recliner, white socks showing beyond his moccasin slippers.

"Vinny, you knocked this guy down, he didn't wanna fight with you. I know, Vinny, we're gonna get what we need to get, a world title. Don't worry about this. Look what you did to Bramble and look where he is now."

Vinny knew Angelo was kidding him and he'd be kidding himself. He could have knocked Whitaker down one thousand times, but he would never have a gold medal. Regardless of how he felt, Vinny knew he had to bury those feelings of disappointment. "I know, Pop, I know." He remembered Whitaker at the

OTC drinking and smoking pot nights before major box-offs and he'd just dominate guys, seemingly going half-speed. But that's what was going to get Vinny over the top, focusing on the positive, diminishing the negative, the proverbial glass always half full. He knew as long as his tools were good enough to get him in the game, his preparation, desire, sheer will, and determination could make anything happen. Focus on what makes you win, not what the opponent has to make you lose.

When Vinny boarded his flight at Boston's Logan Airport to head to Italy, he felt more like a mercenary than a fighter. He was going abroad to fight for Main Events instead of remaining home in the States where he wanted to redeem himself for the disappointing Diaz showing. Lou had other plans. He wanted to showcase Vinny's talents abroad to European markets, more specifically the Italian market where boxing was wildly popular, and second only to their national pastime, soccer. Duva felt Vinny, the flashy up-and-coming Italian-American, would resonate with Italian fans. On November 9, in Riva Del Garda, Vinny easily dispatched of Italian junior-welterweight champion Bruno Simili in his first ten-round fight, finishing him off in three rounds. He now had 11 knockouts in his 13 professional wins.

There were no signs of pain or pause for concern from the lingering hernia operation. Vinny seemed to be back to 100 percent. Three weeks later, it was on to Italy's fashion capital, Milan. Lou penciled in Vinny for an appearance on NBC Showtime boxing and a December 1st boxing date with Syrian Abdelkader Marbi. The fight would be shown on tape delay back in the United States. It was one last fight before a well-deserved Christmas break. Marbi was an unspectacular, but dangerous, fighter. In boxing circles he was known as a billy goat, or head-butt artist. He jabbed and butted, hooked and butted, tied you up from underneath, grabbed your waist and came up from under your chin and butted. As Vinny warmed up in the dressing room, Tommy Brooks held the hand pads as Vinny threw electric combinations, causing firecracker-like sounds to exit the dressing room. "Vinny, step away from this guy after you punch." Brooks demonstrated with close hooks, throwing out his fists and rolling his shoulders. "Give him angles, side to side, don't get tangled up with him." His warnings were in vain because once the fight started, Marbi draped himself on Vinny like a JCPenney suit, awkwardly holding and grabbing him, not allowing him a rhythm.

His boxing style had no rhyme or reason; he was just there in the middle of the ring, unpredictable, coming forward like a crab. Rounds one and two were standoffs, and it was impossible for the judges to get an accurate gauge from all the clutching and grabbing of Marbi. The third started with Vinny bobbing and weaving trying to expose an opening in the outclassed Marbi's stance. As Vinny jabbed forward, Marbi ducked his head and jammed it into Vinny's brow. Vinny backed away from him and wiped sweat from his forehead until it poured down so profusely that he didn't have time to keep wiping. He felt cool air on his forehead, looked down on his glove and pawed at his eyes. He saw the white tape around the wrist of his glove drenched in red. As he looked more closely at his Everlast glove, it was also sopping red. The gash above his opened right eye was about an inch and a half long and about an eighth of an inch deep.

Jesus Christ, Vinny thought, charging Marbi. Baited into his barroom style, Vinny clutched him under the throat, shoving him with his forearm, wailing punches in no sequence, with wild abandonment. Marbi had leveled the playing field. It was suddenly two guys swinging from their hips, hooking blow for blow, now a fifty-fifty shot to win, a puncher's chance.

The bell rung and Angelo climbed the stairs attempting to get at Marbi. Lou held Angelo back, grabbing his red, black, and green Paz corner jacket, tearing the zipper apart. Vinny sat on his stool and tilted his head back while Lou began working feverishly on the cut, loudly giving Vinny instructions above the whistling crowd. "You're boxing beautiful now, baby, do just what ya did in the third. He'll go, I'm tellin' ya. He'll go. Vinny, you need to knock this guy out, ya hear me, Vinny?" Lou stuck a Q-tip deep into the cut, soaking the swab red to the end of the stick, got another and did the same.

Brooks stood on the apron of the ring: "Butt, ref, butt, make the call." If the referee called a butt and the fight was stopped before round five it would be called a no-decision. However, if the fight was stopped with the ruling that a punch had caused the cut, Vinny would lose by TKO. If the fight was stopped after the fifth round as a result of the butt, the judges' scorecards would determine the winner.

The referee shook Brooks off, motioning with his fist that the cut came from a punch, a poor call that changed the complexion of the fight completely. Vinny would need a knockout, because this cut could not be closed by the corner. Following the fight he would require thirty stitches.

Vinny stuck out his tongue for water, looked to Lou and gurgled "aahh." He spit the water into the bucket and looked down as he rose from his stool. His eyes fixated on his boots, then upward to his calves and knees. His blood mingled with his sweat, stuck to his legs and stained his once white shorts a light maroon. Vinny stared at the opposite corner, his arms dangling by his sides, kicking each leg forward trying to shake himself dry, the mat beneath him stained by a puddle of blood and sweat. The sour smell of blood rose as the bell sounded for round four.

Vinny attempted to race to the center of the ring, but Lou held on to Vinny's head, smearing a palm full of Vaseline into the cut in order to stem the flow of blood. The fourth round brought more of the same as the first three, more clutching, holding, butting. Vinny became more and more desperate as a result of the deepening cut. "This is it, Vinny, you hear me? They're gonna stop this motherfucker on ya, ya hear, Vinny?" Lou rallied him. He could see the frustration growing in Vinny's eyes and weighing on his body.

For the first time as a pro, Vinny was being tested. It's not what happens, it's how you respond. He would have to go beyond the psychology of a massive cut. Could he continue to fight with a river of streaming blood blurring his vision, catching punches from unseen places? Would he become apprehensive and tentative, regress into a defensive shell, a basic human instinct to protect oneself? If he went all out now, exerting all his energy trying for the knockout he desperately needed, would he be able to finish the eight rounds or would he run out of gas? All unanswered questions, part of the self-doubt all humans have, but most never have to confront so boldly. Vinny would have to confront his tonight, in Milan.

Finally, in round five, the fight began to sway in Vinny's favor. Angelo always told Vinny, whether playing blackjack or craps, the longer you're on the table, the worse your odds become, and the house gets the edge. Marbi's run against the house was coming to an end. His dirty tactics hadn't ended the fight, and now he stayed too long, unable to take out his opponent.

As for Vinny, he was finding out he had the talent; he was the house. He could stay. He held more chips. And, as each second passed, he knew he belonged, regardless of the blood, the cut, the opponent. Vinny was the house and the house was finding its range, bombing Marbi with right and left hands to the body, walking through the bettor, calling in his chips. He strode toward Marbi now, his hands down, landing punches at will, following him into the corner, flushing the will of response from Marbi. The referee jumped in, grabbing Vinny from his back, pushing him to the opposite corner, waving his arms "fight's over, fight's over." Vinny ran to Lou, arms up in what should have been victory . . . except the referee was stopping the fight on cuts—Vinny's cut.

Marbi was slumped on the ropes, looking dazed and confused, his hand held up in victory like Victor Domyenko's from the blue corner, like Angel Herrera's in the Havana Dome. Again the politics of boxing seemed to be rearing its venomous head to a snake-bitten Vinny. Angelo jumped the apron of the ring, past Lou and Vinny, and reached for the referee. NBC cameras focused on Angelo, center screen. TV analyst Ferdie Pacheco attempted to give play-by-play of the melee unfolding around Vinny, but Angelo drowned out any other audio. "You're in the bag, you cocksucker! I'll kill ya, you fucking thief! You're in the bag, you're in the bag, you ain't robbing my kid!" Again, Angelo extended his arms, reaching out to grab hold of anybody; the first person he reached would be paying the retribution.

This time, Tommy Brooks restrained Angelo. He straddled Angelo's thick, wide frame from behind and held him tightly at the waist. Lou joined in the fracas with Angelo, this time contesting the decision directly to the Italian boxing commissioner, who was on-site. Ultimately, the TKO was changed to a no contest and the phantom punch that caused the cut was ruled a butt. The fight never made it past the fifth round, and as a result, never went to the judges' scorecards. At first, Marbi was declared the winner to both the outrage of the crowd and to Vinny. Only hours after the fight, the Italian boxing commission ruled the fight a no contest because the fight never made it past the fifth round. In short there was no winner.

Incredibly, a couple years later, after Vinny won his first world title, the decision was reversed again in favor of Marbi by the Italian Boxing Commission. The Marbi fight appeared on Vinny's fight record as his first professional defeat by way of TKO as a result of cuts. In the larger scheme of things, the loss would never matter or slow Vinny's progress. The Milan decision was boxing business as usual. But the fight cemented Vinny's maturity and growth in the ring.

Confidence is only gained through demonstrated ability. Vinny answered the open-ended questions of self-doubt and proved to himself he could go on when battered and bleeding. He could command his psyche when in doubt of himself. He would take his game to a higher level if he were pushed. His tools would keep him in the game, and he could rely on his heart in the future.

Following the fight, Vinny faced the longest moratorium of his young career. The thirty stitches he received after the Marbi fight put him out of action for three months. He was in boxing purgatory, unable to train or spar or make a date for his sixteenth fight. On the bright side, he was able to spend Christmas at home and sport around town in his brand new black BMW 318i, license plate PAZMAN. He had become a Rhode Island celebrity by now and everybody who liked Vinny was in some way affiliated with him. Strangers claimed to be family members or friends. In Rhode Island, it wasn't enough to just root for the guy, there had to be some affiliation or self-interest. They weren't just going to give him their hearts, just yet. "Yeah, you know, I'm tight with Vinny, he's my aunt's sister's cousin's friend's friend. I'll get ya tickets."

Conversely, with Vinny's growing celebrity and success the Louie Barones of the world were beginning to surface. They were put off by Vinny's brashness and ironically by his clothing. Guys were standing on corners or hanging in social clubs discussing and dissecting Vinny's wardrobe. These were not real fashion plates mind you, with salmon-colored Sansabelt, double-knitted waistband slacks, and turquoise Members Only jackets, finished off with white shoes and four-seamed black nylon socks. In Rhode Island, Labor Day never comes.

"This kid thinks he's a *muli* [derogatory slang for a black person], with that *muli* car of his and his blue leather pants, sunglasses, cowboy hats . . . the whole world's upside down. His father's gotta talk to this kid, he ashamed he's Italian or what?" The "or what" was usually rhetorical. "You think Marciano or Willie Pep would dress like that, or put fringe or tassels or what the fuck ever on his shorts? Get in the ring, fight, and shut up." But *they* shut up as soon as Angelo came around. Most didn't have the gall to criticize Vinny in front of Angelo. Plus, now they felt like they had to eat shit if they were rooting against Vinny. He was 14-0, he was fighting on national television, and he was close to being internationally ranked by one of the two boxing councils, WBA or WBC. Being a Main Events fighter carried that kind of weight. And of course Angelo was still going on about Vinny being the next Willie Pep.

On March 27th, Vinny went back to work in his other hometown of Atlantic City. His twelve-week hiatus from the ring seemed to re-energize him as he easily discarded Antoine Lark in three rounds. There were no ill effects from the layoff or from the scar tissue that thirty stitches left behind. It was on to bigger and better things and a fight with a cock-strong country boy from Elkhart, Indiana, by the name of Jeff Bumphus. Bumphus was

19-2 and had never been knocked out or down. His only loss over his last 17 fights was to future lightweight world champion Greg Haugen. Haugen and Vinny were on a collision course to meet in high-stakes matches, but neither had ever heard of each other at the time.

Bumphus was a real warhorse who always made the final bell. He fought on the obscure Midwest circuit in places like Springfield, Missouri; Davenport, Iowa; and Troy, Indiana. Many of his opponents were suspect, but it was Vinny's first ten-round fight, and that held the real significance. The ten rounds were a potential burden in this fight. Vinny was going to be able to outslug and outbox the bullish country boy, but could he last the ten rounds? Was his body programmed to go that far? Did he prepare properly? Again, those debilitating questions of self-doubt crept up. But Vinny thought of the Marbi fight and his demonstrated ability. He made it through that bloodbath; he could make the ten rounds.

The Bumphus fight went according to plan: a ten-round decision followed by a Thanksgiving date with a top-ranked fighter by the name of Melvin Paul on USA's *Tuesday Night Fights*. Paul hailed from New Orleans, a good omen for Vinny. Timmy Raban, the mountain Vinny defeated at the national sports festival, hailed from New Orleans.

But unlike Raban, Paul was an experienced pro with 30 fights. He had 22 wins and had already fought for a world title against Charlie Brown, losing a fifteen-round split decision. In addition, he already had 5 ten-round fights to his credit. He fought anybody who was anybody in the lightweight division, including tough-as-steel Tyrone Crawley, crafty counter-puncher Terrence Ali, and the great Hector Camacho. Paul was far and away the most talented and experienced fighter Vinny had seen. He was a slick counter-puncher who was patient and calculating. He capitalized on mistakes and made you pay dearly for them.

The Paul fight was Vinny's third fight of 1985. As the year progressed, the training camps became less grueling, albeit lonely. The result was a remarkably fresh and focused Vinny. Lou limited the sparring with Bramble and Lockridge because he was beginning to recognize Vinny might be a keeper and ready for big-time boxing. But Melvin Paul would find out before Lou.

Prior to the fight at the Sands Hotel and Casino, Vinny drank a very large espresso and the caffeine rushed through his system. He dressed in white trunks lined with red, white, and green glitter. He bounced to the music in the background. Lou held the hand pads, and his arms flew back as Vinny's punches ended with a crisp finish. Lou reassured him: "Beautiful, baby, beautiful, you're gonna be a thing of beauty out there tonight." Even to Lou, Vinny's hands felt heavier than normal. They just had an extra snap to them. His back rolled from side to side smoothly with little wasted motion. Angelo rubbed Vaseline above Vinny's eyes, paying special attention to his scar tissue.

Father-son relationships in boxing don't usually work. What happens is one of two things, and both are spun around the notion of warped objectivity. In the first scenario, the father may be so emotionally attached that he can't bear to watch his offspring being hurt, and as a result doesn't push the fighter far enough or helps him with excuses to justify losing. The father cannot draw the distinction between son and fighter. The second scenario, and the more dangerous of the two, is the overly antagonistic father who thinks his offspring is a reflection of himself. He lives his life's frustrations, whatever they may be, through his son, pushing him over the edge farther than he needs to be pushed, the classic Little League dad, fulfilling his own unrealized dreams through his child.

But Angelo didn't fall into either category: He seemed to straddle the fence perfectly. He supported Vinny in tough times, through long training camps and tough fights with affection and fatherly love, taking care of his cuts, by his side watching his son piss blood from wicked body blows in hospitals, and faraway hotels. He grounded him when Vinny was beginning to live on his 16-0 laurels, always reminding him, "you ain't won nothing yet, Vinny." And on the outside he was still the father behind the fence, like he was at the Cranston Stadium, this time selling

Vinny to Lou and Shelley, this time protecting Vinny from the Duvas, making sure his kid got equal billing and equal attention with the Olympic kids Whitaker, Taylor, Holyfield, and Breland. "You'll see, Lou, my kid's got more balls than all of those guys, he's gonna outlast 'em all," Angelo promised.

When Tommy Brooks finished gloving Vinny up, he stormed the dressing room. He weighed 135, but felt like he was carrying heavyweight fists in his gloves. By the second round, Melvin Paul would have thought so too. As he jabbed with Vinny, he neglected one of the essential rules of boxing, bringing back your hands. His jab was listless and lazy like his Louisiana counterpart Timmy Raban. Vinny just dotted a little to the left and a little to the right, slyly measuring his opponent. He whirled his right hand in a circular motion hypnotizing Paul with it for a split second and *wham*, a looping overhand right that twisted Paul's jaw to the right side of his shoulder. His head swung like a gate in a storm, then it corkscrewed back facing Vinny. A glazed faraway look in his eyes, Paul's arms stiffened to his front and his paralyzed torso flopped onto the Budweiser logo.

Vinny was 17 and 0, with a nationally televised knockout of a top ten guy. It was the 1985 *KO* magazine punch of the year and knockout of the year. Thanks to the Melvin, the new name for Vinny's sweeping right hand, the Pazmanian Devil entered the den of big-time boxing.

10   Little Joe and a Big Draw

In the early to middle 1970s, Sylvester Stallone buried himself in his Hell's Kitchen apartment and wrote the screenplay to *Rocky*, an American classic, a true to life Horatio Alger, rags to riches story that symbolized the essence of our country's history, values, and ideals. It reflected and reaffirmed a constitution of beliefs ingrained in our hearts and socialized into our psyche. The notions of freedom, integrity, work ethic, opportunity, and self-determination were bedrocked within the film. But those fundamental American principles, which defined the character still in Stallone's head, were being re-examined in this turbulent decade.

Ten long years of struggling during Vietnam, Watergate, feminism, and the civil rights movement had worn out and shredded the fabric of our nation. America's soul was purged and its ideologies were under attack with the assassination of President John F. Kennedy, his brother Robert, Martin Luther King Jr., and Malcolm X. We were a nation polarized by the establishment and anti-establishment. We were a nation divided among ourselves.

A heavyweight championship fight in 1971 mirrored all the political discontent of a country in turmoil. Ladies and gentlemen, the ring announcer: "In this corner, from Louisville, Kentucky, weighing 210 pounds, the left corner, representing the anti-establishment, the Commies, the activist reformers, the subversives, The Greatest, Muhammad Ali." Ali was a member of the Nation of Islam; he was a conscientious objector to the Vietnam War and was stripped of his heavyweight title belt in 1968. He would find out four weeks following his legendary March fight with Smokin' Joe Frazier if he was going to prison. He represented instability. The announcer went on. "And in the right corner, representing the right, the establishment, the status quo, his opponent weighting 202 pounds from Philadelphia, Pennsylvania, the undisputed Heavyweight Champion of the World, Smokin' Joe Frazier." Frazier was born in South Carolina, the son of a sharecropper, and he was truly living the American dream. He was a transplanted apolitical Philadelphian who strolled into one of Philly's many gyms. He became a fighter who won the gold medal in Athens, Greece in 1964, and fought himself out of poverty, lifting himself up by his bootstraps. He was Horatio Alger with a brutal left hook. He was Rocky Balboa, the embodiment of stability.

Fast-forward five years to 1976: Sylvester Stallone helped heal a nation. The Vietnam War had ended, racial tensions had calmed, and feminists had won Title IX. Americans were looking for a diversion from the misery of the past decade, and trying to find a way to put the broken pieces of the puzzle back together. As the country celebrated its Bicentennial, *Rocky* hit theaters. The story of Rocky Balboa, getting his chance to improve his lot in life, reaffirmed what was good about our country. Stallone's character had the virtues that both Ali and Frazier held: idealistic and principled, determined and unwavering, caring and fragile. Rocky Balboa was a caricature of them as men, and of America as a nation.

Now one of those icons, and one of Sylvester Stallone's inspirations no less, Smokin' Joe Frazier, was coming to Providence, Rhode Island, on February 5th, eight years after Vinny almost got bounced from the Park Cinema. He was coming to Vinny, who of course became a fighter because of Rocky Balboa, and whose story was woven closely to the very real life of Joe Frazier.

Vinny's world was coming full circle. Of course Vinny wasn't going to fight big Joe Frazier, who had retired and outweighed him by about 90 pounds. He was going to fight Little Joe Frazier, who was the spitting image of Papa Joe.

Little Joe was square and stocky; his head was round and small. He took short forward steps, shimmying his shoulders and bobbing his head. And of course, he always finished with a pronounced, classic, short jaw-breaking left hook, just like his father. When Lou brought the idea of fighting Joe Frazier Jr. to Angelo, he was thrilled. Vinny was getting the attention he was due from Main Events. The fight was at the Providence Civic Center, the largest venue Vinny had ever fought in. Angelo saw great potential for filling the seats. He knew Vinny was going to be awe-inspired, meeting Smokin' Joe, the man who knocked down and defeated his boyhood idol in Madison Square Garden while the world was watching. Moreover, Angelo knew how disappointed Vinny was after the Diaz fight in West Warwick. Now he could come home and atone for that lackluster show.

And that he did. Vinny turned in a dazzling performance, TKO-ing Joe Frazier Jr. in the seventh round, more than making up for the Diaz fight. The fight was beyond the fevered crowd's expectations as Vinny brought the house down, first with his entrance into the ring with a huge entourage and a boxing robe lit up with lights, and then with his masterful boxing lesson as he defeated Joe Frazier Jr. Joe Frazier Sr. was impressed. The ever-pessimistic Providence crowd was impressed. But were Main Events and Lou Duva impressed?

As Lou walked Vinny down the tunnel and into the ring, he was in awe of almost twelve thousand people who filled the Civic Center on this night. Expecting a crowd of three to four thousand people, he never imagined in his wildest dreams that Vinny would sell out the joint. Or should I say that Vinny and Angelo would sell out the joint. For weeks before the fight, Angelo, like in the amateur days, humped the fight all over New England.

He made contacts in Boston with ticket agencies, talking up his kid. He prognosticated tirelessly on the street like an Italian Don King, espousing Vinny as the second coming of his friend Willie Pep. Pep was along for the ride as well with Angelo, selling the fight on radio talk shows, in articles in the *Providence Journal*, and anywhere else people would listen. Angelo even paid for advertising out of his own pocket, supplementing the more conventional practices of Main Events, who paid for the bulk of promoting the fight. Angelo didn't give a shit about the money; it was going toward Vinny's career, and what was good for Vinny was good for Angelo.

Prior to the fight, Vinny woke up from his pre-fight nap at the Holiday Inn, which abutted the Providence Civic Center on the edge of Interstate 95. He pulled back the curtains from his fifth-floor room and looked down to see, to his amazement, locals in bunches hustling past the hotel into the arena. *Are these people here for me?* he thought to himself. The knock at the door would give him the answer. It was the 320-pound, bigger-than-life Henry "Fat Clemenza" Broccoli, with two boxes, one full of hats and the other full of pictures. "Henry, what are you doing with that shit up here now? I'm fighting in two hours."

Broccoli explained as he caught his breath and wheezed. "Vinny, your father is selling out like there's no tomorrow. All your shit's gone, hats, shirts, pins, pictures."

"I signed over a thousand of those things already." It was beginning to hit Vinny; this show was a turning point. Olympic obscurity was a thing of the past. One show, one great fight, one box-office bonanza. Tonight he would get everybody's attention: his home town; the WBC, IBF, and WBA boxing commissions, who would each give him a top ten international ranking; and especially the Duvas, who would now begin to view Vinny in a different light. It was the same light that was shining on Holyfield, Whitaker, and Taylor.

Fans and friends gathered at the post-fight party held at Jimmy Birchfield's Classic restaurant. Angelo celebrated, buying bottles of wine and rounds of drinks for friends, fans, and hangers-on.

Joe Frazier Sr. sang Marvin Gaye's "You're the Man" on stage, and Vinny finally entered to a chorus of cheers. He was wearing a gaudy full-length, black mink coat, a gift from Lou Duva. Angelo knew the score. He did the numbers in his head over and over. As Vinny the fighter shook hands, Angelo the businessman focused on those numbers. Fourteen thousand paying customers at an average price of forty dollars a seat . . . he turned to Jimmy. "These swindlers give my kid $25,000 and a piece of shit fur coat, while they're gonna gross a half a million from the gate!? Vinny did the fighting; we for all practical purposes promoted the fucking thing, and they make the score. We'll see what they come up with." Money-wise they came up with nothing, but that was the trade-off for being with Main Events. Sure they would loot the gate and make more money than the fighters on the boxing shows they ran, but in return, Vinny got recognition, was ranked by three reputable boxing commissions, and within just seventeen months after fighting Joe Frazier Jr., Vinny was matched with Greg Haugen for the Lightweight International Boxing Championship.

Before the Haugen fight Vinny would face and defeat No. 1 contender Ecuadorian Nelson Balonos, who came to Providence undefeated at 33-0, but left defeated. Vinny had beaten over-the-hill but still dangerous pros Harry Arroyo, Roberto Elizondo, and Roger "Going Down" Brown, making him a matinee idol on NBC's Sunday afternoon boxing show. Haugen had won his championship just months earlier, upsetting International Boxing Federation champion Jimmy Paul. Haugen was an iron-jawed lightweight who made his reputation, believe it or not, winning tough-man competitions in America's Great Northwest. But "Mutt," as Haugen was known, also was an accomplished boxer, and he too came to Providence undefeated at 19-0. Haugen later would go on to beat Hector Camacho, a formerly retired Ray Mancini, and other top lightweights and junior-welterweights.

Vinny went into training camp weighing over 160 pounds. The fight was scheduled for June 7, 1987. By the time he stepped on the scale, the morning of the most important day of his life, he had sucked down to 134 pounds, 25 pounds less than his natural weight. The morning before the weigh-in he was feeling the ill effects of "drying out." When a fighter dries out, he doesn't eat or drink for at least forty-eight to seventy-two hours: no food, no water, no ice cubes, nothing. Not only did Vinny dry himself out nutritionally, but he worked out concomitantly in the three days leading up to the fight. He ran with plastics under his fleece sweatsuit, he shadow-boxed, and he sat in steam rooms next to old men at the Providence YMCA, all in his attempt to make the lightweight 135-pound limit. If he didn't make weight, he couldn't fight, period. His title shot might be gone forever. NBC might never return to this old industrial city if Vinny had to be scratched from the fight.

A listless Vinny stepped off the scale as the media snapped pictures, and he made his way over to a Puma gym bag. Inside that bag was his return to normalcy: Gatorade, chocolate, Power-bars, and fruit. In a furious attempt to rehydrate his body, Vinny gorged himself until he soaked up all the necessary carbohydrates to allow him to fight a fifteen-round fight, until he felt he could think clearly again. This was his first world championship fight, which meant it was his first 15-round fight. It was yet another hurdle he had going into this fight.

Instead, his binge crippled him and put him in a sick bed just three hours before his first championship fight. His temperature rose to 103 degrees. He had diarrhea and vomited furiously. Vinny was now covered in blankets in his dressing room in the bowels of the Providence Civic Center. The ten thousand people filing in were clueless, and luckily so was champion Greg Haugen. But NBC executives saw Vinny's condition and were ready to cancel the fight. Of course, Vinny pleaded with the suits and guaranteed them he would be ready for the two o'clock bell, a bell he would answer ready or not.

When the bell for round eleven sounded, both fighters rose from their stools and both were bloodied. Vinny's nose had been broken as well as his right hand. They had begun the championship rounds and the fight was virtually deadlocked. The man who could endure the next five rounds physically and emotionally would climb through the ropes with the belt hanging from his waist. But somehow, something wasn't quite right. The slick boxer people had come to see the last seven years seemed to be fading away more and more each round. Vinny had entered the fight a 2 to 1 favorite. Most boxing experts leading up to the fight felt Vinny was too fast and talented for Haugen. But the former tough-man counter-punched Vinny beautifully, halting his advances with a jackhammer-like jab, which Vinny ran into repeatedly in his attempt to corner Haugen. "Goddammit, Vinny, side to side, use your angles, use your legs," Angelo hollered. But Vinny, by now, had abandoned boxing. He instead plodded straight ahead, throwing punches that seemed to be coming from his hip. Some missed wildly, but more landed. Vinny was planning to win by attrition: out-tough-guy the tough guy.

Vinny followed Haugen back to his corner at the end of round thirteen. "I ain't going nowhere," he said and then walked backward to his own corner, never taking his eyes off Haugen. The crowd watched and wondered why he was resorting to this new style, the style of Jake LaMotta and Ray Mancini. They were great fighters, but it was a take two punches and give one punch kind of style, a style fighters had to choose out of default, because they had real skill limitations, and unfortunately the kind of style that ends a career sooner rather than later.

Was it the dehydration? Was it the weight loss? "Two more rounds, champ, two more rounds and you're champion of the world," Angelo rallied Vinny. And Vinny responded. Over the next two rounds Vinny's pace quickened and he unleashed combinations of body blows and thwarting straight right hands that kept Haugen in a defensive shell, backpedaling on his heels. The tough guy from the Great Northwest wilted under Vinny's pressure and his championship reign faded with each passing minute.

Vinny would outlast Haugen. In six minutes, he would hear what he had been waiting a lifetime to hear. Ring announcer Frank Carpano . . . "And the new Lightweight Champion of the World . . . Viiiiiinnnnnnnyyyyyyy the Pazmanian Devil . . . Pazienza."

Vinny fell into Angelo's arms and raised the belt above his head, too tired for tears. Angelo wept for them. His arms clutched Vinny, not ready to share him and their elation with the world. The Civic Center's crowd rose from their chairs to their feet chanting *Vinny . . . Vinny . . . Vinny.* The ten thousand Pazmaniacs, who now flooded the Devil's Den, serenaded Vinny and Angelo into the night.

When he awoke at 5:00 a.m. on Monday June 8th, he had two closed purple eyes, yet another broken nose, and a soft cast on his right hand that stabilized his broken right hand. He got in his car and drove to Dunkin' Donuts to get a paper, four honey-dew donuts, and a coffee. The four donuts were symbolic of his freedom—no training camps or diets.

He turned the pages of the *Providence Journal* awkwardly with his left hand until he got to the headline that read VINNY PAZIENZA: IBF LIGHTWEIGHT CHAMPION VINNY GOES FROM A SICK BED TO TOP OF THE MOUNTAIN. Longtime journalist Bill Parrillo wrote a glowing post-fight commentary on Vinny's will and courage as well as a blow-by-blow description of Vinny's pre-fight ordeal and the fight itself. Parrillo quoted Vinny's response to the questions from press row about his injuries, his sickness, and his determination to become champion. "Just like Rocky, just like Rocky." Vinny reveled in the victory and immersed himself alone in the article, sipping his Dunkin' Donuts coffee, just as he had been alone in the ring about sixteen hours earlier, reading every line ever so slowly as to savor the win, unwilling to let it get away just yet.

11 Making Weight

Just when Vinny thought all was right in his world, he faced one of his most difficult dilemmas. Vinny had finally achieved his end, a world championship. But it had come at both a physical and an economic cost. Following the Haugen fight, Vinny was rushed to Rhode Island Hospital and given two bags of intravenous fluids; he was severely dehydrated. His nose was broken and his right hand was in a soft cast. He would be out of training for at least three months. Financially, he still was not making a great deal of money. To lure Greg Haugen to Providence, the champion had been promised the lion's share of the fighters' earnings, making a bit over $150,000. With good reason—it was his belt. Vinny, on the other hand, would make only $40,000. After paying Lou Duva a third for his management fee and 10 percent for his training fee, another 28 percent toward taxes, well, you get the picture. As Angelo would often say, Vinny still wasn't making lubini beans.

But now Vinny had a decision to make. The rematch with Greg Haugen could be Vinny's biggest payday. ABC and the

Wide World of Sports came calling with an open date, February 7, 1988, trying to steal the rematch from NBC. They were going to bill the fight as the next great boxing rivalry and compared it to the legendary 1950s Rocky Graziano/Tony Zale fights. ABC offered Vinny $350,000, by far the biggest payday of his career. Here it was, October, Vinny had already been inactive for over five months because of his broken hand, nose, and assorted other injuries . . . and he weighed close to 170 pounds. The real problem was he wasn't fat. It was his legitimate weight. Sure it looked like he could drop to about 160, but to 135? If he didn't take the fight, he could move up to junior-welterweight at 140 pounds or even welterweight at 147 pounds. But there was no way he would ever be able to make $350,000 without defending his belt.

Training camp opened for Vinny on December 1, 1988. He would have nearly nine weeks to prepare for his rematch with Haugen, and more important, nine weeks to shed over 35 pounds. By Christmas's end, he was still hovering in the high 160s; the weight did not want to come off. He was training as hard as ever: tedious 5-mile morning runs, followed by lightweight training routines, and then back to the gym for sparring, every evening, through New Year's Day and into January.

As camp broke and Vinny headed to Atlantic City for the final week of training, Angelo seemed as worried as I'd ever seen him about Vinny's career. The final sparring session with local boxers Billy Hartman and Ray Oliveira took place on the Wednesday before the Saturday afternoon fight in one of the Trump Plaza's oversize ballrooms. The national media was on hand as well as Main Events executives and Lou's sons, Danny and Dino. When the sparring session had mercifully ended, Lou, Danny, and Angelo exited the room heads down, wondering to themselves.

As Vinny and I played cards on that Friday night in a luxury suite at Trump's, ten hours before the official weigh-in, he chewed a wad of gum and spit into a bucket. He paced the room, his skin chalky white, face unshaved, and by now gaunt looking. He had been "drying out" as usual, and walked into the bathroom every fifteen or twenty minutes to get on the scale. This was something he did alone, and nobody ever asked about his weight. He was too ornery and pissed off at the world after losing 23 pounds. That's right, 23 pounds, and if you do the math, that meant Vinny still weighed 147 pounds.

I watched him go toe-to-toe with local sparring partners for the last nine weeks in the gym. If someone from the outside world watched, they would have never known the difference between the champion and the sparring partner. It was the reason that the Duvas and Angelo hung their heads leaving the ballroom two nights earlier. Finally, Tommy said it, what had been on his mind for eight months leading up to the fight. "That's it, kid, enough is enough; Vinny, you can't do this anymore. You can't put your body through this anymore. How the fuck are you going to lose 12 pounds by tomorrow morning?"

Vinny rose from his chair and threw his cards on the table, not saying a word. He took out his sweat clothes from the dresser drawer and began to cut a circle in the top of a green plastic bag. The plastic bag would be worn under his fleece sweatsuit to extract the pounds of water he needed to draw from his body.

At sunrise he was on Atlantic City's famous boardwalk, jogging east to west as the sun rose behind his right shoulder. His feet pounded on the splintering wood as the beads of sweat ran down his wrists, leaving a trail on the ground. When he was done running, he discarded his drenched sweatsuit and climbed into a hot tub with a temperature of 106 degrees. At 8:30 a.m. he made his way to the scale set at 135 pounds. If it moved upward, he would have to return to the hot tub or the boardwalk. Vinny stepped on the scale, taking a deep breath, which is an old trick jockeys use to manipulate the scale in their favor.

Somehow, some way, Vinny lost 12 pounds in eight hours.

Ten hours later, Vinny was being held the very same way Angelo held him in Providence months earlier. This time, however, he guarded him, not ready to share their pain with the world. Together, they were experiencing their first loss of Vinny's professional career. This time they cried together, the championship belt now gone. Tasting the bitterness of defeat for the first time, they had never imagined it would be so difficult to swallow. Vinny had taken the worst beating of his career, in the last recorded fifteen-round fight in boxing history. He had finally earned a real payday as a fighter, but he paid the ultimate price—his title.

12 End of the Road?

As Vinny returned to Providence without his belt, the worst kind of Italians were calling for his retirement. Even the *Providence Journal*, the state's only circulated newspaper, which had always been more than supportive, intimated that maybe it was time for Vinny to quit. An article written on February 9 by *Journal* columnist Bill Reynolds, PAZ REACHED HIS GOAL; NOW IT'S ALL SEQUEL, gave mostly a positive account of Vinny's career to date. But Reynolds wondered in his piece if Vinny remembered an earlier interview done in 1986 in which Paz stated, "If I accomplish what I set out to do I'd quit today." Reynolds went on to say, "I hope Vinny remembers this."

What he had set out to do was to win a world title, which of course he had already done. Were local sports pundits calling for his retirement at age 25, with only 25 pro fights? Vinny knew Willie Pep, his father's friend, had 250. Granted he had had two very tough fights with Greg Haugen, but not only was quitting not an option, the idea to Vinny was ludicrous and insulting.

In a previous article by Reynolds written on February 7— THE RENT FINALLY CAME DUE ON THE DREAM AND PAZIEN-ZA'S FANTASY LIFE GETS PUT ON HOLD—the writer again was complimentary to Vinny in almost every way: his heart, his almost Hollywood-scripted life story, even the way Vinny responded in defeat, like a champion with no excuses. Reynolds quoted Vinny. "'I fought a stupid fight today, I just didn't have it today. I'm very sorry,' Vinny said softly, 'I let a lot of people down.'" He depicted Vinny as a gracious loser that night, and he was. Vinny hugged Greg Haugen on national television, even ingratiating himself to the fans of Tacoma, Washington, Haugen's hometown fans who suddenly found themselves converted into Pazmaniacs. Later in the year Vinny would attend and be the city's honorary guest at Haugen's first title defense of his old championship. Vinny received a standing ovation at, of all places, the Tacoma Dome.

But in all, Reynolds article, though far from venomous and certainly fair, was still reflective of Vinny's past thirty rounds in the ring. There simply was an underlying negativity surrounding Vinny's career. Reynolds called Atlantic City, where Vinny lost his belt, the citadel of broken dreams and a tired old beach town. Was Reynolds implying Vinny was all done? Or his dream was over? Probably not, but it was negativity by association. And Vinny and negativity was not a good mix.

But from 1988 to 1990, his critics' arguments gained merit and momentum: Vinny's career had gone into a tailspin. His Willie Pep–style seemed forever gone. He fought nine more times defeating un-notables and up-and-comers like Felix Dubray, Jake Carollo, and Vinny Burghese. Even though he outlasted and defeated Greg Haugen in their non-title rubber match in Atlantic City, he lost in his three attempts to recapture a championship. He had moved up to junior-welterweight (140 pounds) from lightweight but was still losing over 30 pounds to make weight. By this point, it seemed like the blind was leading the blind. In fact, it probably was: Lou blinded by profit, while Vinny and Angelo were blinded by trust.

After Vinny lost his belt to Greg Haugen in February 1988, Vinny had found himself at a crossroads. His pace up the boxing rankings ladder and to a world championship had been feverish. Since 1983 he had averaged 5.2 fights a year, or a fight about every two months. Physically and emotionally he needed a break from the sport. But the anxiety after losing his belt brought great consternation, as well as a return of the question marks that had haunted his career dating back to before he had won his world title.

On June 1, 1987, Vinny had appeared in *Sports Illustrated* in an article entitled THE PAZ THAT REFRESHES (subtitled VINNY PAZIENZA MAY BE THE ENTERTAINER BOXING NEEDS), a feature story written by Douglas S. Looney. Looney begged for the real question that had to be answered: "Can Paz fight a whit, or is he suffering from delusions of competence?" He intimated in the article that all Lou Duva's fighters are protected from tough fights and face fighters, and "Paz remained suspect." Looney acknowledged that Vinny was a great entertainer, but possibly no more than a cartoon character. He said Vinny did devious little things like an eighth grader, such as stepping on opponent Nelson Balanos's foot and throwing him to the canvas during a fight. Looney quoted Vinny as saying, "Once I saw Nelson's legs go weak like spaghetti I was on him like the sauce." He noted that Vinny gave former Ohio policeman and tough lightweight Harry Arroyo a whistle prior to their bout because he was going to see to it that Arroyo return to work as a policeman.

His story was less about boxing and more about the hype that surrounded Vinny. He questioned Vinny's credibility in the ring and questioned whether a middle-class kid from an Italian-American family had the desire to fight against street-hardened opponents. He poked fun at Vinny's family outside of the ring too, stating that Angelo's full-time job had become to exaggerate his son's abilities. Looney quoted Angelo: "'There's no way they're gonna stop my kid!' Angelo shouts. Angelo always shouts.'He has my genes!'" He also quipped that Louise had more religious artifacts than The Vatican, large prints of da Vinci's *The Last Supper*, and illustrated copies of The Lord's Prayer. He completed his

Shecky Greene–like routine about the classic Italian family by stating that Louise sprinkled holy water on his notepad.

Vinny was so infuriated about the article that he called out Looney immediately after the first Haugen fight in his post-fight live NBC interview. With bloodied eyes and fifteen hectic rounds behind him, he thought of Douglas S. Looney first. "This [win] is for Douglas S. Looney of *Sports Illustrated* and all the stupid things he said about my family." He called out Looney on two fronts, one for doubting his ability, and especially for the derogatory way the writer had portrayed his family. "We fed him and opened up our home to him and he impugns my family and my heritage. My mother made him the best meal he'd ever have and that's her thanks," Vinny told his friends after the disappointing article came out. Vinny felt betrayed. The street-jaded Angelo just called him a rat bastard and left it in the rearview mirror of his Chrysler.

Vinny had also appeared on the cover of *Ring* magazine in June of 1987, shortly before his first fight with Haugen, with a caption that read "phenom or phony?" He appeared in a gold lamé robe set in a purple backdrop. Again, the article was written questioning both Vinny's opponents in terms of quality, as well as his true boxing talent and skill level. Vinny wondered whether those questions would resurface after his loss, or if they were they put to rest on June 7, 1987, the day he won his title.

It was only natural that he started to question his own ability. When fighters lose their first fight, their notion of personal invincibility is also lost. If they are true to themselves, which most fighters are, they often give themselves a cognitive-emotional examination. They get to know themselves perhaps more so than any other athlete, because they are alone in the ring, wholly independent, and not reliant on others to pick them up on a bad night. Because their self-truth is peeled off in the ring layer by layer, round by round, punch by punch, until they can no longer rationalize their feelings or their will or their truest intent. One way or another, self-confidence is organic: It will grow or fade away, sometimes never to return. Even if he had answered the questions of his critics, with a championship win, he now had to confront the seemingly endless self-imposed questions that would play over and over in his head, at any time under any circumstances. The silent but heavy question would arise during a night at the movies with friends or watching a ballgame with Angelo. Is it over?

When Vinny returned to Father and Son's Gym in April of '88, there were no cameras, no opponent in line; in fact there was not even a trainer, only a break- dancing 43-year-old new friend from Fall River named Stevie Powers. Powers was a friend of Nikki's from her hometown. He looked bedraggled, with a deep orange sun-bed tan one does not acquire on the streets of the Northeast in mid-winter and stringy long blond hair with deep black roots and a shade of light green tint. He was so orange that I joked that I had a craving for duck. He wore lots of gold ornaments, chains, bracelets, and rings. He was lit up like a Christmas tree and wore tight 1980s hair-band clothes and a mullet, all draped upon a 120-pound bantamweight's frame.

Every so often Vinny would befriend people who would leave me and the ever pessimistic Tommy Mart shaking our heads. If you wanted to make friends with the optimistic Vinny, he'd be your friend. Period. If you were nice to Vinny he was nice to you. Period. The friendship glass was always half full. To me and Tommy Mart the glass wasn't half empty; it didn't even exist. Vinny was the last friend we made and that was in 1973. When we saw Stevie Powers doing the robot in the ring to the beat of Michael Jackson's "The Way You Make Me Feel" coming from Vinny's blurring boom box, while Vinny shadow-boxed on the side of the ring, Tommy Mart and I knew we had no need to re-examine our isolationist policy.

To our surprise, Powers claimed to be a former kickboxer who was at the gym to "help Vinny out in training." A de facto trainer/ friend/dance choreographer? In reality, though, he was a JAG— just another guy looking to latch on to Vinny, be around the spot-light, the women, and for him maybe even the money. Stevie was a guy with a little inherited money from a dead aunt and a big ego, who did a short bid at Walpole State Prison for some two-bit beef.

Tommy and I called for a meeting with Angelo and asked him what was going on with this guy. We huddled next to the recliner. Tommy and I certainly didn't screen Vinny's new friends, but we were more concerned with the fact that Powers was calling himself Vinny's new trainer. We whispered as I looked over Angelo's shoulder through the door into the boxing area of the gym. Powers was still dancing. I told Angelo, "He's poppin' now."

"What the fuck is 'poppin'?" Angelo shot back and looked at me, puzzled. I started to explain.

"It's a jerking motion that break-dancers do to the beat of . . ." Tommy Mart burst out laughing in the middle of my explanation. "Ange, get him the fuck out of here. He's a stone jerk-off," Tommy Mart pleaded. Tommy Mart and I laughed a little more.

"He's harmless, let him hang around," Angelo thought aloud. "He ain't gonna get nothing from Vinny, don't worry. Let him help."

"But he looks ridiculous," Tommy said.

"Wow, you guys are tougher than me," Angelo said, "I'll just, no, we'll keep an eye on him."

It all seemed a little funny at the time, but in retrospect, three months earlier the Stevie Powers of the world would have never gotten into the gym, never mind a guy like that putting a claim on Vinny. Although Stevie's claim to be "the trainer" had no legal teeth and did not provide him with economic recourse, a guy walking around the small streets of southeastern New England like a white M.C. Hammer, squawking up a storm that he was Vinny Paz's trainer (which he did) could be damaging and tarnish Vinny's reputation as a world-class fighter and commodity. In short, it was also embarrassing.

There were more undesirables who slithered through the cracks of the streets and into the gym, each offering their services to Vinny. Some were legitimate economic opportunities, but most were not. There was a commercial spot for a pig farmer-turned-waste-management millionaire, who claimed he could punch harder than Mike Tyson. He was harmless and at least Vinny made five thousand dollars. But there also was a nondescript karate "expert," who after watching Vinny work out on an April afternoon argued that Greg was a bum, the same Greg Haugen who had taken Vinny's title three months earlier. Two minutes later the karate "expert" was fittingly thrown out of the gym after being knocked down in eleven seconds by Vinny with a left hook to the kidneys.

Again, three months earlier the karate "expert" would have never gained entrance to the gym, never mind into the ring with a world champion. Vinny would have never allowed such a thing. The ring was his place of work, where champions hone their skills. Boxing was his trade and he was proud of it. It was never to be taken lightly. Those who had previously gotten into the ring with Vinny had earned their place, their right if you will, by either winning fights or leaving their blood and sweat in the ring. It wasn't a place for boxing wannabes or dabblers. But after the loss Vinny was becoming a little more vulnerable and insecure about his place in the axis of the boxing world and in the Main Events stable. Angelo was growing insecure too. More and more, people who simply did not belong were breathing Vinny's rarefied athletic air.

By the end of the month, the Stevie Powers act was growing tired. Angelo had always told me, if you really wanted to get rid of a guy, just ask him for money. So I put my plan into effect on the way to Vincent's Dance Club in Randolph, Massachusetts. On I-95 on our thirty-minute ride north, I asked him for a loan of $200,000 for a gym venture Vinny and I had our eye on. I told him we had the spot, the deal was in place, all we needed was the money—his money. Of course, there was no gym or no venture, but it was the end of Stevie Powers. He got lost in the crowd at Vincent's, never to be heard from again. Vinny never knew of the plan I borrowed from Angelo, but every time he asked us, "Whatever happened to Stevie Powers?" I got a wink and a you-learned-well smirk from Angelo.

13　The Master Plan

To his credit Angelo recognized that Vinny was in a funk. Team Pazienza now consisted mostly of friends. With Main Events stretching themselves thin with their stable of elite fighters and megafights, Vinny was on his own. Main Events was putting in place a championship fight for Meldrick Taylor against Buddy McGirt, which was to take place in September of 1988. Evander Holyfield captured the cruiserweight championship (190 pounds) in Las Vegas in the first part of the year, and he was making his move up to heavyweight as Main Events booked a July 16th date with former Mike Tyson rival James "Quick" Tillis. After defeating Tillis in five rounds by TKO, Holyfield would fight a third time in 1988, defeating contender Pinklon Thomas. Lou was also busy with Pernell Whitaker. In March Whitaker challenged Jose Luis Ramirez for the WBC Lightweight Championship in Levallois, France. Whitaker suffered his first loss when foreign judges awarded a controversial split decision in Ramirez's favor. Moreover, the 1988 Summer Olympics were coming up in Seoul, and that meant a frenzied recruiting period for Main Events and Lou to ensure that their cupboard of fighters stayed full to secure the financial stability of Main Events, and to ensure the Duvas' stay atop their empire in the boxing business world.

Lou was awarded World Boxing Association Manager of the Year in 1987 for the work he had done with Evander Holyfield, Pernell Whitaker, Meldrick Taylor, and Vinny. And in 1988 Lou wanted to keep his momentum going. But Lou's momentum meant less time for Vinny, especially with Holyfield moving up to heavyweight. Vinny could beat all the lightweights in the world, and sell out the Providence Civic Center every night of the year, but his purses could never equal that of a heavyweight contender with an Olympic background. As a result, Vinny found himself freelancing, sparring alone in April with little instruction.

With Stevie Powers gone, I for the most part worked Vinny's corner against local fighters who were called into Father and Son's to give Vinny rounds. My instruction was rudimentary and nothing more than reminders to a former world champion. "Vinny, keep your hands up, don't back straight out, use your jab," I would yell from the corner. His local sparring partners offered little in terms of fruitful boxing work. They were for the most part cheerleaders, very happy to be in the ring with Vinny or happy to tell their friends and family they were among boxing elite. They'd throw punches that lacked bad intentions, which Vinny walked through at his convenience. Vinny would punch when he wanted to punch, rest when he wanted rest, and dance when he wanted to dance. He controlled the pace and worked at his own discretion. It's at these times poor habits seep into fighter's muscle memory and these poor habits condition the fighter in a negative way. No need to move your head, no need to faint, no need to set up your opponent because the sparring partners might as well be dance partners that were led around the dance floor deferentially. Vinny simply was not going to pay in terms of getting hit for the mistakes he made in the ring, because these guys he was sparring with didn't have the wherewithal. With the lack of experienced professional instruction I offered and the lack of professional sparring at hand, coupled with Main Events' laissez-faire attitude, Angelo knew he had to make a move. But what would that move be?

That move would come from Angelo's past. On a visit he made to see old friend/wiseguy "Pro" Lerner at the Rhode Island Corrections maximum-security unit in Cranston that spring, Angelo reached out to his old friend and told him of Vinny's boxing troubles. He explained that he didn't have a trainer to work with Vinny day to day and that Main Events was paying more attention to Holyfield than anybody else, and they were distracted, keeping their eyes on the biggest prize. He started most sentences with three simple words, "those fucking Duvas."

Lerner, a guy in his late 40s serving a life sentence, had a solution. Lerner was a former Massachusetts star athlete, who was in the Cape Cod Amateur Baseball League when he got the nickname "Pro." Maurice was his birth name: He earned his handle because he was considered a very good professional baseball prospect. His former life as an athlete before he turned to crime led him to become a fitness nut. He ate well, kept his body in peak condition, and loved to talk and read about fitness and training. So much, in fact, there was talk on the street that he invested some of his money from prison in an up-and-coming new type of weight-training gym called New England Nautilus in the early 1980s. He supposedly partnered there with Paul Katz, who oversaw the operation and growth of the gyms in southern New England. That's when he began telling Angelo about a transplanted martial arts Grand Master from the Far East, North Korea to be exact, who migrated to America to escape the Communist country and who now trained people out of his gym in Merrimack Valley, New Hampshire.

Lerner really talked up the trainer and boasted about his great credentials. According to Lerner, Master Seo worked in the training camps of former heavyweight champion Larry Holmes and junior-welterweight champion Aaron Pryor, the great lightweight Alexis Arguello, and tennis pro John McEnroe, both as a nutritionist and conditioning guru.

This piqued Angelo's curiosity, and Lerner later put in a call to Seo's home to arrange a call between Angelo and the Master.

When Angelo got back to the gym he immediately got on the phone with Master Seo, and Angelo heard all things that he truly wanted to hear, probably above and beyond boxing. Seo told Angelo he had seen Vinny's last two fights and he was sure Angelo was agonizing as a father. "Mr. Pazienza, I am a father too, I would not like to see my boy in that state. My son being hit like that would be unbearable. For Vinny to be hit like that, it is unnecessary."

Angelo liked what he heard, as Master Seo went on to promise Angelo that with Vinny's speed and boxing ability, coupled with his teaching and training techniques, Vinny would never get hit again; he would no longer bleed and his weight problems would disappear.

"I'll be having your son, the champion, slipping punches again and throwing more punches, too," Master Seo pressed on, vying for the job like he was on a big-time job interview, making sure he didn't leave any stone unturned. "I train Larry Holmes, heavy-weight champion, and Aaron Pryor. Mr. Pazienza, I trained Alexis Arguello." Seo went back to the subject and his rambling solilo-quy. "I can train your boy, he will throw 300, 400, 500 punches per round no question. He has the talent, I can make him better and keep him safer, the ring is too dangerous of a place."

Angelo hadn't spoken, which he was unaccustomed to, but he finally interrupted Master Seo. It all sounded so good, but he knew he couldn't make a decision without Vinny.

"I'll talk to Vinny, okay. Let me see what he thinks. If you think you can bring all these things to Vinny, we'll see then." Master Seo spoke again, confidently. "Mr. Pazienza, I don't think I can straighten out your son, I know I can."

Angelo reached over his recliner and put the green phone down on its cradle, which wobbled on a shaky tin television tray. He rose from the chair and walked around the gym, mopping the sparkling cement floor out of habit more than anything else. He leaned the mop down against the wall and went over to the trophy case. As his eyes moved from right to left, he read press clippings from his Vinny's amateur days and took in shots of Vinny posing before his pro debut. The pictures were so clean, Vinny's face so unmarked, his nose so perfectly straight. There was no sign of scar tissue above his eyes, or no sign of a hard life. The pictures brought Angelo back to a place of innocence in Vinny's life, and suddenly they started to make him feel old. He realized more so at that moment that Vinny's life was his life and that he had to do what was best for the both of them. Maybe this is what is meant by a father being too close to his son in a boxing relationship. Maybe Angelo was making a decision with blinders on, blinders that he hoped would keep danger out of Vinny's sight. Maybe he was making a decision based solely on the notion of keeping Vinny out of harm's way with the promises made by Master Seo, rather than making a sound boxing decision, contemplating the hiring of a boxing trainer who worked in the camps of champions, but never was the leader in those training camps or fighting corners. Maybe Angelo was closer to Vinny's career than he should have been, but he was there and there was never a doubt about that.

One week later, just like that, Master Seo was Vinny's new trainer. Master Seo sold Vinny with his dignified personality and dress, always wearing all white. He was a diminutive man who spoke softly in a judicious broken English. He also sold Vinny with his background as conditioning coach to three future Boxing Hall of Famers, his use of meaningful Chinese life proverbs, and lastly a Chinese meal at Kings Garden in Cranston that led Master Seo to say after he observed Vinny eat two egg rolls, a big bowl of wonton soup, a basket of bread, a full order of fried rice, and an order of shrimp with lobster sauce, followed by six fortune cookies: "Binny, you train very hard, you need to eat more."

That was music to his ears. And the fact that he called him "Binny" made Vinny smile. Vinny took another sip from the friendship glass as Master Daeshik Seo officially became Vinny's trainer and friend in May of 1988.

Master Seo was formally "unveiled," according to the *Providence Journal,* as Vinny's "new secret weapon" at a press conference at the Civic Center on June 9, 1988. "Together I know the two of us can't be stopped," Vinny boldly predicted at the podium, as

Master Seo soaked up his newfound fame by telling the media that his dream was to make "Binny" the next junior-welterweight champion of the world, and by telling them of his journey from Korea to the United States in 1975, how he had been an accomplished physical therapist, educator, and athlete, having once been an amateur boxing champion in his native Korea. He stressed the importance of health, nutrition, and the tranquility of mind, body, and spirit. Master Seo also boasted that "he'd not caught a cold since 1954." The fact that he articulated his 1954 cold line like the straightest of straight men resulted in a roomful of laughter from press row and Vinny's friends. The fact that he stared ahead stone-faced, genuinely stoic to what caused the laughter, made him look like he was borrowing shtick from Bob Newhart. But it was no shtick; his language and cultural nuances were often lost in translation. Seo spoke softly, integrating old world proverbs that didn't always translate well, and when things often moved so fast especially around an always amped-up Angelo, he seemed to be an intellectual step behind.

In large part, little was actually known of him, giving Master Seo a mystical presence, even if an underlying stereotype bolstered that presence. It made for good copy by the *Providence Journal* as they ran with VINNY'S SECRET WEAPON as a headline on June 10th.

There was clearly a cultural divide between Master Seo and the press. And if there was a cultural divide between Master Seo and the mainstream, how was that cultural gap going to be bridged with Angelo, who himself still hadn't been fully Americanized from his Quacino roots? As Master Seo always had an air of tranquility surrounding him, Angelo always seemed to have an air of chaos surrounding him. Could these two really coexist for months on end in the day-to-day rut of a training camp? Because where Vinny went professionally, Angelo went professionally. Totowa, Houston, or San Remo: If Vinny picked up a boxing glove, Angelo was there. If Vinny jumped rope or shadow-boxed, Angelo was there. If Vinny tried to get laid during training camp, he tried to sabotage it.

And if that relationship wasn't odd enough, how would Vinny respond to Seo's personality? The two seemed to have little in common, wrote Sean McAdam of the *Journal* in a follow-up June 26th article. "Vinny was flamboyant, Seo was reserved, Vinny was naturally carefree, Seo is so serious, Vinny is 26, and Seo was generations apart at 47." But the two developed a mutual affinity for one another quickly. They had training in common, and that outweighed their differences. What trainer Master Seo loved to do most was condition athletes, and Vinny was a workhorse who loved to train.

When the press conference finally broke up, reporters did one-on-one interviews both with Seo and with Vinny. Vinny told reporter Sean McAdam that the hiring of Seo was not intended to be a slight on Lou Duva, who was really nowhere to be found. "You don't see the Duvas here because it's solely my decision," Vinny went on. "Lou's still my manager," Vinny assured McAdam. Lou's daughter-in-law and Main Events publicist Kathy Duva was contacted by the *Journal* later in the day. "Vinny's happy with him [Seo] and we're behind him 100 percent. He's doing it with our blessing. It was like Lou was an interim trainer who lasted a long time," Kathy said. Vinny reaffirmed what Duva said to McAdam, and bit his tongue in the process. "I didn't have a trainer so Lou was only helping out."

Privately, Vinny was hurt that Lou was paying so little attention to him. And Angelo summed up the Pazienzas' feelings best when he started his sentences with those three telling, growling words: "Those fuckin' Duvas."

14   The Hampshire Hills

Vinny had been training at Hampshire Hills for four weeks before the June 9th press conference that introduced Master Seo. When Vinny left for New Hampshire he had done so the same way he always left for all training camps, with tight lips and a frown. Coincidentally, the day Vinny left for camp, Tommy Mart and I spotted Angelo's car on 95 North about three car lengths ahead of ours. We were on our way to McCoy Stadium in Pawtucket to watch the Boston Red Sox Triple-A affiliate Pawtucket Red Sox play a matinee game against the Toledo Mud Hens. Angelo was driving his Chrysler, packed floor to ceiling with Vinny's boxing gear. More suitcases, six weeks' worth, filled the open trunk as only a thin piece of rope held the Louis Vuitton luggage intact between Angelo's car and the highway.

We sped ahead catching up to the car's port side, but reached Vinny before Angelo because he was sitting in the backseat. He just sat there looking sad, his head bent straight down morbidly looking into his lap like a 10-year-old kid being dropped off at summer camp against his will. I blasted my horn as Tommy Mart yelled out of the window, "*Cugi, cugi.*" The wind swallowed up his words. "*Cuug,*" Tommy hollered again, this time waving his arms and sticking his body halfway out of the passenger window. Vinny sprang up from his slouch, waved back, and pointed and smiled; his eyes reached to us as if he were receiving a governor's pardon or as if we were about to rescue him from eternal damnation.

I blew the horn more, this time ceremonially as we passed Angelo and left Vinny still waving from his backseat. Tommy put his fingers to his ear, miming a phone call. "Call ya soon," Tommy yelled, as Angelo drove Vinny northward, past the Pawtucket exit out of Rhode Island, toward Master Seo's and their first training camp together.

To their credit Main Events had lived up to their part of the managerial/promotional bargain, showing no ill will toward Vinny for the hiring of Seo. They scheduled a June 26th fight in Providence against Felix "The Cat" Dubray. Dubray was a Native American with an obscure boxing record. He claimed to have a 13-1 record, but *The Ring Book,* the self-proclaimed bible of boxing according to the *Providence Journal,* didn't know he existed. His name didn't appear on any of the 1,145 pages of its 1987 edition. He was a member of the Sioux tribe and a former resident of the Black Hills Reservation who now lived in Omaha, Nebraska. The fight would be Vinny's debut as a junior-welterweight (140 pounds) and the Duvas wanted to restore Vinny's marketability and confidence by bringing in Dubray, who because of his background had a good storyline but little else. Vinny would be the live co-feature on June 26th at the Civic Center, while the real main event would be the closed-circuit showing of Mike Tyson's annihilation of Michael Spinks.

When Vinny moved into Room 417 of the Hyatt Regency in Milford, New Hampshire, he was preparing for his June 26th date. He was comforted that he was only 90 miles north of Cranston. He was only about 90 miles north of Louise's eggplant and his friends, and even more important to Vinny, he was only about 90 miles northeast of Nikki, which of course worried Angelo. His prior training camps had left him in seclusion; whether they were in Colorado Springs, Totowa, or Houston, he was pretty much cut off from his friends, lovers, and family.

Some fighters embrace the isolation of trainings camps. Some even thrive in desolation. According to Bob Pace of BobPace boxing.com, former Brockton middleweight legend Marvin Hagler, now "Marvelous" Hagler, "often went to the ends of Cape Cod more than three months before fights, away from family and friends to lose weight and to dry out from the party life." Vinny didn't need to dry out. He didn't live the party life. In fact, Vinny didn't sip his first taste of alcohol until the time he was 24 and that was only for a championship toast at The Classic's post-fight party.

His new digs were also only about 2 miles from Master Seo's unassuming but comfortable white ranch house where Vinny was always welcome day or night, and about 3 miles away from his new training headquarters, the Hampshire Hills Sports and Fitness Club. Hampshire Hills was a sprawling 115,000-square-foot facility, on 119 acres of forest land, the multidimensional upscale fitness club that catered to the area's weekend warriors, who engaged in tennis, squash, racquetball, weight training, soccer, and swimming. It was a place where soccer moms dropped their kids to work with tennis pros or lacrosse coaches while they relaxed in the spa or had a day of fitness pampering.

Hampshire Hills was only 90 miles away in Milford, but worlds apart from Father and Son's Gym, which was sandwiched in between the crime-ridden, gang- and drug-infested Hartford Housing Projects and Angelo's old hard-bitten neighborhood of Silver Lake. Compared to the coziness of Hampshire Hills, Father and Son's was a gym that hosted hard training sessions and guys with hard luck, faded bricks that soaked up faded dreams, guys beaten up by Vinny and guys Angelo knew had been beaten up by life.

But if the posh exterior where yuppies parked their Saabs and Volvos told one story, the upstairs at Hampshire Hills told another. Walking up three flights of stairs and above the Olympic-size pool, the tennis courts, the Jacuzzis, and the many juice bars, one was transported into the fitness club's attic, now known as Vinny's new training area. With each step you took from bottom to top the temperature rose incrementally, slightly at first, then in waves until you reached the door where a backdraft of heat engulfed your body when you opened the door. If it were a cool 75 degrees outside, it was a steamy 95 in the attic. If it were 85 warm degrees downstairs it was a 105-degree steam bath upstairs. And if it got to be 95 degrees in front of the attic door it became a breathtaking, depressing 113 degrees behind it.

Vinny's training sessions began in mid-May when Vinny had been given word of his opponent and date by Lou. He had six weeks to get ready for his opponent and the scale. He was hovering at middleweight, weighing more than 165 pounds, and Master Seo was going to see to it that Vinny make weight at least one week before the fight to avoid last-minute drying out, which often led to his post-fight dehydration problems, a scenario Vinny was all too familiar with.

Each day at Hampshire Hills started the same with Master Seo and Vinny. Before any shadow-boxing Seo would stretch Vinny out for at least one half hour. He'd lay Vinny on his stomach and stretch his legs to his back, focusing on his hamstrings and glutes. He'd pull his arms to the center of his frame from behind and hold for a twenty count. Seo would lay Vinny on his back and put Vinny's size 8 foot on his own shoulder and walk forward toward Vinny in tiny, meticulous steps, focusing again on stretching Vinny's hamstrings, quads, and glutes. The trainer would slowly lift Vinny's arms up beyond his shoulder blades around to his lower back and hold, first his right arm then his left. Then Master Seo would stretch his neck ever so slowly, instructing his fighter to look slowly right and relax and breathe, then slowly left, relax, and breathe. And Angelo would observe. Unable to sit still, he mopped the floor, tightened up the speed bag, or tightened up the ropes of the ring he transported and restaged from Father and Son's, all the while keeping an eye on Master Seo's new training regimen.

Vinny poses at Ocean State Boxing weeks after first seeing *Rocky*.

Vinny poses with manager Lou Duva before the Roberto Elizondo fight.

Vinny celebrates after defeating Jake Carollo at the Trump Plaza Hotel in Atlantic City on April 14, 1989.

Paz-Haugen fight in Atlantic City, August 5, 1990. Paz won in a unanimous decision.

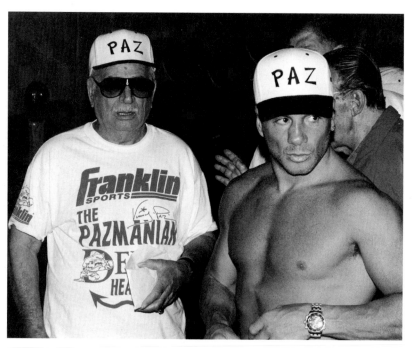

Vinny makes weight with Angelo by his side.

Vinny defeats Ron Amundson for the U.S. Boxing Association title.

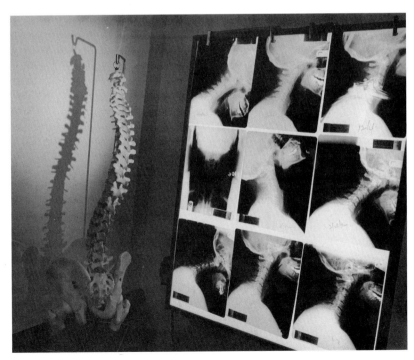

X-rays from the November 14, 1991, car accident that broke Vinny's neck.

Vinny trains for the comeback trail at a local gym in Warwick, Rhode Island.

Angelo celebrates his birthday at the Classic.

Vinny strengthens his neck in his basement gym.

Vinny celebrates with his idol, Muhammad Ali, and *Rocky* actor Burt Young. Vinny was awarded Comeback Fighter of the Year in 1992.

The stretching would continue until Vinny was in a deep sweat and Master Seo said it was time to move on to boxing-related drills. He would order Vinny to start off shadow-boxing for five five-minute rounds with the one-minute break between rounds to be replaced with jumping jacks or running in place. This he insisted would keep Vinny's heart rate up and at a maximum level. Vinny was then laced up with 14-ounce gloves while Angelo turned the timer on, and Vinny would spar ten to fourteen rounds with rotating sparring partners who either he or Main Events had requisitioned to Milford. The usual sparring partners included Classy Clarence Coleman from Newark, New Jersey; Sammy Young from upstate New York; Franco D'iorio from just outside of Boston; and Mike Austin, who was a visiting Aussie.

Of the four, Coleman was the most seasoned and clever, a 5'10" puncher with a quiet demeanor and an average record. He was getting ready for a title shot in July against Frankie Warren, and would go on in the coming years to fight for championships or against impressive champions Rafael Pineda, Saoul Mamby, Freddie Pendleton, Charles Murray, and against tough guys and top contenders Boston's "Irish" Mickey Ward and an always tough Tony Martin. Coleman had great talent, but could not quite get over the hurdle as a result of an overriding desire to earn street cred"; this, Vinny thought, diverted his attention from boxing. Coleman bragged he always carried an M&M with peanuts, which on the streets of Newark translated to a 9-millimeter semi-automatic handgun.

Sammy Young was a part-time fighter, small in stature and big in mouth. He was only about 5'6" and he talked and rah-rah'd his way through each sparring round and each sparring exchange with, "Yo, good job, champ, yo, good shot, Vinny, I'm comin' for ya now, ya hear?" When Vinny landed a good body punch, he'd respond with, "That's it, baby, my turn now." Young was also a fighter who lost way more than he won. His part-time job at a car wash kept his family fed.

Franco D'iorio had been an up-and-coming New England fighter but never made it out of the regional circuit. D'iorio was a real tough guy who liked the idea of fighting a little more than the actual fight, a guy who liked to say he was a fighter. He appeared on many of Vinny's undercards in Providence and did reasonably well. He was becoming a fan favorite, but Franco was always "saving himself" in training and never wanted to "Burn himself out." Vinny, who left every bit of himself every day in the gym, would always ask, "Burn yourself out? How? Kid, you're 25!" For some guys the thought of coping with the fear of failure was more frightening than the actual beating they might catch in a loss. Franco may have been one of those guys. When he came to Hampshire Hills a muscled-up 155 pounds on a 5'8" frame, he just mostly watched all the fighters train before he gave Vinny three or four rounds in the ring. Ironically, years down the road, when the two were a bit past their prime and shopworn, D'iorio would fight Clarence Coleman twice, defeating him both times.

And lastly, Mike Austin wandered into Vinny's Providence gym sometime that spring. He entered the gym as a fan and as an amateur boxing veteran from Australia, seeking an autograph, and wound up a fighter being quasi-trained by Vinny through sparring sessions. Austin was put on the June 26th card by Main Events at the urging of Vinny, where he would be making his pro debut. He was blond-haired and blue-eyed and looked like he would be more at home on an Australian 12-meter yacht in Newport racing for the America's Cup against Dennis Connor's *Star and Stripes*, instead of eating left hooks from Vinny in a downtrodden part of Providence or in an attic in the woods of New Hampshire. And despite his gleaming white teeth and straight nose, Austin proved to be up to the task. He gave Vinny solid rounds of boxing in which he would do everything he could not only to fend Vinny off but also provide enough offense that Vinny had to be careful with him. Because the Aussie could punch, and with his right hand, Vinny knew Mike could put a guy down under.

Following the twelve rounds of sparring, Vinny was already more than two hours into his workout. But there was more to come, much more: five rounds of speed-bag work, five rounds of heavy bag, five rounds of pad work, and five rounds of jumping rope. That brought us to the three-hour mark, when Master Seo allowed him about ten minutes to change into dry workout clothes. The sparring partners were done and they were sent back to their room or off to lunch, or to the pool to relax and get their rest. Vinny was headed down to the weightlifting gym for the next hour, where he would do repetition upon repetition of weight-training exercises and calisthenics: pullups, dips, situps, dumbbell presses, bench press, situps, pushups, etc., followed by back, biceps, triceps, and thighs, until the routine took Vinny into the fourth hour and into his 5-mile run into Milford's wooded hills, shadow-boxing in spurts and backpedaling up against the rugged terrain. When he got to the top of a hill he sprinted down the other end of it, blocking out sounds of the beating of his heart and the short-ness of breath with pounding music in his ears from his Walkman. His roadwork was done daily to build his endurance to take him through the later rounds, and to keep his weight in check.

That 5-mile run would irrevocably be followed by twenty 100-yard wind sprints on the soccer field of Hampshire Hills. Wind sprints build leg muscle and build the fast-twitch muscles in the body and ultimately the speed that would help Vinny in the ring—fast punches followed by fast feet and dotting angles, explosive punches, and coiled recoveries.

The daily five- to six-hour routine was the norm, not the excep-tion. Each day of work would end with Vinny sitting exhausted in a 106-degree hot tub, his hands hanging over the sides with Mas-ter Seo facing him in a baseball catcher–like position massaging his aching hands.

Master Seo was giving Vinny the first-class attention he craved and was not getting from Lou, and in return Vinny gave his trainer first-class effort. No matter how draining those five- to six-hour training sessions became, Vinny was out to prove to Master Seo that anything he threw at him he could endure, and that those training sessions would not be in vain. Somebody would have to pay for his pain.

On June 26th, Felix Dubray paid, as Vinny dismantled him with an alarming body assault for three rounds before turning his attention to Dubray's head. He broke his opponent's nose in the fourth round and ripped through the Black Hills native's defense with uppercuts and lead right hands, until Dubray drooped to his knees, head down, his long black hair covering his face and the blood from his nose splattering onto the canvas. Fight over. To nobody's surprise Vinny dispatched of Dubray easily.

But after all the grueling training and seven day a week, six-hour workouts leading up to the fight, Vinny still had lost a battle with his other opponent: the scale. Vinny weighed in at 144 pounds, 4 pounds over the junior-welterweight limit. Bruce "The Mouse" Strauss, Dubray's manager and a longtime friend and fan of Vinny's, allowed Vinny to fight, although he hadn't made weight. His reasoning was probably threefold. His first reason was probably guided by self-interest because if he didn't allow Vinny to fight, Main Events would have probably called off the show, thus Dubray wouldn't have gotten paid and in turn The Mouse wouldn't have gotten paid. Secondly, maybe just maybe, Vinny was all done or his face was giving out on him. The scar tissue that now built up thickly along the ridge of his brow from the brutal battles of the Haugen wars and the head butts of Marbi could lead to a blood-letting. Possibly the past rigors of his trade would catch up to Vinny and Dubray could get a victory via TKO by a stoppage on cuts. A win over Vinny could earn Dubray a top-ten ranking and maybe even a title shot. Thirdly, Bruce Strauss just liked Vinny. He referred to Vinny the week leading up to the fight as an "honest fighter," a fighter who never cheated himself or the fans. But the fight went on and the victory immediately landed Vinny a ranking in the junior-welterweight top ten.

And he was one fight away from a shot at reigning World Boxing Council Junior-Welterweight Champion Roger Mayweather. But first he had to head back to Hampshire Hills and the Spartan-like six-hour training sessions—after a two-week break.

July and August in New Hampshire meant serenity and calm to those who visited and hiked Mount Washington, water-skiied, and boated around Lake Winnapuasakee, or for the L.L. Bean crowd who shopped in North Conway bargain outlets. And just to the east, less than 100 miles from Vinny's training camp, was Hampton Beach. But for Vinny it was anything but summer fun. It meant preparation for his October fight against journeyman Rick Kaiser and a tentative championship date of November 7th against Roger Mayweather. If Vinny defeated Kaiser, he would star in the co-feature at Caesar's Palace in Las Vegas with Sugar Ray Leonard and Leonard's attempt to win the light-heavyweight championship against Canadian Donny Lalonde.

The summer sessions with Master Seo meant long days and lonely nights for Vinny. Angelo headed back to Providence and he and I would make weekend visits only. Nikki occasionally made secret visits once Master Seo dropped Vinny off at his hotel after a long day of training. From Fall River a few minutes past midnight, after a day's work in a clinical office and a night's work at The Classic at her waitressing job, she'd get in her (formerly Vinny's) Jeep Wrangler and drive northeast on 495, up Route 128, onto Route 3 north past Lowell and into New Hampshire, pay the 50-cent toll and arrive at Room 417 for an hour of loving, no questions asked by Master Seo and no dealing with Angelo. Not to mention the fact that it was all being done under the radar made it that much more exciting. No harm, no foul.

The greatest harm would be done to Rick Kaiser in Chicago on October 4th. Kaiser was a legitimate middleweight who weighed more than 160 pounds. He sucked down to 147 pounds in order to roll the dice against Vinny. Kaiser's hopes lay in the same formula Dubray had hoped to use to upset Vinny: cuts, cuts, and more cuts, hoping he could steal a TKO victory against a big name. The fight was made at the welterweight limit of 147 pounds to accommodate Kaiser. But Vinny entered the ring at the limit of 147 pounds. He looked thick through the back and his shoulders were wide. This worried Lou; it was the heaviest Vinny had ever gone into a fight and sometimes extra weight can mean sluggishness and a loss of speed. At the weigh-in, Duva for the first time started to outwardly question Vinny's time with Master Seo. "Why the fuck is he so heavy, goddammit. He's too fucking big," Lou growled to Angelo as the scale kept tipping upward, from 144 pounds to 145, 146, and it finally rested as Vinny held his breath to make the 147-pound limit. "Why don't you spend more time up there yourself with Vinny, you fat bastard," Angelo said. He moved toward Lou and stopped only when he heard a plea coming from Vinny in his leopard underwear to calm down.

But Lou was concerned on two levels. One, that Vinny would weigh 154-plus pounds against Kaiser on fight night, because he knew Vinny would gain at least 7 to 10 pounds after the weigh-in and into the ring. And he knew that the November 7th date with Roger Mayweather was looming, and Vinny was still having trouble making the 147-pound weight limit, never mind the 140-pound limit he would have to make in just five weeks. And on November 7th there would be no "take a few." (The expression "take a few" referred to a clause in many contracts for non-title fights that allowed boxers to come in at a weight either a few pounds lighter or heavier.) It was a title fight, which meant make the 140-pound limit or lose the opportunity to fight and lose the $300,000 purse that went along with it. Two, Lou was immediately concerned whether or not Vinny could hold that kind of weight in the ring. Fighters who carry excess weight for the first time in a fight, whether it be fat or muscle, tend to lose hand and foot speed, become lethargic in the ring, and run out of gas faster because their bodies and hearts aren't accustomed to carrying the extra weight. And what contributes more to the unknown of carrying extra weight is the fact that no matter how much good sparring does a fighter in terms of sharpness and the fighter avoiding ring rust, sparring can never simulate the speed and stress of a live fight.

But Lou need not have been concerned, on this night anyway, as Vinny dispatched Kaiser easily, looking like he was punching harder than ever. His opponent flew to the canvas twice in the second round and three times in the third. Each time Kaiser went down he landed back first, feet above his head, and a loud thud filled Park West. The punches were so emphatic and Kaiser was so animated in his knockdowns that Vinny stared into his gloves in his neutral corner, as the journeyman struggled to his feet, with an "am I punching that hard tonight?" look on his face.

It was once again back to Hampshire Hills where Vinny would begin his quest for a second world championship against the Las Vegas bookmakers' odds, as he was immediately installed as a 3 to 1 underdog against the WBC champion. But as he left the ring victorious on Chicago's South Side, he weighed more than 154 pounds and he had less than five weeks before he met his lifelong nemesis, the scale. In Vegas that nemesis would be followed by another nemesis, a brooding Roger Mayweather.

When Vinny and Angelo got back to New Hampshire on October 11 after a week off, Vinny seemed more ornery than usual. He was back up to 164 pounds and he needed to shed 24 pounds in four weeks: 6 pounds per week. True, a championship fight was only four weeks away and most times ornery was good. But this ornery seemed to be different. His extra weight and the five- to six-hour days seemed to be wearing on him emotionally as well as physically. Master Seo's three-a-day workouts rolled into one weren't getting Vinny's weight down a week prior to fights as promised. On top of that he had been in training camp for over four months with some short breaks in between, and the every-day bumps and bruises were starting to take their toll. Vinny's right hand became permanently disfigured somewhere between the Arroyo fight and the end of the first Haugen fight. It looked as if a baseball had been stuffed between his thumb and index finger and then shoved back tightly under his skin toward his wrist. Jumping rope became a chore because it was difficult for him to hold the rope. The days of running long winding hills on hard bumpy roads gave him shin splints and the constant concern of diet was eating at him.

Master Seo wasn't letting up at all, and after a long sparring session one afternoon in October he ordered Vinny to throw at least 1,000 punches per round. And when Vinny wasn't able to throw 1,000 punches in the round, Seo counted only 200. So, Seo ordered him again to throw 1,000 punches in the next round. Again negative. Master Seo chastised Vinny for his poor performance. "Binny, no good, no good, 225 punches no good, you need 300 punches! Three more minutes." Again Vinny heard those words, "no good, no good, no good, no good." Although Master Seo probably only said "no good" once, his voice became trapped in Vinny's head, a 33 record stuck on an old Victrola, "no good, no good."

Vinny tore off his headgear, tearing through the buckled strap and throwing it to the canvas, kicking it through the rope and spitting out his mouthpiece. "No good?" he choked on his words, "no fucking good?" He questioned Master Seo questioning him. "It's impossible, you hear me! It can't be done . . . a punch a second is only 180 punches." Vinny's voice raised with each word. For the two prior rounds Vinny had respectfully appeased Master Seo, but he had done the math in his head beforehand. One thousand divided by 180 seconds [one round] is 333 punches per 60 seconds. It can't be done.

But now he called Seo out when he started to question his work ethic, his character. Angelo cut his tape and unlaced his gloves. "All right, Vinny, that enough, that's enough." Vinny walked past Classy Clarence and Sammy Young: "Go get 'em, champ," Sammy said. Young's words brought Vinny back slowly from his building anger. He went to the jump rope and skipped, then stared straight ahead and skipped some more. He threw punches intermittently with the ropes still clenched in his hands: "Bop, bop, rhh, bahhh!"

It was the first time in five months that Vinny had questioned his trainer. Perhaps the six-hour, seven-days-a-week schedule was getting to Vinny. Perhaps the immersion of boxing was drowning him. Perhaps it was just the strain of leading up to a career crossroads fight, where a loss could cost him his career or certainly hurt his marketability in the boxing futures. Perhaps it was something more.

The something more became evident in Las Vegas on fight night. After Vinny succesfully shed the 24 pounds to make weight, his body craved bread, steak, and rigatoni. And Master Seo and Lou Duva craved the spotlight as the two got into a self-serving shouting match after the weigh-in, in Vinny's room the night before the fight. Angelo played impartial referee at first between Seo and Duva as Vinny sat at his long, modern dining-room table sipping hot wonton soup with a cup of white rice. Lou had allowed Master Seo to work Vinny's corner against Felix Dubray and Rick Kaiser. They were lesser opponents and Lou knew both were easy work for Vinny. But now the spotlight shined and a pay-per-view fight with Sugar Ray Leonard as co-feature meant millions of viewers all over the world. There was no way Main Events was going to let a little-known boxing trainer who spoke broken English and who had never been a lead trainer in a world title fight call the shots, while Lou, the megamanager and WBC trainer of the year, held a spit bucket.

Master Seo found himself in the same place Freddie LaFazia had been in years back at the train station: on the outside looking in. Angelo had one concern, the same concern he had on track 19 with Freddie LaFazia and the same concern Angelo had in Edgewood, for that matter the one and only concern Angelo ever had: Vinny. And with Vinny now embroiled in the argument of who was going to work his corner, Angelo had seen enough.

The truth was, Vinny was losing faith in Master Seo and the six-hour training days that left him dehydrated and sapped his strength, but left him still unable to make weight. The gaffed-up corner instructions from Seo and the orders that Vinny throw 1,000 punches a round insulted his boxing intelligence. As far as Vinny was concerned, the eating of wonton soup before one of the most important nights of his life, after a double-digit weight loss and after already making the 140-pound weight limit, and Seo's draconian training and dieting methods had exposed him. When Angelo saw that Vinny had had enough of Master Seo in that audacious Caesar's Palace suite, he did the same thing he always did, this time a little more handily. As Master Seo continued his argument with Lou in a high-pitched mix of Korean and English, Angelo jumped from his chair using its brown oak arms for extra leverage and swooped down on Master Seo, putting him in a bear hug from the back, splitting the seams of his hounds-tooth jacket, exposing his burgundy silk shirt beneath, and dragging him to the door of the room, along the way talking to him in a warning whisper. "You're not welcome here no more, you fucking phony." Angelo caught his breath and talked some more. "You fucking fraud, you're killin' my kid." Vinny jumped up from the table to restrain his 71-year-old father, the porcelain bowl spilling over the table's side and smashing to the black marble floor, but it was too late, as Vinny arrived to the slamming door. As quickly as the relationship between Vinny and Master Seo had started, the end came just as fast as it was Seo who held the spit bucket on fight night, not Lou Duva.

Twenty-eight hours after the acrimonious split between fighter and trainer, in the desert climate of Las Vegas in the early hours of November 8th, Vinny was facing yet another life-threatening bout of dehydration. The uncompromising training over the past six months resulted in another title opportunity lost, and another period of his career without a trainer, but more important it resulted in Vinny fighting for his life at Sunrise Medical Hospital. After losing a unanimous decision to Roger Mayweather in Las Vegas for the WBC Super-Lightweight Championship, he left the ring lightheaded and nauseous. His heart raced and his pulse slowed. His skin was dry and ashy white behind the red welts left behind by Mayweather. He was rushed by ambulance to the hospital where he seemed lethargic and was becoming incoherent, unable to answer reasonable questions from emergency room doctors.

Dehydration can be fatal if not treated swiftly. The body can go into ketosis, which is when there simply is not enough body fluid to keep the body's organs operating sufficiently. The decrease in total body water reduces the number of blood cells in the body. This negative fluid balance results from decreased intake and increased output of fluids and long periods of depleting your body from its natural water and caloric intake levels. The very functioning of essential organs like the brain, heart, kidneys, and nervous system is compromised without sufficient water or minerals. This was the consequence of Vinny following Seo's training regimen and continually trying to lose weight over the preceding six months.

As dehydration progresses, hypovolemic shock can ensue, which can result in heat stroke, organ failure, or even death. Vinny remained in the hospital for seventy-two hours, where he was rehydrated with glucose and electrolytes. The IV had to be inserted in his ankle because the arteries in his arm were so dense as a result of his dehydration. But things worsened before they got better. His pulse and blood pressure tumbled downward far below their norms. Making matters worse, the last bit of fighting Vinny had in him was left at Caesar's Palace. He drifted off, his mind in the clouds and thought: "Fuck it, I lost the fight, in front of Stallone. What's wrong with my body tonight?" His body felt as if it was drifting further away from him, detaching, his mind pushing him away from his own body.

A thermometer was placed in Vinny's ear near his eardrum, a measurement that quickly registers the temperature of internal organs. It was 96.1, 1.1 degrees above the hypothermic level. A male nurse's voice rang out as he strapped a Velcro wrap around Vinny's arm and pumped a ball at its end. "Blood pressure's dropping badly, 110 over 58, pulse rate down to 40 beats," he yelled out openly to four emergency room doctors surrounding Vinny.

"Mr. Pazienza, we're losing him, we're losing him," another emergency room nurse said, looking to Angelo for help. The doctors moved in slow motion, far too slow for Angelo anyway. Angelo grabbed Vinny's damp hooded sweatshirt and started to shake it, raising Vinny's head from the gurney. "Vinny, wake up. Vinny, wake up, let's go." Angelo shook some more and brought in Vinny to his chest. "C'mon, Vinny, don't worry about a fight. You hear me, Vinny."

The lights above Vinny and the hospital metal doors shone in Vinny's eyes as he felt himself coming back to his body. His father's face came together in pieces as the emergency room staff called out more numbers, numbers that were not significant to him, but numbers that alerted Angelo that Vinny's vital signs were improving.

Angelo hugged Vinny again: C'mon, Vinny, stay with me." He held Vinny tighter. "We're gonna be okay, Vinny, we're gonna be okay." Vinny lay his head on Angelo's chest, smelled the familiar scent of his father, and experienced the familiar feel of his body and the familiar sound of his protecting and loving voice. Again, like always, Angelo was there.

15   King's Con and Kevin Rooney

Weeks following the Mayweather defeat, Main Events called heavyweight champion Mike Tyson's recently fired trainer Kevin Rooney to see if he had any interest in training Vinny. Rooney was fired in the latter half of 1988 around the same time Angelo showed Master Seo the door. Tyson's mentor Cus D'Amato died in November of 1985, and D'Amato's upstart protégé, Kevin Rooney, had taken the reins. Together, Tyson and Rooney dominated the heavyweight division and boxing for that matter, crushing opponents and breaking live gate attendance and pay-per-view records from 1985 onward. But when the undefeated heavyweight champion decided he had to restructure his boxing management team, going from longtime managers, the late Jimmy Jacobs and his partner Bill Cayton, to Don King Promotions led by "Con Man" Don King, as Kevin Rooney would forever refer to him, Rooney would be odd man out.

Tyson's personal life was in shambles and it was intruding on his professional life, as he was in the midst of an ugly divorce from soon-to-be-ex-wife actress Robin Givens. Rooney, being a fiercely loyal friend and trainer to Tyson, was asked a question in an interview regarding Tyson's marital bliss and according to Rooney, he "just answered the question honestly." "Mike didn't need her," Rooney said, meaning Givens in Tyson's life. This was the comment that got Rooney fired. Rooney maintained that King filled Tyson's head with notions of "anti-white paranoia and suggestions that Tyson shouldn't trust white doctors, bankers, managers, accountants, lawyers, and boxing trainers." According to Rooney, the $100,000 tax-free cash King delivered to Tyson in a black briefcase also may have played a role.

Tyson's Aphroditean misery and misfortune became Vinny's fortune, as the now unemployed and ostracized trainer was looking for work. Rooney maintained that Lou first floated the idea of hiring Kevin Rooney to Angelo before ever speaking to Vinny. Angelo was desperate. He knew he had to atone for the hiring of Master Seo. He knew it was he who had brought Seo to Vinny. He also knew it was he who set Vinny's career back almost a year. He also knew he also had brought death by dehydration to Vinny's dressing room door, as a result of the burn-out training methods exacted on his son by Master Seo.

Angelo loved the idea of hiring Rooney. He knew of Rooney's boxing pedigree. Rooney was a fighter himself who was closing in on a world title opportunity before being knocked out by Alexis Arguello in two rounds at Atlantic City's Bally's Place, never to be the same. His coconut eternally cracked. His career ended just two and a half years later at the age of just 29 with a 21-4 record. All four losses came by way of knockout.

If the championship belt eluded Kevin as a fighter, it certainly didn't elude him as a boxing trainer, as he guided Mike Tyson to a world heavyweight championship at the earnest age of 30. Rooney was from the legendary teaching school of Cus D'Amato, who had guided Floyd Patterson to the heavyweight title during the early 1960s. D'Amato had converted an old rundown police station into a boxing gym in the Catskills. Staten Islander Rooney migrated to the country after his boxing career to learn his craft under the birds-eye tutelage of D'Amato.

Rooney used D'Amato's peekaboo style of fighting to finish the raw skills of Tyson. One minute he would be a flat-footed, fast-footed, deceptive, defensive boxer and the next minute he would burst into an offensive explosion, each movement of the head setting up the next punch. Never stop moving your head; never let a punch miss without a response, the next punch thrown setting set up the defense to end again in an offensive posture. Angelo also loved the fact that Rooney was a big name and Vinny would be his most well-known fighter. But he also knew the style of boxing Kevin taught, and he just didn't know whether that style was right for Vinny, who was not a flat-footed boxer.

When Angelo took the news to Vinny he was ecstatic. First, because it was a sign the boxing world wasn't writing him off. There was almost no talk of retirement by the local press or Main Events, no sanctimonious story lines about a fighter walking away into the sunset or theatrical parallels with his boyhood idol, Rocky Balboa, and no postmortem press conferences. Second, Kevin Rooney was a throwback trainer who trained throwback fighters. Because beneath the sequined shorts and the gold lamé robe, Vinny defined himself less by wins or losses and more by the ability to pick himself up when he was down, more by his blue-collar roots and less by the showmanship persona that preceded his "gone-Hollywood" reputation.

Vinny brought Tommy and me the news, but first he played a game of guess who. "Guess who my new trainer is?" he asked me and Tommy Mart on the way to a fundraiser for The Impossible Dream, an organization that brought the dreams of terminally ill children to reality. Vinny's brother-in-law's father, John Florio, had started the charitable organization a few years earlier. "I don't know, who?" I was never one for games. "Come on, guess. One guess."

"I don't know, but he better at least speak English after that last disaster."

"Fucking guess, already." Vinny became excited.

"Eddie Futch."

"No. Guess again."

"Angelo Dundee."

"Good guess, but no."

"You back with Georgie Benton?"

"Nope, Kevin Rooney," Vinny finally said. He was busting and couldn't wait another second.

"He's gonna train you in Providence?"

"No, Catskills. Home of heavyweight champion Mike Tyson."

Tommy Mart chimed in. "Back to the woods. Kid, sorry, you're not cut out for the woods. Neither is your father."

"Stop, stop, don't be a black cloud. I'm with Kevin Rooney now." Vinny couldn't contain his energy as his BMW picked up speed into the parking lot, his life headed in another direction.

When Rooney became Vinny's trainer, he was shocked to see Vinny actually weighed 170 pounds. After their first workout together in the worn-out police station, Kevin asked his new fighter why he was fighting junior-welterweight. He told Vinny the first thing he should do before he threw another punch was to move up to middleweight. Vinny told Kevin he asked Lou many times to move up to welterweight (147 pounds) but each time he was denied. "Forget welterweight, Vinny, you're a middleweight, you can't lose 25, 30 pounds and expect to be any good, you're a dead man walking." Kevin insisted. But Main Events insisted on Vinny losing the weight. Lou thought Vinny was too small and not disciplined enough at the table, often making light of Vinny's weight troubles and telling the press Vinny had to stay away from Louise's pizza and pasta. Kevin Rooney was a trainer only. He wasn't a manager, a promoter, or a matchmaker. Main Events owned Vinny's contract and they would tell him where, when, and whom to fight. And if he didn't oblige, he didn't fight. And if he didn't fight he didn't make a living, pure and simple. So he continued at 140 pounds.

Although Angelo liked the idea of moving up in weight, he wasn't sold on the idea of middleweight. Even a move to 147 was a stretch, Angelo thought, and maybe he had a point. Simon Brown was dominating the division before he won the title in the early part of 1988 defeating Tyrone Trice in fourteen rounds, then unifying the belt with a win over Maurice Blocker. He would go on to defend his title nine times until he finally lost in 1991. During his reign he was generally accepted as one of the top-ten pound-for-pound fighters in the world, not a guy you'd want to face when trying to get your career back on track. Angelo kept Simon Brown off Vinny's radar.

Marlon Starling was also a welterweight whose style worried Angelo. He wasn't tall, but his arms were long and his neck and torso were a mix of elastic and rubber. He was patient and defensive, a counter-puncher who might lull Vinny's frantic style to sleep the same way he had put Simon Brown to sleep a few fights earlier.

So Vinny trained with Kevin for two fighters with similar Italian-American lineage but nothing else. First, he disposed of Jake Carollo in two rounds in Atlantic City on April 14, 1989. Vinny walked the Chicagoan to his corner, spun his back to the ropes, and ducked under a Carollo right hand and *peekaboo*, like Kevin had taught him, jumped up with a thwarting left hook knocking Carollo out and simultaneously splitting the seams of his black lightweight trucks down the middle. Vinny left the casino crowd with a victory and with a towel wrapped around his waist.

Almost eight weeks later, on June 11th, Vinny faced off against his namesake Vinny Burghese. Burghese was 17 and 1 and had become a regular on USA Network's *Tuesday Night Fights*. He was a South Philly kid who was marketed as The Next Rocky, because "he shared the streets with Balboa." All the promos and spots leading up to the fight for NBC were shots of Burghese running up those famous Philadelphia Museum of Art stairs that Rocky ran up guided by that same Bill Conti music. Burghese posed next to the statue of Rocky, as if NBC was marketing him to be next in the line of Italian-American warriors pushing Vinny, their former matinee idol, from that mantle. Behind the scenes, Burghese's father worried that maybe his son wasn't ready just yet for an experienced fighter like Vinny. He'd already lost to John Rafuse, a Boston fighter Vinny had regularly worn out in sparring through the years at Father and Son's Gym. It was rumored that Burghese's father begged him not to take the fight with Vinny Paz. This time Burghese's father was the guy behind the fence, trying to protect his son, trying not to get him hurt.

Burghese should have listened to his father, because he wasn't ready for what Vinny brought that day: too much experience, too much skill, and too much of Vinny as he fought to retain his mantle as the best Rocky-like story NBC had to offer.

Burghese lost all ten rounds before being knocked out, just like Jake Carollo with a peekaboo left hook that left him staring straight into the rafters as his father jumped through the ropes to save his son from any more Pazienza punishment.

Five months later on November 27th, Vinny knocked out another wannabe, Eddie Van Kirk, in five rounds in Providence. A win is a win is a win, and this fight had greater significance than the previous two. It was a tune-up fight for 36-0 left-handed magician Hector Camacho in a fight that would be billed as "Put Up or Shut Up." The three wins against Carollo, Burghese, and Van Kirk were nothing more than staging to reach another plateau; they were guinea pigs for Kevin Rooney's imprint on Vinny and a new fighting style, stepping stones toward another run at a big money fight and a world title. A Camacho fight offered both of those things. Camacho was putting his WBO junior-welterweight belt on the line in a fight that would captivate the boxing world.

Fifteen months after his loss to Roger Mayweather, Vinny was once again seeking redemption in front of a roaring, pro-Vinny crowd of fifteen thousand–plus people, this time at Trump Plaza in Atlantic City.

Hector Camacho could be the perfect opponent. He was a huge gate draw with a huge Hispanic following. He was a flashy and charismatic fighter who transcended boxing into the mainstream sporting world. He evoked emotion: People loved or hated him after seeing him, and few fans remained ambivalent. He came out of the dressing room and walked down the aisle like a runway model walks the catwalk at a Ford or Elite Party, dressing in an array of different costumes, from an American Indian with a full-feathered headdress and moccasins or as a peacock, all the while dancing to the song "Macho Man" by the Village People. Boxing purists often seemed repulsed by his act, but they could never argue with the outcome, because he was so very talented. He had come away unscathed in all 36 fights up to that point, outclassing just about any fighter he'd ever fought.

He was a sharp-shooting southpaw with hand speed the likes of Ray Leonard and the craftiness of Pernell Whitaker. When people referred to great legs in the ring, Camacho was their poster child. And Vinny said aloud what most people didn't give Camacho credit for. "He could punch." According to Vinny it was simple physics: Speed generates power. Camacho had defeated Ray "Boom Boom" Mancini via split decision eleven months earlier in Reno, Nevada, and had two fights after against un-notables to keep busy while waiting for Vinny.

His résumé was a lightweight who's who of boxing: Cornelius Boza Edwards, American Olympian Howard Davis Junior, lightweight champions Edwin Rosario and Jose Luis Ramirez. All great fights, and all fell under the W column on Camacho's boxing dossier. But many in the boxing world, including Main Events and Lou, thought Camacho was ripe for defeat. Lou felt that he had lost his swagger after defeating Edwin Rosario in 1986 in a controversial split decision, when Camacho was rocked by a Rosario left hook. He seemed never to recover from that. Lou and others felt that he had lost his greatness that night and it never returned. He turned into a runner as a result of that left hook and refused to stay in the pocket, forfeiting his punching power, just happy to win fights on his skill and craftiness. Las Vegas bookmakers agreed as Vinny was installed as a 2 to 1 favorite.

Vinny wasn't about to take a backseat to Camacho in terms of drawing power, as Angelo helped Trump Plaza set up junkets from Providence to Atlantic City. Rhode Islanders followed Vinny down to the Jersey shore in the dead of winter six thousand strong, by junket, train, and from I-95 south, over the Tappan Zee Bridge or through New York City to the Jersey Turnpike southward. Italian-Americans came out in full force to support Vinny.

In his proverbial corner that night, the Greatest Living Ballplayer Joltin' Joe DiMaggio, retired Oakland Raider Phil Villapiano, Ray Mancini, president of the Italian-American Sports Hall of Fame George Randazzo, Sylvester Stallone, and many others.

They would all leave disappointed as Vinny lost the first four rounds. Vinny was done in by Kevin Rooney and Mike Tyson's peekaboo style, choosing to fight flat-footed instead of like his whirlwind self. Vinny played the role of the bull while Hector Camacho comfortably played the matador. When Vinny changed his strategy and became elusive and unpredictable in rounds five through twelve, he dominated the action, winning five of the last eight rounds. But it was too late: He lost a frustrating unanimous decision on points. Judges Jose Salcedo and John Rupert had the fight scored similarly, 117-116 and 115-112, while Richard F. Murray had Camacho a runaway winner, 119-109.

A perfect storm of circumstances seemed to be conspiring to end Vinny's career after he had lost three straight high-profile championship fights. The weight battles, his transitioning style, and his bleeding face all raged in the eye of the cloud hovering over Vinny's career. Although his weight for the Camacho fight didn't seem to be an issue on this frozen February night, it certainly had been a major factor in his two previous losses against Haugen and Mayweather.

He was also caught in between boxing styles, both in a physical sense and a philosophical sense. Rooney's style, which Vinny was still learning, betrayed Vinny as he gave up an insurmountable lead. Losing the early rounds seems to work better for one-punch knockout artists, a style better suited for heavyweights who throw minimal amounts of punches, but who generally can end a fight with one heavy blow. That was never Vinny's forte. He could be that one-punch knockout guy against the Jake Carollos of the world, but not against the class of the division. Could he learn Kevin's style in mid-career and win another world title? And was this style suited for Vinny? These were the prevailing questions. Only a non-title, ten-round unanimous victory over Greg Haugen in August of 1990, again in Atlantic City, seven months after the "Put Up or Shut Up" fight, kept Vinny's career flickering.

But on December 1, 1990, his face had given way in Sacramento, California, trying to wrestle the WBA Junior Welterweight Championship away from champion Loreto Garza. Losing on all scorecards from the onset, Vinny, in a futile attempt, frustrated and bleeding, hoisted the 6'2" Garza to the top rope, picked him up between his legs, and Garza held on for dear life as the referee Larry Rosadilla slid in amid the mayhem and pulled Vinny away, disqualifying him.

In the corner, trainer Kevin Rooney nursed yet another massive cut, this one below Vinny's right eye. It was thick and meaty as Kevin pressed three Q-tips bound together into the cut to stop the hemorrhaging, his face torn up by Garza's jabs and his other recent wars. The putrid maroon blood spattered on his shoulders and coagulating in his hair fight after fight was becoming unbearable.

His body and his face seemed no longer willing to cooperate with his mind. He was now 29-4 and had lost four championship fights in a row. He was 6 and 4, little more than a .500 fighter since winning his title, and had defeated only one top-ten fighter in that span, losing, regardless of the perfect storm of circumstances, to the top fighters of the lightweight and junior welterweight divisions.

Kevin again questioned Lou Duva and Angelo as to why Vinny was sucking down to 140 pounds to fight. Again, Kevin pressed Angelo openly for him to move up to middleweight.

For Lou, the reason was obvious. For almost the last three years, Vinny had still been a huge draw, even though he had won only 7 of his last 11 fights and had lost in his three bids at regaining a world championship. Whether Vinny won or lost, it almost didn't matter to Lou because he always bled, he always entertained, and the turnstiles always spun. But after the Garza fight, they had seen enough. At the post-fight press conference, which Vinny did not attend as he again was at an emergency room getting his face stitched, Main Events and Lou Duva called for Vinny's retirement. Lou prefaced it by saying all the right things. "Vinny was a true warrior, a tough guy by anyone's standards, but his better days are behind him." Behind the scenes, Lou and Danny were beginning to think Vinny's ability and the drawing power of his name were declining. Plus, their cupboard was stocked full with champions and title contenders, Holyfield, Breland, Taylor, Whitaker—all earning seven figures for Main Events. The fact that Lou called for his retirement outwardly to the press following the Loreto Garza fight without consulting him was an embarrassment and according to Vinny, "the first act of betrayal."

Vinny's troubles continued at home as well. One week before the Garza fight and with Vinny already in Sacramento, Father and Son's gym caught fire on a freezing, ice-ridden stormy night. Luckily, the boxing ring, heavy bags, speed bags and all of his belts and memorabilia were salvaged because the fire was contained to the second floor. Unfortunately, Angelo took the biggest hit. He lost thousands of dollars of "merchandise" he had already paid for, his Christmas inventory including Hugo Boss suits, Bally shoes, gold chains and charms, colognes, perfumes, and even five full-length mink coats. Of course, none of those things were insured, because in reality they didn't exist. Providence Fire Department investigators quickly identified the fire as accidental and as an "electrical malfunction," and any notion of foul play was put to rest.

16   The Banking Crisis

To Nikki's credit, she recognized that Vinny was reeling. His career seemed to be slipping away, his gym had almost burned to the ground, and those things were beginning to take a toll on their relationship. She surprised Vinny with a Christmas vacation and a chance to get away, a trip to Las Vegas, and this time Vegas would be solely for pleasure. They would leave the day after Christmas, celebrate New Year's Eve at Caesar's Palace, and return New Year's Day evening, just in time to celebrate the holiday with the family and the Italian tradition: For good luck, the Pazienzas and Nikki would be having their annual lentil soup.

After the Chino Rivera fight in 1983, Vinny not only procured greater skill in the ring, he also refined his skill as a blackjack player. His six-hour run on the Caesar's Palace blackjack table started after his New Year's Eve dinner at Caesar's Palace, and ended in the wee hours of the dry desert morning. Onlookers gathered around Vinny's table, and two good-looking couples in their late 20s, dressed to the nines, stopped and positioned themselves behind Vinny. He was the lone player on the table, one on one, Vinny versus the house. Sensing excitement was brewing, after each winning hand Nikki raised her arms in the air and draped herself on Vinny's shoulders from behind. Vinny gave high-fives to strangers and tipped the revolving dealers handsomely for their generosity. As his pile of purple $500 chips grew, so did the curiosity on the casino floor. By this point the crowd around the table was three deep. Vinny upped his ante playing multiple hands at once, splitting cards, and doubled-down every opportunity he had. He had over $55,000 of chips on the table and gave $20,000 of them to Nikki to put in her purse.

"Don't give these back to me, no matter what," he instructed Nikki, knowing he might have all the discipline in the world when it came to boxing and training, but gambling, especially blackjack, was another story. Moreover, he figured he could now take a shot with "their money." It was house money, so according to Vinny if he lost the $35,000 it wasn't really his anyway. And who knows, maybe he thought he could parlay this $35,000 into $50,000, $100,000, or . . . .

For two more hours the crowd stayed and Vinny was once again on stage as he entertained his new fans: $2,500 hands, $5,000 double downs, and $10,000 split hands. At one point Vinny was up well over $50,000, but as many gamblers do, like so many fighters (see Abdelkar Marbi), Vinny stayed too long and the house got some of its money back. But Nikki still had the $20,000 in her purse, and now it was time to go. Vinny was unaware at the time that the $20,000 in Nikki's purse might be the only money he had left.

Walking away from a blackjack table with $20,000 was comparable to Vinny earning a $100,000 payday. After paying taxes, promotional fees, management fees, trainers' fees, and sparring partners, his gross earnings were usually ravaged. But this time the whole $20,000 was his.

Before leaving, Vinny treated Nikki to a shopping spree at Caesar's Coiffures on the hotel's ground floor before they took their 11:00 a.m. flight back to Rhode Island. Nikki bought $800 knee-high leather Chanel boots, a $1,000 North Pacific electric blue leather jacket with a matching leather beret, and finally, to cap the outfit off, a $750 Fendi bag with a bad attitude. She wore her new garb for the trip home.

When Nikki and Vinny boarded the Boeing 747 for their return flight to Providence on New Year's Day 1991, their relationship suddenly didn't seem so strained. They sat in first class, in luxurious tan leather reclined seats and sipped mimosas with California strawberries. Their seats were upgraded, compliments of player rep Jimmy Longo and Caesar's Palace. Vinny had $17,000 tucked in his boot, à la Angelo, and all seemed good in the world. Vinny put aside $3,000 for Louise as an added Christmas gift that could now go along with her new food processor and state-of-the art VCR.

"God, Nikki, you look so fucking hot," he said. He pulled Nikki close and ran his hand upward beyond her knee-high boots and underneath her miniskirt. He ran his other hand above her head, took off her hat, and ran his fingers through Nikki's silky straight black hair.

"Vinny, we can't," Nikki said, breathing heavily. She looked around and behind her.

"But you're so fucking beautiful," Vinny said and caressed Nikki more. He grabbed a blanket and put it over the two of them, and in one swoop he lifted Nikki and she got on top of him. They acted as if it was a loving hug and nothing more than an affectionate moment.

A now content Vinny thought it was a good time to call home and make sure Angelo and Louise knew he would be there for lentil soup. But when Vinny called his mother 37,000 feet above the Rocky Mountains to tell her the good news about his winnings, Louise uncharacteristically answered the phone somberly and with the weight of the world on her shoulders.

"Ma, Ma," Vinny spoke loudly over the plane's hum into the phone, "I won $20,000 last night, tell Dad . . . I'm gonna give you and Dad—"

Louise interrupted him. "Vinny, listen to me sweetheart. I got bad news for you."

Louise, like every other Italian mother, was known for her drama and hyperbole, so Vinny responded lightly, especially with the high he was riding. "What? C'mon, Ma, I just won $20,000."

"Vinny, the banks are closed down. Nobody can get their money. All the credit unions, Vinny, it's all over the papers and on the news." Vinny remained silent on the other end of the phone. "The governor closed all the banks this morning, and nobody can get their money," she repeated herself. "You gotta get home."

"Ma," Vinny's ire rose, "I'm on the plane, 40,000 feet in the air, I'll be home by eight o'clock." Vinny hung up the phone and just stared straight ahead, shaking his head.

"What's the matter, Vinny?" Vinny continued thinking silently. "What the fuck's the matter?" Nikki asked again. "Answer me! Is everything all right with your mother and father?"

Vinny told Nikki what was going on back home, and that all the money he had to his name was in a credit union that now was officially closed. Only two weeks earlier over breakfast, I had told Vinny what a great interest rate he could get at Cranston Municipal Credit Union. "8½ percent, champ! What do you get at Citizens Bank?"

Vinny didn't know, but he quickly inquired, and by the time Cranston Municipal Credit Union closed that day, Vinny's $300,000 worth of blood money, literally, sat with my $3,000 of tuition money in the same bank, the same bank that was now closed with a 6-inch chain link lock and Rhode Island state troopers guarding it.

The day before Bruce Sundlun was to be sworn in as Rhode Island's forty-first governor, he realized he had to do what no other governor in the state's history had to do, close forty-five banks, in particular savings and loans and credit unions. Sundlun had learned prior to his taking office that the state's credit unions were going into receivership, thus freezing the assets of 211,000 families. It was Rhode Island's personal savings and loan debacle. When President Reagan deregulated the banking industry in the early 1980s, it opened up a legal economic windfall for bankers, developers, loanees, and politicians, both on a national and local level.

In Rhode Island there were entangling alliances involving bankers who were lending out high-risk, collateral-free loans that ranged into the hundreds of thousands of dollars and sometimes millions to quasi-business partners, friends, political cronies, and Rhode Island mobsters. To the layperson it all seemed so illegal. But in fact, such dealings were legal, albeit unethical. All the players seemed to be connected in this murky superficial veil of secrecy that was maintained in the polluted, stench-filled backrooms of banks and boardrooms. Developers and business leaders were getting million dollar nonguaranteed loans for building projects that were unlikely ever to come to fruition. In return, those loanees would give kickbacks to politicians for legislative favors and to bankers to procure their loans. At the center of the scandal was Joe Mollicone, aka "Puppy Dog," who for years was president of the Heritage Savings and Loan, a post he had inherited from his father on Providence's Federal Hill. The family had longtime ties to the Rhode Island underworld and also to the Rhode Island legislature. Coincidentally, "Puppy Dog" Sr. had taken part in many of Angelo's craps games on Decatur Square years earlier.

The economic and political graft added up to banking and ethical malpractice, especially because these financial organizations had to meet few of the federal guidelines and mandates previously instituted during the Great Depression that applied to traditional banks. To re-instill confidence in the nation's banks, the Federal Deposit Insurance Company [FDIC] had been created. This was part of Franklin Delano Roosevelt's economic reformation, put in place by the federal government to insure all banking procedures.

But credit unions and savings and loans in Rhode Island were not insured by FDIC: they were insured by the Rhode Island Share and Depositors Insurance Corporation (RISDIC). In short, forty-five banks were insured by the state and RISDIC, and both were going into receivership. The failure of RISDIC meant that the funds insured in those institutions were no longer insured, and by state law, the institutions could not continue to operate without insurance.

As a result, among Sundlun's first official acts as governor on January 1, 1991, he ordered the immediate closing of the banking institutions insured by RISDIC. They were to remain closed until such time as they could obtain insurance from the federal government [FDIC] or the National Credit Union Association (NCUA).

The principal response of the Sundlun administration was the development, introduction, and passage of legislation entitled The Depositors Economic Protection Act. This legislation created a government agency, the Depositors Economic Protection Corporation (DEPCO). The function of this agency was to restore funds, as quickly as possible, to depositors whose accounts were frozen. DEPCO would work with officials and depositors of closed institutions to assist them in getting federal insurance or to assist them in finding other banking institutions willing to purchase and reopen the closed institutions. If either option wasn't feasible, DEPCO was empowered to assume their assets and sell the institutions in order to get funds to depositors. The agency would ultimately recover millions of dollars through lawsuits and negotiations, enabling the state to pay off the bonds it floated. The goal was to reimburse all or at least some of the money to the people who had been victimized when the credit unions closed.

But at the time there were no guarantees, and panic quickly spread throughout the state. There was even discussion from the Sundlun administration about calling out the Rhode Island National Guard to secure the banks. Thousands of Rhode Islanders rallied in front of their particular banks on this New Year's Day and over the coming months demanding access to their money. They walked the highways and exit ramps halting traffic and marched to the white-domed Rhode Island State House calling for a general strike among workers. They were in the same exact position as the apolitical Vinny. All of their hard-earned life savings was possibly gone, not through any fault of their own. The bottom line for Vinny: He was out $300,000.

17   Vinny the Middleweight

When Vinny arrived back home, the 1991 New Year's Day celebration went on as planned in the Pazienza household. Louise got to serve her lentil soup, but the family gathered quietly with a sense of heaviness looming over the table.

"Champ, pass the bread." Angelo dunked the heel of the bread into his bowl. Louise assured Vinny everything was going to be fine and that the governor would get the banks open fast.

"That's what he said," Angelo said, bending over to pick up his jug of homemade wine from the floor, pouring a glass for Nikki, then one for himself. "Remember what I told you, Vinny, everybody is out to make a buck, no matter how they get it. Those crooks downtown, they don't even leave the crumbs for the people. That's why I did what I had to do for all these years. Nikki, nice outfit, is it new?"

Vinny didn't need a lesson in political science or the human condition, nor did he need his father's sarcasm toward Nikki. He needed money; he needed a fight. Vinny needed Lou Duva, who by all accounts had retired him and at this point really did not want to represent him. Money-wise, all that Vinny had left was the $17,000 from Caesar's Palace. When Nikki and Louise started cleaning the table, Vinny moved his chair closer to his father.

"Dad, what am I going to do?"

Angelo reached behind him and put a platter of wine biscuits and leftover Christmas cookies on the table, preparing for coffee. He shook his head as a sign that he had no answers.

"What would you do?" Vinny asked.

"Well, champ, I would get that $17,000 and get back on that plane to Vegas and take a shot with it, but that's me ... and you're not me, and you're not gonna make the same mistakes in your life as I made. We're gonna call Kevin, I know in your heart you want to keep fighting, and if you want to move up to welterweight that's what we'll do. And if it has to be without that fat bastard [Lou], so be it. Let's call Kevin."

Not wanting to waste any time, Angelo and Vinny called and spoke to Kevin later that night. As they huddled around the phone, he urged the two of them to forget welterweight. Kevin's point was why move up 7 pounds to 147? Vinny would still have to lose over 23 pounds to make weight. Kevin believed Vinny should just move up to middleweight or at the very least junior-middleweight, 154 pounds. Losing 10 to 15 pounds is much more manageable than losing 23. Plus, with the fights being nontitle, they would have the "give or take a few" option to come in a little lighter or heavier. Those five words have tremendous meaning in a fighter's life. In many cases, it's the difference between winning and losing, or fighting and not fighting, and in Vinny's experiences, living or dying as a result of dehydration.

Kevin also believed if Vinny moved up in weight, he would bring along the punching power that went along with the added 15 to 20 pounds. He maintained that many of Vinny's cuts along his eyebrows and cheekbones were a result of his sharp features that were no longer protected by a natural layer of skin. Instead, his skin became elasticized when he "sucked" down in weight.

As for Lou Duva and Main Events, they were nowhere in sight. To them, the issue was resolved after the Garza fight. They felt Vinny should not be fighting at all. For over six weeks, Vinny did not even know whether he was still being represented by Lou. In 1987, his written contract with Main Events had expired and they were operating by a handshake agreement.

Kevin Rooney phoned Angelo the next day at the gym, after talking privately to Vinny during a late New Year's Day phone call. Vinny and Kevin agreed it was time to make the move up to middleweight. Kevin truly cared about Vinny and the direction of his career. Moreover, their relationship by this point had evolved into a genuine friendship. Kevin admired Vinny for his old-school tenacity and Vinny for his part admired Kevin for his training ability and his loyalty. Kevin felt Vinny should either make the move up to middleweight or not fight at all. And Vinny recognized Kevin's integrity, because it didn't matter if Vinny fought at 135, 147, or 160 pounds: Kevin was still going to make his 10 percent cut whether Vinny won or lost. But Kevin wanted Vinny in the ring at his best. If not, according to Kevin, Vinny should "pack it in and retire." And that would cost Kevin money.

Angelo, conversely, wasn't sold on the idea. While talking to Kevin he paced around the gym on his cordless phone. The gym still smelled of the remnants of the fire that had occurred less than a month earlier. Angelo was there again, still cleaning the mess.

"Middleweight? Marvin Hagler fights middleweight, Tommy Hearns and Iran Barkley fight middleweight. Kevin, for Christ sake, those are big fucking guys! I don't know, I just don't know." Angelo leaned his mop against his fading reclining chair. Angelo felt if things weren't working at 140 pounds, how could they possibly work out at 160 pounds? Middleweights were bigger and stronger. More weight usually meant more height; more height usually translated to more punching power because taller fighters can leverage their weight against shorter opponents, opponents like Vinny, who stood at 5 feet 7 inches.

Unbeknownst to Vinny or Angelo, Kevin had made a trip down to East Orange, New Jersey, before Christmas to see Lou. Kevin again argued on behalf of Vinny.

"Lou, I'm telling you, this kid still can fight. I see him in the gym before he blows that weight, before he becomes emaciated. Get him a middleweight fight. What do you have to lose?" Kevin continued. He put it in business terms for Duva, knowing few managers care for the personal interest of their fighters.

"Lou, one more shot, if he wins he'll do what nobody expects him to do, and . . . if he loses, he's supposed to lose . . . right? Big deal he's a fucking lightweight, so you don't look bad. And if you put the fight in Providence he's still gonna draw, you're still gonna make your end. It could be his farewell fight . . . or who the fuck knows, just maybe we may have a middleweight."

Lou chomped on his half-lit stubbed cigar, which hung from the side of his mouth, leaned back in his chair and turned to Danny who walked in on Kevin and his father.

"What da ya think?" Lou inquired.

"I think he's right, what do we really have to lose. We'll run the show in Providence? If he wins, fucking A, but if he loses, we did our best, we move on . . . and I still think he could draw in Providence, now out of curiosity."

Danny gave Lou the okay from the promotional side of Main Events. Now it was solely up to Lou. "I'll get back to you, Kevin." Lou turned his chair and picked up the phone. He immediately called his moneyman and business partner Shelley Finkel, and the two started putting out feelers. So by the time Angelo and Vinny got their New Year's Eve/Day phone calls from Kevin, the wheels were already in motion with Main Events.

Angelo was taking his twenty-minute afternoon power nap when the ringing of the phone woke him. It was the first time he had heard from Lou in six weeks.

"Angelo, it's Lou," Lou barked in the phone. Angelo pushed the bottom of the recliner in with his legs and made his way to his feet.

"Eh!!! Where the fuck you been? I been looking for that face of yours on milk cartons . . ." Angelo walked to the television and waited for Lou's response as he turned down the volume on *Days of Our Lives*.

"All right, all right, we don't talk in a few months and that's my greeting? Listen, I got Vinny a fight at middleweight," Lou continued, "on USA."

Angelo interrupted. "What!? I don't know about this, Lou. I told Kevin—"

Lou interrupted. "Fight's in a few months. This kid Ron Amundson's got a broken hand, he needs some time to heal up. But the fight's in Providence, for the United States Boxing Association's [USBA] title. The kid's ranked eighth in the world." This worried Angelo further.

"Tell Vinny the kid can fight, he's tall and rangy. I'll be sending you guys tapes of 'im."

Angelo now had to go tell Vinny the news. Moving to middleweight was a nonissue for Vinny. He didn't care about how tall middleweights were, how hard they punched, or for that matter what their names were. You could roll out all the Marvin Haglers or Roberto Durans in the world, his toughest foe over the last three years was still his weight. He wanted to get in the ring and simply feel like the fighter he used to be. If he did that and still didn't succeed, well, then it was over, and that was okay. But he wanted to go out firing, and in his words, "in a blaze of glory."

18   Richie Cunningham and Vinny Paz

Ron Amundson landed at T. F. Greene Airport in Warwick, a suburb of Providence, about 15 minutes south of the city. It was June 24, 1991, and only eight days before the fight. Angelo was curious to see what Vinny was getting them into, so he volunteered to pick up Amundson and his handlers at the airport and drop them off at the Holiday Inn in Warwick. Before he took them to the hotel, he extended some good old-fashioned Rhode Island hospitality. He treated the North Dakotans to an Italian dinner at Joe Marzilli's Old Canteen in Providence. Tommy Mart accompanied Angelo and his guests to dinner. After appetizers he excused himself and went to the pay phone to call Vinny.

"What's he like? How big is he?" Vinny asked.

"*Cug*, you got nothing to worry about, you're fighting Richie Cunningham. He's white, whiter than white." Tommy laughed into the phone. Vinny laughed harder. "What do you mean?"

"He's fucking Richie Cunninghan and Howdy Doody rolled into one." By this point they were just laughing at each other laughing. Besides the comedic value, they were probably laughing out of relief. Vinny felt no "white boy" could ever beat him, regardless of the weight. He also felt no "white boy" could match his style or his intensity. Vinny learned from his experiences with the black and Hispanic Olympic kids at Colorado Springs that he was the "crazy *Italian*," not the crazy white boy. Minorities didn't view Italians as white. From that point on, Vinny redefined himself ethnically, at least as a fighter. It sounds racist, but that's just the way it was. Few white fighters rose to the elite ranks of the game from the 1960s onward.

Of course there were a few, but could you name them? Moreover, the boxing game has always been a microcosm and reflection of socioeconomic status in the United States. The ethnic and racial groups on the bottom rung of the economic ladder have always dominated the boxing game, from the Irish, Polish, Italian, and Jewish immigrants in the first half of the twentieth century to the largely black and Hispanic domination from the 1960s onward. This trend in boxing nearly represents a cultural group's upward social mobility: The better an ethnic group has fared economically and socially, the less likely they have shown to be drawn to the brutal sport of boxing.

In short, white fighters and the aforementioned European fighters simply were not as hungry as their lot in life improved. When white fighters did rise to the top, their style was usually predictable and easy to solve. Vinny and a few others were the exception, not the rule.

The old Vinny's style could not be solved so easily because the old Vinny fought so unpredictably, since he rarely knew what he was going to do in the ring. How were his opponents supposed to know what he was going to do? But would the old Vinny or the Vinny of the last three years appear in the ring with Ron Amundson on July 2nd?

By round two Ron Amundson found out firsthand. Vinny was nowhere to be found. He was only felt by Amundson. The eighth-ranked middleweight in the world was getting hit with unconventional lead left hooks to the jaw, followed by double left hooks to the kidneys. When he punched back, he hit air.

Vinny was gone, like Willie Pep, turning his back to his opponent and pivoting his left foot, then reappearing behind him, spinning him to his front, throwing lead uppercuts and jabbing backward on his heels. The old Vinny remained the rest of the way, for eight more rounds without relenting. Angelo hollered from the corner, "Willie Pep, Willie Pep." Angelo was not using his name as a noun, but as an adjective, reminding Vinny to fight that "Will-o-the-Wisp style." It was a style with the premise of hitting while not being hit. Move your head, your feet, and your hips. Throw punches in combinations from all angles. And if you can do what Willie Pep did, actually win rounds without throwing a single punch, making your opponent chase you around the ring, making him look amateurish, then you're fighting like Willie Pep. The result of Vinny implementing Pep's style: no cuts, no blood, no marks. Vinny was barely hit by the middleweight, who was mesmerized by Vinny's speed, cleverness, and by the sheer number of punches he threw.

As the fight wore on Amundson's body began to wear down and his pace slowed, which is natural for most middleweights. Except the middleweight he was fighting was mentally and physiologically conditioned to fight like a lightweight, and actually was getting stronger as the later rounds came.

And Kevin was right all along. The extra twenty pounds Vinny took into the ring that night did translate into greater punching power, along with the great speed he brought up from lightweight. His hooks and straight right hands were able to generate power because his legs were stout and firm beneath his torso. There were no signs of dehydration or exhaustion, the two hindrances that had plagued Vinny for three years.

Vinny only had to lose 13 pounds to make weight (154) on July 1st. In the year prior to the Amundson fight, state boxing commissions across the country had made some reforms to promote boxing safety. One of those reforms was to make the weigh-in the day before the fight, at least twenty-four hours in advance. As a result fighters like Vinny who had to lose weight could properly rehydrate their bodies.

By the time Vinny entered the ring at 11:00 p.m on Tuesday night, July 2, he weighed 166 pounds, fully hydrated and feeling like the fighter he used to be.

And the "old crowd" appeared, ten thousand strong, cheering on their reborn lightweight, who moved up three weight classes to win a unanimous decision. The final tally of the three judges' scorecards: 100-90, 100-90, 101-89. Vinny won every round on all three cards and, to use a baseball reference, pitched a shutout.

In the dressing room, Vinny celebrated. He hugged his father as the two called home to Louise, telling her the good news. And *pop* . . . a bottle of Asti Spumanti was opened and poured over Kevin's head.

Vinny stood on a chair, his hands still taped, his glass raised, his black trunks trimmed with white fringe with MOM AND DAD inscribed on each leg soaked with sweat and the sweet smell of cheap champagne. With the North American Boxing Federation Championship belt around his waist, he hollered over the celebration. "To Kevin Rooney . . . And don't say we're back, because we were never gone!"

Of course, Main Events took notice. They now had to begin to rethink their retirement plans for Vinny. USA Network and Tuesday Night Fights were sure to come calling again. Dan Duva the promotional guru and Lou the matchmaker would once again have to take notice.

19   Roberto Duran and Vinny Paz

Main Events did go back to work for Vinny. Three weeks following the Amundson fight, Vinny was on his way to a mortgage closing. Vinny took Angelo's advice. He didn't go back to Las Vegas with his $17,000; instead he used the money for a down payment on a new home in Warwick, his first real investment. Vinny was finally ready to leave his tiny bedroom and his childhood posters of Muhammad Ali, Farrah Fawcett, and Roberto Duran behind. Buying the house in and of itself was a risk, because the only money he had made after the banking crisis was the Amundson payday, and he only netted $20,000.

The mortgage closing was at 2:00 p.m., and he was already fifteen minutes late. But a package in the mail sent via Main Events would make him a bit later. The package contained three VHS tapes of his next opponent, WBA junior-middleweight champion Gilbert Dele, with a note attached from Main Events: "Are you ready to become the WBA Middleweight Champion of the World?" Vinny retreated back into the house and hurriedly cut through the oversize envelope. He quickly called his attorney Everett Petronio and told him to start the closing without him.

Each tape of Gilbert Dele he put in the VCR was more impressive than the next. He watched a middleweight from France who simply did not beat his opponents, he demolished them. He was undefeated in thirty fights, with 29 wins and 19 resounding knockouts. He had one draw early in his career. And they weren't just knockouts: They were *knockouts* that called for paramedics, smelling salts, and stretchers.

Dele was, as Vinny described him, "nasty." He was as Kevin Rooney called him, when Kevin saw the tapes in his Catskills home. "He's a cocksucker, a real cocksucker," he said when leaving a message on Vinny's answering machine. Coming from Kevin, that was a compliment of the highest order, because "cocksucker" in Kevin's world meant he he was good, very good, dangerous, a fighter you had to be careful with in every exchange through every second of every round. And if you weren't, you were gone. Just like that, your lights were out.

Kevin couldn't afford to pull any punches with Vinny. Kevin knew a "cocksucker" when he saw one—he trained Mike Tyson.

When Angelo saw the tapes of Dele, he was oddly quiet, not commenting at all. In fact, almost everyone Vinny showed the tapes to over the next few weeks was eerily quiet. Even guys around the gym who often told Vinny what he wanted to hear to bolster his confidence were tight-lipped. When Vinny pointed the remote at the television after watching the tapes of Gilbert Dele in the gym with the guys, the clicking of the TV was the last sound he heard in the room. After again witnessing the destruction Dele had put forth on his opponents, Vinny looked around the room. Angelo's face was deadpan as he looked straight ahead, and Cipolla and Tommy Mart were stoic. I excused myself to the bathroom, grinning as I walked by Vinny. "I'm glad it ain't me."

"Eeehhh!!! What the fuck, are you guys kidding me or what," Vinny said laughingly.

But the laughing wasn't masking his doubt, which was only natural.

Fast-forward to September 24, 1991: I had gone to Peter Manfredo's boxing gym in Pawtucket undercover, just another fighter in training, in a dull, dreary boxing gym. Manfredo knew me, but he was a longtime friend of both mine and Vinny's and he wasn't going to tip his cover to the Dele camp.

What I saw that evening at Manfredo's confirmed what Vinny saw on the tapes, but I saw a problem even bigger than his punching power. Dele was much more athletic in person and in much better condition than any fighter I had ever seen, Vinny included. He danced around the ring in perfect harmony, round after round in his yellow and red Canali trunks. He threw punches from odd angles and his balance was perfect. He knocked down two sparring partners that night, one with a left hook to the body, the other with an overhand right to the temple. The champion jumped rope and shadow-boxed simultaneously, alternating exercises. His routine went on and on . . . and on. After twenty-five rounds of sparring and floor work, it looked like he still had a lot more left in him.

When I got back to Father and Son's Gym later that evening, Vinny sat drenched in his puddle of sweat following his workout, his white-tasseled Pony boots unlaced as he awaited the scouting report. When I walked through the door, Vinny read the expression on my face like a dime-store novel.

"What, what now?" Vinny asked, his arms opened wide as he stood from the ring apron where he'd been seated.

I shook my head back and forth. "He's good, real good. . . . Fuck, he's great."

"C'mon, what the fuck, Tommy Jon? He's great? How fucking great can he be?"

"I don't know. I know he just looked fucking awesome," I countered.

"Awesome or great, which is it?" Vinny's now ready to kill the messenger.

"Both," I said, brutally honest. "What the fuck, it ain't my fault."

"He's gotta have some fucking weaknesses." Vinny was getting even more pissed off.

"I don't know, maybe . . . math, cause he doesn't have any boxing weaknesses." I toyed with Vinny's anxieties while bringing down his intensity.

Tony Cipolla and Kevin roared out loud, laughing hysterically.

"Champ, you're on your own on this one," Tommy Mart chimed in.

Angelo took the towel from Kevin's shoulder and patted down Vinny's wet shoulders and head. "Don't worry, champ, I got our back, forget about these guys, rat bastard Benedict Arnolds."

The laughs eased Vinny's tension. But Vinny knew Gilbert Dele was not Ron Amundson/Richie Cunningham, and this time there would be no laughing for Vinny.

Gilbert Dele agreed to fight Vinny. He was in Providence because many European fighters need to market themselves abroad, especially in the United States. For Dele, Vinny was the first hurdle on his way to unifying the junior-middleweight championship with WBC middleweight champion Terry Norris. Perhaps the only real weakness Dele had was his mind-set, because he bought into the idea that Vinny was "a small guy, a blown-up lightweight," who had lost his last three world championship fights and was not a real test for a legitimate middleweight.

As good as Dele was, he miscalculated when he chose Vinny as his opponent. Vinny was not a blown-up lightweight. He was now a legitimate middleweight with a heavyweight heart. And Vinny was no longer a middle-class suburban kid in the comfort of his parents' home. He was fighting to keep his new home and fighting for his career. Moreover, he was doing so in front of his friends and his fans in Providence, a place in which he never lost. When Dele entered The Devil's Den on October 1st, he too, like all of Vinny's previous opponents, lost to the Pazmanian Devil.

20 Side by Side

Angelo woke up alone on the waiting-room couch. Louise, Doreen, and everyone else had gone home. It was November 15, 1991. Angelo's hair and clothing were disheveled as he reached for his eyeglasses, which rested on scattered *Time* magazines on the coffee table next to him. One cover in particular stood out to Angelo. The headline read: A DAY OF INFAMY, DECEMBER 7, A FIFTY-YEAR ANNIVERSARY TRIBUTE TO PEARL HARBOR. You ain't fucking kidding, he thought to himself.

Dr. Cotter stood above him as Angelo cleared his head. This was real. It wasn't a nightmare. Cotter told Angelo he could join Vinny in his room on the second floor if he'd like. Vinny was sleeping, Dr. Cotter informed him, but at least Angelo could be with his son. The doctor continued. "Angelo, don't be alarmed, Vinny's been equipped with his halo. It's striking at first, but remember this is going to get him better."

Angelo walked into Room 209 quietly and pulled up a chair beside Vinny's bed. Under the blanket, Vinny's legs trembled and his hands twitched as his mind raced in his sleep. The white

Lincoln Town Car traveling southbound on Post Road was barreling toward him again. This time Gilbert Dele was driving and Nikki was in the passenger seat. Vinny, alone in the gray Camaro, braced himself behind the steering wheel. Faster ... faster ... faster ... the White Lincoln picked up speed. He heard Nikki's voice, "Just give him his belt back," and right before the *crash*, Vinny was jolted awake.

Angelo rubbed Vinny's hand softly. "Champ, it's okay, it's okay. I'm here, champ." He slid his hand down to Vinny's thigh. "Champ, you're dreaming."

Vinny awoke groggily. "I've been dreaming all night." Vinny cleared his hoarse voice. Angelo poured a cup of water from the yellow hospital thermos and bent the straw toward Vinny's parched mouth. "Dad," Vinny whispered, "where's Ma?"

"Home, Vinny, I sent your mother home late last night. She's okay, she's with Doreen," Angelo assured Vinny.

"How about Kurt, how is he?" Vinny asked more questions.

"Kurt's okay too, Vinny. He's banged up, with stitches, but he's up and walking around."

Angelo tried to keep his emotions in check and continued on, knowing what was important to Vinny, his belt, although at this point it meant little to Angelo.

"Jimmy talked to Lou late last night from here, he should be here sometime today. I guess he's gonna have some answers for us about an extension."

Vinny, feeling some relief, closed his eyes and licked his lips as he slowly fell back to sleep. Angelo took a warm blanket that rested above a radiator and covered himself as he sat in the chair next to Vinny, his legs stretched in front of him. Angelo quickly joined his son in the shared comfort of his sleep.

When I arrived at the hospital later the following day, I was met by Angelo, who stood outside Vinny's door, making sure no media or strangers gained access to the room. He shook my hand and gave me a quick hug. "How's he doing?" I nervously asked.

"Tom Jon, go in. He's been asking for you and your cousin Tommy," Angelo urged.

Stay strong, I thought to myself as I opened the door.

Vinny was sitting up in a baby-blue recliner. He welcomed me like a mourner at his own wake. "Tommy Jon, Tommy Jon. Do you believe it, do you believe this?"

For the first time in my twenty-six years, I saw no spirit and sensed a massive vulnerability in my childhood friend. Vinny's body looked small. What had happened to his broad back and thick neck, his thick legs and rounded fists? They all seemed to have withered away in less than twenty-four hours. The adrenaline to fight off the accident and the pain had worn off and Vinny was left with an uncertainty that already seemed to have overtaken his body and his will.

One by one Vinny's room began to fill as Louise, Doreen, Nikki, Tony Cipolla, Jimmy Birchfield, and Tommy Mart each made their way through the door with Angelo's permission. For Vinny it seemed as if there really was no time to rest.

But then Robinson, a tall, muscular 215-pound Haitian nurse entered the room.

"Mr. Angelo, I'm not sure all these people should be in here. Vinny needs some time to himself. Should I show them to the waiting room?"

Angelo agreed. "All right, everybody out. Follow my friend here." Angelo rolled up a ten-dollar bill and handed it to Robinson. "Thanks, take care of these guys and get a coffee for yourself."

The friends visited Vinny in pairs throughout the day. In the waiting room they commiserated, talking about the past, the medical present and inevitably, Vinny's boxing future. Though boxing was really their last concern, it still was an issue that piqued their curiosity because they knew Vinny. Jimmy Birchfield, who had some past financial dealings in Vinny's career, pulled Angelo to the side and reminded him that visiting time was almost over. It was 9:00 p.m. and there was no sign of Danny or Lou Duva, or anyone else from Main Events.

When Vinny awoke the following morning, Robinson was taking the filled urinal from the bedside table. It was only 5:00 a.m. of Vinny's second day in the hospital and the room was already filled with flowers, prayer beads, and get-well cards from his fans.

"Goodness gracious," Robinson said, "Mr. Paz, look at this room, it looks like a greenhouse. You should see what's been going on outside. The lobby is filled with gifts from your fans. This hospital has been a madhouse since you've arrived, hundreds of people calling and even stopping by, Mr. Paz." Robinson laughed. "They look up to you, be strong for them and Mr. Angelo."

The mention of Angelo raised Vinny's suspicion. "Why my father?"

Before and after many of Vinny's fights, Angelo would break out with the shingles, a condition brought on by nerves. If fights gave Angelo a viral reaction, Vinny could only imagine what the last thirty-six hours could have done to him.

Robinson answered Vinny directly. "Mr. Paz, your father is next door. He was admitted into the hospital late last night after you fell asleep. He's got the shingles, and he's hooked up to antibiotics to fight his infection."

Vinny needed to see his father and asked Robinson to help him out of bed.

"I'm not sure that's such a good idea right now, Mr. Paz," Robinson said. "I'm not a doctor—"

"C'mon, get me up," Vinny insisted. "It'll be okay."

Within seconds, Vinny lifted both legs from the bed and placed his feet gently on the floor. With the help of the ambivalent Robinson, Vinny straightened out his legs and took his first uneasy step out of his room and toward Room 208. The halo hovered awkwardly above his head but was much lighter than it appeared. Robinson stayed close to Vinny's side as Vinny approached his sleeping father.

Vinny giggled as he approached the bed. "Look at ya, ya bum ya," Vinny woke up Angelo, quoting *Raging Bull*.

Angelo's back and head rose from the bed as he rested on his right elbow. "Champ! Champ! You're up? Champ!" Angelo grabbed Vinny's arm this time with force and held it tightly, an ear-to-ear smile across his face.

"Robinson, look at the champ," Angelo exclaimed.

Vinny sat, getting the feeling of his legs beneath him. Over the next hour the father and son shared steak, eggs, and toast in Room 208. Angelo sent his steak back twice, the first time because the steak wasn't 6 ounces. He specifically wrote on his menu card the night before that his breakfast steak should not be 8 ounces or 4 ounces. Angelo wanted the steak to be 6 ounces. There was no give or take a few. Angelo watched his weight, and now even more so because he was going to be laid up in the hospital for a couple of days. The second time he sent it back because it was overcooked.

"Will you just eat the thing?" Vinny yelled at Angelo. He then apologized to the 20-something Spanish orderly.

"Don't worry about it, Paz." The orderly just seemed happy to be there. Slowly and suddenly things seemed to be getting back to normal.

By two o'clock that afternoon, Vinny was making his way to a microphone before a jam-packed conference room for the first press conference since he had broken his neck. Cameras from all the New England news stations and major newspapers attended, including the *Providence Journal*, the *Boston Globe*, the *Boston Herald*, and the *Hartford Courant*. Photographers snapped pictures and fought for space along the walls and in front of the dais with the cameramen from ESPN, CNN, WBZ Boston, and many others.

Vinny's attorney Everett Petronio approached the podium with Vinny. He spoke into the microphone. "Good afternoon, ladies and gentlemen. As you know, this is Vinny's first public appearance. He will be making a statement and if he feels up to it he may do one-on-ones, but that will be at Vinny's discretion."

Vinny took his place at the microphone. His halo rested on bars that were attached to a white plastic vest lined with sheepskin fur underneath to avoid irritation to his skin. He was sleeveless, his bare arms exposed. He began speaking.

"Me and my family would like to thank you for all of your support, all your prayers and your letters and your kind thoughts.

And to whoever sent over the eggplant parmigiana . . . it was great." There were some laughs from the crowd.

Vinny continued. "And I'd like to thank Dr. Cotter and all the wonderful people of Kent County Hospital. As you know I had a procedure on Monday and I promise I will be back in the ring to defend my title. I'm gonna make this happen or I'm going to die trying."

Vinny's statement was not what the written or electronic media expected to hear, even though most of them were accustomed to Vinny's grandiose predictions. Looking the way he did physically, with the halo screwed into his skull from four sides, even his greatest supporters would find his words difficult to believe. Hours later, after the press conference and visitors departed, Nikki remained in the hospital room alone with Vinny. Angelo, at the urging of Michelle, a nurse in her mid-20s, retreated back to Room 208. He was still receiving antibiotics for his shingles, so Angelo had to remain in the hospital.

"C'mon, Michelle, you come with me." Angelo made his way out the door. "It's already seven o'clock. I gotta call Mondo the Egg for tonight's basketball lines."

"Isn't that illegal, Mr. Paz?" asked Michelle knowingly.

"Only if you get caught or if you lose. And you're not gonna rat me out, right?"

Nikki looked at Vinny, as if to say, your father's out of control, but she said nothing. She was about to learn the apple really did fall close to the tree. Vinny shrugged his shoulders. "I know, I know, what are you gonna do? He's an old-time Italian."

As Nikki rearranged the plants and the greeting cards around the room, Vinny made his way to her from behind and grabbed her hips with both hands. He leaned over and began kissing her, trying to move his lips to her neck, but was held back by the front bars of the halo. Vinny repositioned himself in front of Nikki and pulled Nikki to him.

"Vinny! Stop!" Nikki warned. He continued like she had never spoken and moved his hand up to her right breast. He continued kissing Nikki's ear, breathing heavily into it. Vinny slid his left hand down the front of her velour sweatpants and rubbed himself against her from behind. Vinny lifted his hospital gown and moved Nikki forward. Nikki, too excited to protest, put her arms in front of her against the closed door and spread her legs while Vinny pulled down her sweatpants and white cotton panties. Vinny moved closer as Nikki braced herself, and he put himself inside her. The two moaned and soon found a rhythm. Vinny bit her ear harder as she pushed herself back and sighed.

Suddenly, Dr. Cotter pushed on the door. "Son, are you okay? Vinny is everything—?"

"Doc . . . doc . . . I'm okay." Vinny pulled his gown down.

"Shit, Vinny I knew it," Nikki said and quickly pulled up her pants.

Vinny pleaded with the doctor not to come in. "One second, Dr. Cotter."

As Dr. Cotter entered the room he stared dead-on at Vinny, and then his eyes surveyed the room. Nikki propped up her sweats in the chair next to Vinny's bed and hid her face behind a *People* magazine, too ashamed to face the distinguished Dr. Cotter.

The doctor looked at his chart and shuffled some papers on his clipboard. Dr. Cotter took off his eyeglasses and rested them on his chest. "Son, you've got to be kidding me," Dr. Cotter said, looking at Vinny quizzically.

"What, doc? I broke my neck, everything else is fine," Vinny defended himself. The doctor paused and gave a long sigh before he spoke. "I think you're going to be all right, son. We should start thinking about you going home."

Vinny woke up early the next morning. His disposition was changing and his spirit was resurfacing. He walked by Room 208 to check on his father, who was snoring loudly, and closed the door quietly.

Vinny saw Robinson and told him he would be going for a walk. "Excellent, Mr. Paz, would you like some company?" Robinson was instinctively protective of his patients.

"No, I'm good, thanks. Don't worry. I'll be fine." As Vinny continued his walk, he made his way into the children's wing. Several children were gathered together playing games. Some had shaved heads because of their chemotherapy, others were in wheelchairs or leaned on their walkers. Unlike the rest of the hospital the children's wing was lively and the children were happy despite their conditions. Jenny, a girl in a wheelchair, noticed Vinny first.

"Hey, mister, what's that thing on your head?" she asked. All the children took notice. They were not startled, just curious.

"It's a halo," Vinny answered.

"A halo like an angel?" Jenny asked.

"Yeah, but I ain't no angel. I'm the Pazmanian Devil." With that, Vinny smiled.

"Whatever," Jenny said and turned her wheelchair away.

Twelve-year-old Bert, also in a wheelchair and Butler, 13, an African-American boy on crutches, made their way to Vinny. They both were sports fans and knew of Vinny. "Yo, my brother said you were in the hospital." Butler turned to the other kids. "This is Vinny Paz, the boxer. But my brother knows karate and he said you ain't that tough."

"Oh, yeah! Where is he?" Vinny joked.

"He's home," Butler responded.

"I'm only kidding. What are you guys playing?" Vinny was ready for some competition.

As the hours passed Vinny engaged in a roundtable game of Battleship with the kids. Everyone was competitive and before he knew it, the day had passed.

Doris, a 50-year-old nurse who had been watching the game, gently broke it up. "It's dinnertime for the kids and the grownup too."

They all begged for more time, Vinny included, but the rules were the rules. As Vinny said his goodbyes, Butler asked one final question to his newfound friend. "Hey, Vinny, you gonna fight again?"

"Definitely!" he answered the kids. "And when you guys get better, I'm gonna have tickets for you when I make my comeback."

Vinny, who for obvious reasons left quite an impression on Dr. Cotter, was discharged after his fifth day in Kent County

Hospital. Before leaving, the doctor warned Vinny that his activity must be limited and his halo must remain on until February 14th, Valentine's Day. Vinny was wheeled from 209 accompanied by Angelo, who had been released from 208 the day before, his shingles now under control.

Vinny was met at the hospital's entrance by his friends and some media.

Joe Rocco from NBC 10, the television station that had broken the story the evening of the accident, shouted above the other reporters. "Vinny, where you going?"

He answered affirmatively, "I'm going home, to my parents. Where do you think I'm going? I love those guys."

Vinny could not stay alone in his Warwick home. He needed an adjustable reclining medical bed, which was waiting for him in his mother's living room in front of the 46-inch television. The medical bed of course could not fit in his former 5-by-8 bedroom.

As they made their way to Angelo's white New Yorker, Nikki lagged yards behind talking on her cell phone, beginning the process of distancing herself from Vinny. She went her way to her own car, a White Geo Tracker 4x4, and sped off before the Pazienzas ever left the parking lot.

21   Home Cooking

For the next week Vinny paced around his parents' home, not knowing what to do with all the free time on his hands. He had always, in his words, "punched the clock," like any other person who had a job. For the past eight years as a professional fighter Vinny had had a structured, regimented day. He'd wake up every morning at 7:00 a.m., do his roadwork, go back in his house or to the gym, and do some weight training and eat breakfast by 9:00 a.m. He then would rest until noon, open some fan mail, have some lunch, take a power nap, and prepare himself for his late-evening workout. If a fight was on the horizon, he would have to undertake the arduous task of sparring anywhere from 100 to 150 rounds over the course of six or seven weeks. It was the unglamorous part of his life that most people never saw. But it was his life and now it was gone.

Beside his mail, all that Vinny had was time. And time could be this devil's playground. After waking up to reruns of *Gilligan's Island*, *I Dream of Jeannie*, and *Bewitched*, Vinny would make his way down to his old gym in the basement, next to Angelo's broken-down barbershop chairs and Louise's old wigs. He'd just stare at his old dumbbells, exercise bike, and heavy bag.

Louise would call from the top of the second-floor stairs, "Vinny, what are you doing down there?" She was getting suspicious. Doreen, who lived on the first floor, would reaffirm her mother's suspicion with a louder, deeper holler, "Vinny, get upstairs. Ma's calling you." And when he didn't answer, Louise would make her way to the cellar in her housecoat. She warned Vinny: "I hope you're not thinking of working out, the doctor said you can't do anything for three months. You could hurt yourself worse."

"Ma, I'm just bored, plus how worse could it be? I've got a broken neck," Vinny argued.

"You wanna end up a cripple? If you're bored come upstairs and help me peel potatoes."

"I ain't that bored." Vinny waved his index finger at his mother.

By 11:00 a.m., he'd be back upstairs making serial phone calls to Nikki at Dr. Nelvin's office where she worked as a dental technician. Vinny would make other phone calls to all his friends at their jobs and at their homes. He'd check in with his lawyers, doctors (nose and hand), and his accountants. And Vinny would have long conversations with cold-calling telemarketers who promised him free Caribbean vacations, as Bob Barker awaited contestants who made their way down the aisle and the musical theme from *The Price Is Right* played in the background. He was in housewife hell.

Fortunately, the mail kept coming, because it kept him sane and at least gave him a sense of accomplishment as he responded to every letter. There were outpourings of support from celebrities like Sylvester Stallone and James Caan, and people from the athletic world like Muhammad Ali and football coaches Bill Parcells, Bobby Bowden, and Joe Paterno. There were also letters from people who were in a similar position as Vinny, and letters from those who were terminally ill or whose family member was facing a similar fate, urging Vinny to stay strong and positive. There was still, however, no sign of Lou Duva or Main Events.

When the dust settled from the car accident and the hospital stay, it was finally time to confront Vinny's financial future. He had a new home and a mortgage to pay. His boxing career was in obvious doubt and he didn't have an income. Making matters worse, Kurt Reader didn't have car insurance and the owner of the white Lincoln Town Car that haunted Vinny was suing Reader, because in all probability Reader was at fault in the accident. Hence, with Reader at fault and carrying no liability insurance, Vinny had no economic legal recourse. If Reader had been insured, Vinny would have been able to sue his driver, for both pain and suffering and loss of wages for his time out of work, or in this case out of the ring. If Vinny could no longer fight, his attorney Everett Petronio could have sought due compensation and negotiated with an insurance company based upon Vinny's future earnings. All of those options became moot when it was learned there was no insurance on the 1984 Camaro. Vinny faced yet another economic hurdle, which paled in comparison to his physical challenge of coming back from a broken neck.

After two weeks of horrific news and new challenges in the Pazienzas' lives, Angelo felt there was only one thing to do—have a private party for Vinny, to lift his spirits. It was Friday night, December 15, 1991, the night before Vinny's 29th birthday. Angelo invited me and Tommy to the house. Tommy Mart and I made our way up the stairs to the sounds of Nat King Cole's "Christmas Song" and the smell of freshly cut salumi, Parma proscuitto, a variety of cheeses, and warm Italian bread.

Tommy Mart and I knocked on the door twice and entered. Louise welcomed us with a warm hug as Angelo raised his hand to greet us. His back was to his guests as he faced the counter and the dark wood kitchen cabinets. He continued cutting sopressata, prosciutto, provolone cheese, and fresh buffalo mozzarella. He added stuffed cherry peppers to the antipasto and cut vine-ripe tomatoes and placed them delicately around the platter. "I hope these goddamn tomatoes are all right, they're not gonna be like our native tomatoes, but what are you gonna do?" Angelo then dressed the antipasto with his imported Edda olive oil from New York's Arthur Avenue. "Gift from a friend of mine, in the city. Fourteen dollars a gallon, wait till you guys taste this stuff." He took a dish towel, or as Angelo calls it, a *marpene*, that hung from the waist of his brown pants and crocodile belt and first wiped, then shook our hands. "How you been? Let's have a party."

About an hour passed as Angelo and we continued celebrating Vinny's birthday without him. We drank homemade wine and ate before finally realizing that Vinny had never come out of his de facto bedroom, formerly the living room. Angelo crept to the closed door as he heard Vinny talking softly into the phone. His eyes squinted as he trained his ears, then with a look of disgust he walked back to the table and refilled the three glasses to the brim.

"That fucking Nikki," Angelo whispered, "she's no good. He's on the phone with her around the clock, calling, all hours of the night. They're arguing again. She's not been here once since he's been home. Why? 'Cause she might be out of the limelight now, if Vinny can't fight no more, that's why," he answered his rhetorical question. "Why don't you guys talk to Vinny, tell him she's no good. Can't he see that?"

"Ange, he loves her," I interjected.

"Love, after what he's been through? I don't buy it."

Vinny made his way out of the room and looked at our faces red, with the flush of alcohol.

"You guys are having a party, ahh?"

Angelo quickly responded. "Tommy Jon and Tommy Mart are good guests. Sit down, champ. Have a glass of wine with us." Angelo picked up his now empty jug of wine. The three of us burst out laughing, drunk like teenagers.

"I meant you're having a party on me. Talking about me and Nikki. Dad, let it go, will ya?"

Vinny finally joined the party and Louise and Doreen made their way upstairs. All talk of Nikki was put to rest, at least for now. The coffee was brewing as Louise made her way across the kitchen. She balanced the huge chocolate birthday cake with twenty-nine candles as Doreen turned off the lights. The five of us sang "Happy Birthday."

The next evening, Nikki came to the Pazienza home. Angelo was at St. Anthony's and the house was dark; it was about six o'clock. Nikki had rented three movies from Major Video and planned for a long evening in the house, but Vinny was ready to go out socially for the first time. *Terminator 2* was playing at the Park Cinema and Vinny put on his black leather jacket and put Nikki's videos on the coffee table.

"Let's go to the movies, Aah'nold starts at seven," Vinny said, doing his best Schwarzenegger impersonation.

As Vinny and Nikki made their way down the aisle holding popcorn and Raisinets, people in the theater stared and whispered quietly. The theater was almost completely silent, then one voice rang out, "We love you, champ." Another voice yelled encouragement: "We're praying for you, Vinny." By now all the moviegoers were standing and burst into a spontaneous applause, and as Vinny stood, the crowd erupted with a louder ovation. Nikki tugged Vinny's shirt to sit down, embarrassed by the commotion.

After the movie, Vinny and Nikki sat in front of his parents' house. The weather was damp and misty as Nikki kept her 4x4 running, her lights bouncing off the fog, creating a hazy glare. She refused Vinny's offer to go upstairs and lie on his Craftmatic adjustable bed. Nikki also refused Vinny's affectionate advances toward her. He tried a second time, leaning over, rubbing his hands over Nikki's thigh. "C'mon, baby, what's the matter? Something's wrong. What is it?"

"Vinny, I can't do this anymore. I've tried, I really have, but I can't look at you like this. It makes me sick. Not you, but that thing on your head," Nikki said bluntly.

"This thing on my head is making me better, understand?" Vinny responded with a mix of frustration and embarrassment. The inside of the car was silent. The two stared at one another, eye to eye. Vinny knew what was next.

"I'm sorry, Vinny, I can't." Nikki stood her ground.

Vinny opened the door and got out, banging his halo on the door.

"Motherfucka!" he yelled.

Nikki leaned over and told him to be careful.

"Fuck you, Nikki."

He slammed the door behind him and stormed away from the truck, taking long angry strides up his driveway. Once inside the house he raced down to his basement, repeatedly slapping the faded, veneer paneling in frustration.

Still in the dark, Vinny approached the silhouette of the white Everlast heavy bag that hung from the ceiling. He unleashed a wicked right hand; the 100-pound bag filled with sand barely moved, but Vinny's knees buckled, and his upper body cringed from the shocking jolt to his body. His eyes became a mix of fire and water, his desire at odds with his body's limitations. He made his way over to the dumbbell rack and picked up a pair of 40-pounders. Lifting the weight sent vibrating sensations up to the screws lodged in his forehead. Instinctively his hands opened and the dumbbells dropped loudly, crashing to the cellar floor.

Finally, Vinny was quickly recognizing the new physical limitations of the world in which he now lived. He picked up two 5-pound dumbbells and they too felt enormously heavy. He strained but persevered as he began to talk to himself under his breath: "You can do this, you can . . ." He began to curl the dumbbells. The pain was horrific, but he challenged his reflection in the dusty mirror in front of him. He continued on, going a step further. He took a step to his right and picked up the 10-pound dumbbells, again refusing to be beaten by the image in his mirror. He began doing military presses. In agony, he went on, his arms shaking from the pain, but his moans turned to a grimace, and a grimace to a smile.

22   The Comeback

Tony Cipolla woke up early Saturday morning, December 17, to a phone call from Vinny. He rolled out of bed and squinted at his alarm clock, "Champa, it's six o'clock, whatsa the matter?" He yawned into the phone. "Eeh!! Happy birthday, Vinny."

"Thanks, Tony," Vinny replied and then got down to business. He told Tony to pick him up, that he had big news for him, and him only. Cipolla, never at a loss for energy, pulled up in front of the Pazienza house forty-five minutes later.

Vinny peeked out of the second-story window of his parents' vinyl-sided tenement, waiting for Tony to arrive. He grabbed his hooded gray and black Everlast jacket and quietly walked down the front staircase, out of sight or earshot of Angelo and Louise. Vinny jumped in the car before Cipolla could make his way out. Tony had a large coffee from Dunkin' Donuts for Vinny and handed it to him. "Black, noa sugar, champ."

"Thanks, Tony, but forget the coffee for now. Drive."

They drove down the street as Tony looked in his rearview mirror checking for Angelo, sensing this was his and Vinny's secret. Tony was curious; he didn't know what to make of the early-morning call. He was disheveled, his jet-black hair uncombed and still bushy from a night of sleep.

Vinny explained to him they were on their way to the gym this morning and would be every morning from now on to work out, before Angelo arrived and opened up around 10:00 a.m. for his "business"—not gym business. Tony, for the foreseeable future, according to Vinny, was going to be his trainer in hiding.

When Cipolla heard Vinny's plan, he spun his head and looked at Vinny wide-eyed in disbelief. He unconsciously slammed on the brakes of the car, coming to a screeching halt, holding up traffic. Vinny's arms instinctively went out in front of him, bracing the dashboard. Car horns blasted from behind. "Tony, are you out of your mind, man? Calm down," Vinny warned. "I don't need another accident."

"Vinny, noa, I won't do this, and especially nota behind your father's back. *Madonna a mi*, your father," Tony put his hands together as if he were praying and looked upward, "will kill me." As loyal as Tony was, he didn't want to take on the enormous responsibility of guilt if something were to happen to Vinny under his tutelage.

Vinny explained to Tony that he'd been working out on his own for a week in his cellar behind everyone's back. He embellished by six days. Vinny insisted he knew his body better than anyone, including any doctors. Vinny began: "Tony, Dr. Cotter is a great doctor, but he doesn't know me, he doesn't know my body. Believe me. It's no big deal."

The horn from behind blasted again, as Tony steered his car toward the curb. Tony knew it was more than a big deal, it was an enormous deal, with enormous risk, but he felt himself caving to Vinny's pressure. "Vinny, you gotta promise me that . . ." The sentence went unfinished.

When Vinny heard those first four words, he knew he had Tony where he wanted him, cracking under the pressure like Joe Frazier Jr. and like Greg Haugen. Vinny interrupted Cipolla. "Tony, nothing's going to happen, believe me." Vinny had his trainer in hiding.

For the next two weeks, Vinny told Angelo and Louise that he was going to breakfast with Tony, going on an errand with Tony, or going to the post office with Tony. Of course, he went to the gym with Tony. Each day he blared his boom box in his gym to the beat of LL Cool J's "Mama Said Knock You Out," and coincidentally Tony! Toni! Toné!

Before Angelo arrived at the gym, Vinny lifted weights and did pushups and situps, all in his halo. He worked with rubber bands that were fit behind the ring post and punched for rounds, with resistance. Each couple of days, he increased the weight and the tension on the rubber bands. Each day he did more pushups and would do them in sets targeting different areas of his upper body, close-grip pushups for his triceps and shoulders, wide grip pushups for his chest and back. He would work his abdominals to Tony's whistle until his repetitions reached into the hundreds. And before Vinny knew it, an anxious Tony reminded him it was time to go before Angelo arrived.

While Vinny showered, Tony scrubbed the gym floor and fanned out the musty smell of sweat. They turned the lights off and returned everything to its place, the way Angelo left the gym the prior day.

On New Year's Eve, Tommy Mart and I arrived at the Pazienzas for another party. This time however, the party was with Vinny, not Angelo. We entered Vinny's de facto bedroom wearing black tuxedos, white shirts with black buttons, and black bow ties. Our hair was slicked back and we each wore black Bally leather shoes we had bought on the arm from Angelo. Vinny looked at the two of us and lowered the sound of the college football game he'd been watching. "Penn State winning, Vin?" I asked.

Vinny just looked the two of us up and down, and laughed aloud. "You guys look good, shit, like the Italian Siegfried and Roy."

"Ta da, well now you're part of the act." I pulled out a triple-extra-large tuxedo shirt with the neckline cut out so Vinny could fit it over his halo.

"No, no, I don't think so, fellas."

Tommy Mart told Vinny they had a big night planned at The Classic, downstairs in a private room just for the guys. "The limousine is waiting for us outside. Let's go, put on the shirt." He handed the white shirt to Vinny.

When the three of us arrived at the restaurant to celebrate New Year's Eve, Tony Cipolla, Jimmy Birchfield, and the rotund Henry Broccoli were already digging into their appetizers of broccoli rabe and fried calamari. The three of them rose from the table together, made their way over to Vinny, and each greeted him with a hug and attempted kiss on the cheek, but were awkwardly kept at bay by the rods on Vinny's halo.

"I knew you couldn't resist us, champ." The 320-pound Broccoli wrapped Vinny in a friendly bear hug.

"Ohh! Easy, you're gonna crush the guy, we're gonna lose our friend for good," Jimmy Birchfield said, making his way down the stairs with six bottles of Dom Perignon.

"Jimmy, no Asti?" Tommy Mart said to Birchfield in an obvious dig at Vinny's pedestrian taste in champagne, and the party was on.

Vinny teased Tony: "How'd you get out tonight, on New Year's? Your wife's tough."

Tony went on to explain that the two were having a marriage spat and maybe a little more. Tony apparently didn't want to talk about it, but again when it came to Vinny, he easily broke down.

"My wife, she went to the Civica Center to see the cars, she lovesa cars. And while she was there, she met The Fonza."

"Who?" Jimmy asked as he lit his extra long Cuban cigar.

"The Fonza, Fonzie from the TV show Good Days."

"Henry Winkler, *ah fongole*, from *Happy Days, Happy Days*," Tommy Mart corrected him.

"Righta, Fonzie! Well, The Fonza slipped his phone numba in my wife's jacket, and the fucka face asked her out. So I giva her an ultimatum: It's either me or the fuckina Fonz. Could you imagine the fuckina Fonz?"

The table of guys roared out loud, belly laughing, repeating, mimicking Tony, *the fuckina Fonz, the fuckina Fonz*. For the first time in a month Vinny was living in the present, enjoying the night like old times. His head was cleared of the worries of his injury, his financial future, and the uncertainty of his comeback.

As the clock ticked past midnight, the party slowly broke up. Tony spoke quietly into his cell phone schmoozing his wife, getting the okay from her to go home, Fonz or no Fonz. Henry Broccoli nibbled on what was left of dessert and Tommy Mart and I sat with Jimmy in the corner, discussing Vinny's future. And Vinny was doing what he loved most, signing autographs, soaking up the admiration of adoring fans, and making new friends as they joined him at his former table. He guaranteed his admirers, who hung on his every word, that he would soon be back in the ring.

23   The Exam

Vinny could make all the promises he wanted to fans and friends about returning to the ring, but only Dr. Cotter could tell him for certain if he was still a professional fighter. Vinny had made regular trips to Kent County Hospital for routine X-ray tests and to make certain the screws drilled into his skull were tight, and not getting loose, infected, or causing a more serious infection in Vinny's bloodstream. Once or twice a week, Louise used an antibacterial solvent to clean the four reddened holes at the end of the metal rods that entered into Vinny's head from temple to temple. The two prior months of checkups with Dr. Cotter had been fairly routine. But on this day, during this examination, two weeks after New Year's Eve, Dr. Cotter noticed something odd; the screws both in the front and back of Vinny's head had gotten extraordinarily loose. Dr. Cotter washed his hands in the sink, his back to Angelo, Cipolla, and Vinny. He turned around to face them almost as if he knew Vinny and Tony's secret. "Vinny, your halo is awfully loose since our last visit." He reached for the ratchet that he used for tightening up the halo's screws. As the doctor turned the ratchet to its right, the clicking noise of the screws echoed in the sanitized white room. Vinny winced in pain.

Tony attempted to change the subject, fearing Angelo's wrath if his and Vinny's secret was exposed in that office. "*Madonna a mi*, tomorrowa nighta we're a supposeda to a get a foota of snow." The doctor ignored Tony's winter forecast.

"Doc, my son has always had a screw loose." Angelo laughed at his own joke.

The doctor continued on, tightening up the other three rods of the halo, and offered Vinny some advice in the process. "Son, we have one month before our fluoroscopy exam; don't do anything foolish that would compromise the integrity of the natural healing process. One more month, son; you hang in there."

Tony quietly breathed a sigh of relief as he helped Angelo put on his trench coat.

"All righta then, let's go fora lunch . . . my treata." He looked at Vinny from behind as Angelo swung his arms into his coat, giving him a knowing, look-what-we-got-away-with smile.

As Vinny and Tony left the office, Angelo remained with the doctor. "Doc," Angelo spoke softly, "what are the odds Vinny's not gonna need surgery?"

"Mr. Pazienza, this isn't a horse race," Cotter responded.

"I know, doc, but just for the sake of argument," Angelo pleaded.

Dr. Cotter gave in. "About fifty-fifty."

What Vinny and Tony had gotten away with the past few weeks was Vinny upping his workout regimen. The 40-pound dumbbells he could barely lift in his cellar a few weeks earlier were being used regularly as part of his light-day weight-training routine. Vinny was now bench-pressing more than 185 pounds, doing 60-pound flat-bench dumbbell presses and 50-pound cable flies. In the boxing gym he shadow-boxed and hit the speed bag and double-end bag. Vinny added familiar exercises to his floor workout, but he could not jump rope; the pounding would loosen the screws of the halo. Any pounding at all such as jogging or running in place could damage the integrity of the halo. So Vinny found alternatives. He rode an exercise bike and dressed in sweatshirts and sweatpants to keep his weight down. He knew he had to do this, keep his muscles alive, fend off the atrophy, or he would never be able to fight again. Slowly he could feel his muscle memory facilitating a return to the skill level to which he was accustomed.

There were days his body ached and the muscles around his upper back tightened, days his neck stiffened, and days that brought endless hours of anxiety. Vinny sequestered himself alone with his pain. He kept it away from Tony, away from Angelo, from Louise, and from Tommy Mart and me. After workouts he iced his neck and continued nursing himself toward his Valentine's Day date with Dr. Cotter.

When Vinny awoke on Valentine's Day morning he found his mother sitting on the edge of his bed. She was dressed in a black pantsuit and her hair was fixed. "Ma, where you goin'? Why are you all dressed up?" Vinny asked, as he wiped away the night's sleep. "Vinny, before your doctor's appointment today, I want you to come to church with me to say a prayer and light a candle."

Vinny was as areligious as he was apolitical. "Mom, I'll feel like a fraud. I never go to church; now that I need something, I'm gonna go?"

Louise countered, "Vinny, you're a good person, that's all Jesus really cares about, and how often do I ask you to do anything for me?" Vinny, pressured by good old-fashioned Catholic guilt and more than a little self-interest, agreed to his mother's wishes. Moreover, he felt he could use as much help as he could get, especially today.

When Vinny arrived at Dr. Cotter's office a month after his last checkup, he knew that day his life's work hung in the balance. For fourteen years he had defined himself by the thing he loved to do most—fight. He had traveled the world, become a local and then national celebrity, and a two-time boxing world champion. But in just a few minutes, after his fluoroscopy exam, all of those things could be taken away and made part of his past life. His new life might have to be one of a common man, one that did not involve sport or celebrity.

Vinny would be placed in the fluoroscopy machine to see if his bones had fused; if they had, he could continue to have the halo removed from his skull. If the bones hadn't fused, the halo would have to stay on longer, which probably meant the chances of bone fusion in the second and third vertebrae would be a long shot, and an operation to fuse the bones would cut Vinny's range of mobility by 40, 50, 80 percent or more. Not even Dr. Cotter could be certain about how the operation would affect him, but he was certain that an operation would end Vinny's boxing career. This was Vinny's best hope of ever returning to the ring.

Angelo stroked Vinny's shoulder as he sat on the black hospital examination table. The white paper beneath him made loud crackling noises, revealing Vinny's tension as he could barely sit still. "Vinny," Dr. Cotter addressed his patient professionally as always, "it's time, son." Vinny made his way to the machine. The rods attaching Vinny's halo to the vest were taken off for him to move his head up and down ever so slightly. His halo and vest stayed on, for the meantime anyway. He stood at a profile position to Dr. Cotter but directly facing Dr. Kim.

"Okay, Vinny, move your neck for me," Dr. Cotter ordered from behind the machine. Vinny just stared straight ahead. He just moved his eyes up and down. "Keep going, Vinny."

Dr. Cotter again asked Vinny to move his head. Vinny tried again, but barely moved a hair. Dr. Cotter asked yet again but this time in a more irritated tone, almost now challenging his patient. "Son, you're going to have to do better than that."

"Jesus Christ, doc, he hasn't moved in three months!" Angelo took exception to the doctor's ploy.

Dr. Cotter readjusted the machine. "I'm aware of that, Angelo. Listen, Vinny, I know this is difficult, but the only way we're going to see if the bones fused is if you move your head."

Vinny took three long breaths and gathered his thoughts.

Fuck it, he thought as he dropped his head straight down. "How's it looking? How's it looking?" Vinny raised his voice a decibel level each time he asked the question.

Dr. Kim blurted out the results from behind the machine, too excited to wait for the always cautious Dr. Cotter or his nurse. "It's staying stable, it's staying stable," Dr. Kim's voice echoed throughout the room and bounced off the ceilings. "It's stable!" Kim said for a third time.

Tony almost leapt completely into Angelo's arms as Angelo struggled to get to Vinny. Angelo hugged Vinny and gently grabbed him by the sides of his face, kissing him on his forehead and cheeks. Vinny met Tony with a high-five through Angelo's bearish hug. Celebration filled the room as Dr. Cotter and Dr. Kim shook hands with each other, then their nurse. Vinny, at least for now, was still a professional fighter.

Vinny's body anxiety was replaced with adrenaline, and he needed as much of it as he could get because it was time to take off the halo, perhaps the most painful procedure Vinny would have to endure. "Vinny, we're going to give you something for the pain, okay?" Dr. Cotter tried to prepare Vinny.

"No drugs, doc. Please just take this off me," Vinny asked.

Dr. Kim warned Vinny about the halo's removal and how painful it could be. Again Vinny refused the medication. "I haven't even taken an aspirin in all this time, Dr. Kim, so with all due respect, 'cause you know I love ya, I'm not starting now."

Throughout the entire ordeal, from the time Vinny awoke in the triage unit at Kent County Hospital on the day of the accident, he hadn't taken any medication of his own volition. When he was first brought into the emergency room, ER nurses, following standard operating procedure, gave Vinny a low dosage of morphine intravenously to help him cope with the pain of the initial trauma of his accident and to keep him calm to ensure he wouldn't move and cause even greater injury to his spinal cord. When the IV was put in, he was barely conscious. But when he was gaining his full faculties and coming to terms with what had happened to him, and after he had tried to ease the pain Angelo was in, Vinny thought of nothing else but returning to the ring. Laying on his gurney, swollen and stained from his own blood, only hours after the accident, he thought about how fast he could return to protect his title. To protect his title he knew he needed to train, and he knew he couldn't train taking pain medication, Vicodin, Percocet, or whatever other kind of medication people who weren't like him took.

Narcotic painkillers affect specific receptors in the brain and spinal cord. They're prescribed by doctors to help ease their patient's pain or emotional responses to pain. But they also make people weak, tired, and listless, things Vinny knew he couldn't afford to be. Not even way back on November 14th, on the day of his accident and on the day he planned for his second future. Perhaps he was just in a state of denial, unwilling or unable to accept what had happened to him and the ramifications of a serious spinal cord injury. But whether Vinny was in a state of denial or in a state of medical ignorance, it was he and he alone who had gotten himself to this point, both in his career and through his injury. There would be no medication.

Dr. Cotter positioned himself on a chair in front of Vinny. He picked up his ratchet and began to take out the first screw. He began the process. Click . . . click . . . he turned the ratchet to the left. Vinny winced in pain and grabbed the sides of the table. "Whoa! Doc, are you sure you're going the right way?" Vinny questioned Dr. Cotter. The doctor just nodded and breathed softly through his nose, the ratchet clicking again. This time Vinny grabbed Dr. Cotter's leg.

Angelo and Cipolla stood in the back of the room and became concerned, knowing Vinny's great tolerance for pain. "This fucking guy better know what he's doing," Angelo whispered to Tony.

"Doc, you got to be turning it the wrong way!" Vinny raised his voice. The feeling of the screws turning in his head was like a steaming locomotive driving through his brain.

Dr. Cotter continued. He dropped the first screw into a metal bowl. "Three more to go. Vinny, are you ready?" Dr. Cotter asked as he raised his ratchet.

"Let's go, just get them out." A bit of relief filled the room.

With all four screws finally removed from Vinny's head, a nurse began to remove the rods and vest from Vinny's sweat-filled body. Vinny looked straight ahead and awaited orders from the doctors.

24　Houston

D r. Cotter fit Vinny with a soft neck brace before he left his office on Valentine's Day. The doctor suggested Vinny wear the brace throughout the day but told him he could take it off when he went to bed. The doctor also warned Vinny not to engage in any physical activity until further notice.

"Look, doc, I gotta be straight up with you." Vinny was ready to share the last six weeks of his life with Dr. Cotter, a man he'd come to admire and trust. "I've been working out for the last month and a half."

Dr. Cotter looked at his patient, confused, not quite taking in what Vinny was actually admitting to. Ceremoniously, the doctor took off his eyeglasses. "Excuse me, son." Dr. Cotter hung the glasses from the corner of his mouth.

Vinny, expecting the wrath of his neurosurgeon, was preparing to defend himself for his defiant actions. The doctor took his glasses from his lips and reached for his tissues. He wiped the lenses and squinted, then looked up and addressed Vinny. "Vinny, then do what you've been doing. You know your body better than anyone. It's certainly against conventional wisdom, but you've gotten this far and have gotten yourself healthy."

Vinny was astonished at his doctor's answer. Dr. Cotter, with a thorough examination and all the information in hand, gave Vinny a clean bill of health. Vinny could work out at his discretion, but Dr. Cotter still warned Vinny that there was to be no live boxing or sparring of any kind. Vinny gave Dr. Cotter his word.

Angelo, Vinny, and Tony made their way onto Interstate 95 and headed due north, back to Cranston. Vinny was flying from the great news he had just received, but there was one lingering problem. The Pazienzas with good reason had an inferiority complex when it came to the attention that Main Events gave to the Olympic kids. In fact, after years of Angelo whispering in Vinny's ear about mistreatment by Main Events, Vinny the Optimist was finally beginning to buy into Angelo's theory. Now Angelo's suspicions were confirmed, when not one person from Main Events— Lou, Danny, Dino, or Shelley—bothered to visit Vinny in the hospital after his accident, and by all accounts had retired him. Main Events put Vinny on the shelf, according to Angelo, "like a jar of relish." The notion was firmly cemented in Vinny's mind that he was just another meal ticket for the Duvas and they really didn't care whether he lived or died. As a result, Angelo's first business phone call was made to Kevin Rooney.

When Angelo got home he immediately got on the phone with Kevin and told him the great news. With continued rehabilitation, Vinny could start training in the boxing gym, although the actual act of sparring was still some time away. Kevin excitedly told Angelo he was ready to go any time, anywhere Vinny needed him.

The next call Angelo made was to Lou Duva. Angelo repeated verbatim to Lou what he had ten minutes earlier told Kevin. This time, however, Angelo's news was met with skepticism by Lou and Danny. "Angelo, this all sounds a little bit far-fetched to me. Vinny broke his neck, he's not gonna be able to defend his title within the year. If that happens the WBA is gonna strip him of his belt, and if that happens, he's back to square one, no title, and short purses." Duva went on. "Angelo, you guys think this out, is he really gonna be able to fight again? The whole idea seems crazy to me. But if you want, if he wants, we'll send him down to our doctor in Houston and if he gives us the okay, we'll see what we can do," Lou attempted to pacify Angelo.

"All right then, I'll tell Vinny about Houston. By the way, why can't we get an extension on his title?" Angelo asked. Lou told Angelo that there would be no extension; Vinny had one year to defend his title from the date he had won his belt, until October 1, 1992. The WBA champion of any weight class had to defend his title against the No. 1 ranked contender. If he didn't, he would be stripped of his title. Again, Main Events, though it seemed this time by no fault of their own, left the Pazienzas bargaining from a position of weakness.

As always, Vinny did what he did best: He went back to the gym. The business end of boxing was at the bottom of his to-do list. For the next several months he trained like the fighter he used to be. He no longer had to hide from Angelo. Tony could come out of the proverbial closet and was no longer Vinny's trainer in hiding. Vinny moved out of his makeshift bedroom at Angelo and Louise's and moved back to his Warwick home. Kevin Rooney came to Rhode Island more often to get Vinny back to his championship level of boxing. Rooney set up shop in Vinny's spare bedroom, which was now tabbed the Rooney Room.

Vinny was back in action. In his words, he was "punching the clock" the way he used to before his accident. He woke up early, did his road work, got back to his house, and did his weight training. In the afternoon, he attacked his ever-growing pile of fan mail, and at night he, Kevin, and Tony went to Father and Son's Gym for his floor workout. He modified his weight-training routines with the help of former Mr. America and Mr. Universe competitor Mike Quinn. Vinny had become friends with Quinn when the two met at a Cranston bodybuilding seminar sometime around 1989. Quinn was making a guest appearance at the seminar, and the two started talking shop about weight training and nutrition.

From that point on Quinn had offered Vinny his help both as a nutritionist and as a physical trainer.

Having Quinn on hand as part of Team Pazienza was a godsend. Vinny became a prized pupil, following Quinn's weightlifting rehabilitation routine to a T. Vinny lifted heavy weights, not the norm for boxers. But no boxer had ever attempted to recover from a broken neck. Vinny used heavy weights to build up his trapezoids, doing 125-pound dumbbell shrugs, building the muscles located between the shoulders and right below the neck. He wore a customized mask with a pulley system rigged at its end and 25- and 45-pound weights hanging from a 3-foot rope. Facing the floor he raised his head up in repetitions. The first set he did 25 reps, the second set 50 reps, the third set 75 reps. Alone in his basement gym, Vinny did dips for his triceps, pullups for upper-body strength, and three-plate T-bar rows for his back, all core exercises that built muscle density in his upper back, shoulders, and neck. Fighters need the most physiological resistance in these muscles in particular to absorb the shock of punches from their opponents.

Late one night, Vinny was in the boxing gym with Kevin, working on technique, shadow-boxing, jumping rope, and the speed bag. It was all coming back to him. He could taste the mustiness of the gym and feel the sweat of his hands taped tightly inside his gloves, and with that, he could feel his boxing instincts returning. The pain from his workouts was beginning to subside and the hesitancy he felt in the ring upon his return was diminishing almost with each day. The more time he spent in the ring, the more it became his home, and the more he realized how much he had missed being there. He was alone, at peace, where almost nothing else seemed to matter. When he climbed through those ropes, the ring insulated him from the world, the economic worries of boxing, the possibility of being stripped of his title, rogue decisions, and boxing larcenists. The boxing ring became the center of his world; it brought him peace, and he was in it, the same way he came into the world, alone.

At last, Lou Duva called Vinny and Angelo. He set up an appointment for Vinny with his doctor in Houston. Vinny would go through the same rigorous battery of tests that Dr. Cotter had performed a few months earlier. Duva set up the appointment with his team of doctors, led by Dr. Richard Calvo. He was going to meet Vinny and Angelo at the Houston Neurological Clinic on June 27th. Vinny was so excited about the trip that he bought himself and his father first-class airline tickets down to Houston. The fact that Main Events didn't pick up the tab for the tickets was yet another indicator that Lou was beginning to detach himself further from Angelo and Vinny. Duva clearly viewed Vinny's comeback as being as likely as hell freezing over.

As he had done at Kent County Hospital, Vinny took an MRI, X-rays, and a fluoroscopy test for the doctors at the Houston Clinic. He also took his X-rays from Kent County Hospital to Houston. Vinny, Angelo, and Lou sat awkwardly in the room waiting for Dr. Calvo to return, barely exchanging pleasantries. "Why you gotta a moose on?" Angelo questioned Duva's long face and his slouched body language. "What, do ya think you did us a favor by coming here, what? Like, what, we're wasting your time?" Angelo was turning up the heat on Lou.

Dr. Calvo had been gone more than thirty minutes examining Vinny's X-rays and his own fluoroscopy exam with his own team of neurological specialists, and Lou couldn't wait for him to get back, first to get Angelo off his back and second to finally put an end to what he thought was Vinny's fantasy of being cleared to fight. But upon his return, Dr. Calvo confirmed Dr. Cotter's Valentine's Day diagnosis: "Vinny, I'm going to clear you to fight. Dr. Cotter's diagnosis was accurate; your second and third vertebral bones have healed and fused naturally. Your fifth vertebra has also been reset." Calvo continued. "The calcium deposits organically filled in the broken areas of the bones, thus making the bones actually stronger than prior to the accident."

To Duva's shock, after a daylong examination of prodding and probing and endless tests, Vinny was again given a clean bill of health. Again, Vinny and Angelo hugged and kissed. Their dream was coming closer to fruition.

Lou Duva rose up from his chair in one bounding motion. His arms flew out in front of him, leading his words. "C'mon, doc, you gotta be kidding me? The kid's got a goddamn broken neck. How can he fight?" Duva showed his disbelief. "Are you sure about this?" Lou confronted Dr. Calvo with question after question, more self-serving than out of concern for Vinny. "Where's a goddamn phone? Get me a phone," he hollered at Dr. Calvo. "I gotta call Danny." Duva was finally showing his hand. With his stable of champions occupying so much of his time, and earning him so much money, he no longer had any interest in the fortunes or misfortunes of a broken-necked fighter.

Dr. Calvo was Main Events' house doctor, so in an attempt to appease Duva, he even tried to talk Vinny out of his future. "Vinny, I am clearing you to fight, but are you sure you want to do this? There is still great risk. Do you know what can happen to you?"

An infuriated Vinny jumped from the hospital table. "No, I'm not sure I wanna do this. That's why I been killin' myself, busting my ass for four months, lifting weights with a halo on my head, cause I'm really not sure." The veins in Vinny's neck popped stressed colors of purple and red as he pointed to the scarred holes the halo had left in his skull. "Dr. Cotter's a great doctor, one of the best in New England, and he gave me the okay. How could you ask me a question like that. I flew down here and spent two Gs on tickets with my father 'cause I'm not sure. Are you outta your fucking mind?" Vinny pointed to the scars in his forehead again, raising his voice to an even higher pitch, while putting on his sweatshirt.

Angelo had been measuring up Dr. Calvo from the time he entered the room. Knowing the doctor was nothing more than a mouthpiece and puppet for Main Events, he asked: "Look, Lou, if you don't want to be part of this, we'll go somewhere else. But this is gonna be the greatest comeback in sports history. You just gotta decide if you want to be part of it." Now Angelo, not Kevin, was appealing to Duva's business sense. And regardless of how Vinny and Angelo felt about Duva's integrity and loyalty, they knew he still had the connections with television networks and fight venues.

Later that night, Duva met with Vinny and Angelo and this was his message: Main Events would get Vinny a fight, but he would have a decision to make. If he wanted to retain his title, he had to do so before October 1st. The WBA's No. 1 mandatory challenger was from Argentina, Julio Cesar Vasquez. Vasquez was a strong, awkward left-hander who had only lost two fights and was a real up-and-comer in the middleweight division. That meant if, and there was still a big if, Vinny could return to form, he would have to fight Cesar Vasquez after being out of the ring for almost one year, coming off a broken neck, and not knowing if his boxing skills had eroded as a result of the accident. Moreover, if fighters take long breaks in between fights, ring rust can develop. This simply means many fighters lose their timing and their instincts of when to punch and when not to punch, and the ability to slip punches and counter-punch can diminish as a result of inactivity. Regardless of how much one spars getting prepared for a fight, it will never duplicate a live fight where the adrenaline leads to a much faster, physical battle. In a game where timing is a key element, every split second counts. A defensive lapse or a moment of indecision can result in the fighter being knocked out. For Vinny, a fight of this magnitude, with one year out of the ring, was a great risk. Of course, Vinny wouldn't have it any other way.

25 Stripped

Prior to Vinny's trip to Houston, Tony picked up Vinny for what he thought was going to be yet another mundane boxing workout. Kevin had gone back home to the Catskills to train a couple of his future prospects, Kelvin "Moutah" Prather and heavyweight hopeful Jeremy Williams. Vinny and Tony stopped at Dunkin' Donuts, where they picked up coffees, and made their way to Vinny's usually empty boxing gym. But on this June morning, when Tony entered the parking lot, there were two cars, one of which was parked in Vinny's space. No one would dare park in Angelo's spot.

"Whosa this, champ? Whosa here?" Tony asked.

"Nobody, I guess some people from the neighborhood needed a place to park. Let's go, Tony, don't worry about it." Tony got out of the car balancing his and Vinny's coffee on a cardboard tray and snooped around a BMW with Massachusetts license plates.

"Tony," Vinny raised his voice, "don't worry about it. Let's go inside." When they entered the gym, Tony heard music and voices. What's more, he heard the pounding of boxing gloves against the gym's black Everlast water-bag.

"Champa, whatsa goin on? Whosa here?" Vinny again ignored Tony and walked through the maze of the gym until they finally reached the doorway. Tony followed close behind.

"Ray, thanks for coming, man." Vinny shook Ray Oliveira's hand and brought him closer for a hug. Actually, it was a mix between a shake and a hug. On the street, where most fighters gained their credibility, it's called a shug.

"Eeh, Jimmy, how you doing, brother," Vinny greeted Ray's trainer, Jimbo Isperduli.

"All right, champ, how you doin'? You look great," Ray and Jimbo spoke almost as one.

Ray Oliveira was a world-ranked welterweight from the historic old whaling city of New Bedford, Massachusetts, about 30 miles southeast of Providence. He had won his first thirteen professional fights while losing only one and was considered by many to be the best prospect in New England. Ray was tall, almost 5'10", with long arms that dangled almost below his thighs. He threw crisp sharp punches from all angles and did not bother to fight patiently or judiciously. Ray had an iron jaw and had never been knocked out. He had sparred with Vinny in the past, helping him get ready for the Roger Mayweather and Loreto Garza fights.

Vinny took his boxing equipment out of his oversize Main Events gym bag. He meticulously laid his roll of white tape on the edge of the ring, along with his bag gloves and boxing shorts. Next, he took out his You Gotta Have Balls to Conquer the World black t-shirt, with skulls and crossbones trimming the sides, and his black Pony boxing boots last worn defeating Gilbert Dele. Last, he arranged his headgear and mouthpiece case next to the rest of his equipment and nonchalantly started to tape his hands and wrists.

Meanwhile, Oliveira again made his way over to the heavy bag and started throwing a light combination of punches as he took orders from his trainer. He stretched his arms and raised his knees to his chest, holding each to a five count.

"That's it, Ray, keep it going. Make sure you're nice 'n' loose, baby," Jimmy said.

Tony sipped his coffee and surveyed Vinny's equipment on the ring apron. Tony wondered: *Why in the world did Vinny need his headgear and mouthpiece since he never trains with them?* And then it dawned on him: headgear, mouthpiece, Ray Oliveira. He suddenly found himself in the last place in the world he wanted to be. Vinny was going to spar. He was going to box for the first time since the injury.

"Vinny, what the hella you doin'? Don't do thisa to me, Vinny! Please."

"Tony, calm down. Me and Ray are gonna do a little sparring today. Don't worry, it's no big deal." Vinny again promised Tony, like so many times before. "Nothing's going to happen."

"No! Vinny, notta this time, everythinga is no biga fucking deal witha you. Wella, notta this time, fucka this shit!" Tony continued his rant, but somewhere in the middle of his tantrum he changed his language from English to his dialect of Italian, which nobody understood, not even Angelo, who stood behind him in the open doorway. "*Che cazzo di Gesù Cristo perché proprio a me perché proprio a me, perché io sono stupido, che è il motivo per cui.* [Jesus Christ, why me? Why me? Because I'm stupid, that's why.]" Tony pointed to his head and his hands flew out in front of him faster than the words raced from his mouth. Then, suddenly, his Italian turned back to English. "No bigga fucka deal, that's all you say, no bigga deal. I'ma lucky your father didn'ta kick my ass the first time."

Vinny allowed Tony to finish his diatribe, then he just raised his taped hands, held his arms straight in front of him, and nodded to his 16-ounce boxing gloves, which hung from the ring's post. Tony went on, "Vinny, ifa anything happ—"

Vinny interrupted. "Nothing's going to happen. C'mon, lace me up." Vinny bent down, put his hands into his boxing trunks, bent his knees, and adjusted his cup.

Angelo walked up behind Tony. "What are you getting my kid into now?" Tony looked like he had seen a ghost. Angelo smiled, flashing his bright white teeth. "It's all right, Tony. I know you can't say no to Vinny." Angelo took off his Burberry trench coat and threw it on the row of folding chairs. "Don't worry, Tony, I'm here today. Lace him up, let's see how he does." Angelo turned to Vinny. "Just do what you always do. Keep your hands up, and Vinny if you feel anything different or hurting, you stop. You hear me?"

The three-minute timing clock was set and Vinny and Ray touched gloves in the middle of the ring. This was the moment Vinny had been waiting for since November 1st. Vinny danced around the ring and flicked out a jab here and a jab there. Ray's hands never left his guarded position covering both his body and face. Angelo and Tony stood next to the ring post; Tony placed his hands over his brow and peeked up at the ring. Angelo watched for any clue of harm or pain. Again, only Vinny threw punches, landing two double left hooks to Oliveira's body. Again, Ray only responded with a wince and a deep breath from the pain of the body blow.

"C'mon, Ray, you gotta punch, man. Throw some punches, Ray," Vinny hollered out from behind his headgear. Vinny threw two more hard looping right hands, trying to goad Ray into an exchange, but to no avail. The bell sounded, ending round one.

Vinny followed Ray back to his corner. "C'mon, Ray, I gotta see if I can fight. I'm gonna be fine, fucking throw some leather." Vinny walked back to his corner, but then turned and walked backward. "C'mon, Ray. I need you, that's why I asked you to do this for me. You're a warrior like me."

Vinny's words inspired Ray. He came out gunning in round two. He threw five stinging jabs to Vinny's forehead. Vinny barely attempted to get out of the way. Two more jabs followed, then a right hand that landed against the side of Vinny's head. "Yeah! Ray, that's it brother. Load up, man." With that, Vinny began to bounce around the ring. The two fighters exchanged punches for three more rounds, neither fighter getting the best of the other. Vinny continued landing his pounding left hooks and Ray kept firing at Vinny's head. By round four, Angelo proudly watched

Vinny revel in his labor and Tony took his hand away from his forehead.

The electronic bell signaled the end to round five. Tony gingerly removed Vinny's headgear as he spit his mouthpiece to the ring canvas. Ray walked to Vinny's corner and patted him on the ass. "You were great, champ."

"Thank you, Ray. Thank you, that was great."

Vinny jumped from the ring and cut the tape from his hands. He grabbed his conventional jump rope and started to skip as the timer signaled round six. As Vinny jumped rope, he looked to his father and winked. "Just another workout, champa," Tony hollered, as he put Vinny's cassette into the boom box. "No biga deal, right?" Tony picked Frank Sinatra's "The Best is Yet to Come," an apt choice that would hopefully foreshadow Vinny's future. Vinny, in the private peace of jumping rope, reflected on the turbulent past six months, the most important sparring session of his life, and what was to come.

What was to come was a Penthouse Pet named Leigh Anderson. When Vinny had come back to Providence from Houston, he had immediately packed his bags and gone to Florida, partly for a vacation, partly as a celebration, and partly for some national publicity. He had gone to visit a longtime Providence friend, Anthony Manzo, owner of Anthony's Jewelers. Manzo had designed five WBA Championship rings for Vinny after he had defeated Gilbert Dele. Manzo, as a gift to Vinny, did not charge him for the customized rings, which were inscribed VINNY PAZ WBA MIDDLE WEIGHT CHAMPION 1991. The rings were all 14-carat gold. Vinny handed the rings out to Team Pazienza as a gift for their hard work, dedication, and loyalty to him.

Vinny planned on spending some time with Manzo at Florida's finest beaches and nightclubs, but he was also going down to Miami to let it be known that he was still the WBA Middleweight Champion of the World. Vinny felt his comeback needed some exposure, and perhaps he could buy some time from the WBA. If they knew he was training toward a fight, they'd be less likely to strip him.

In his first day in Miami, Vinny packed his gym bag and went to work out at Dundee's Gym, owned by the legendary fight trainer Angelo Dundee. Dundee had guided the greatest of boxing greats to world championships, including Muhammad Ali, Sugar Ray Leonard, and many other notable world champions. Anthony Manzo called the Miami press upon Vinny's arrival at the gym, and reporters showed up full force to cover his floor workout, guided by the legend himself, Dundee. As Vinny intended, word was getting out that his boxing career was far from over. Vinny promised the press during one-on-one interviews that he would defend his title against Julio Cesar Vasquez by summer's end.

On his second night in Florida, Manzo and Vinny headed north from Miami on Route 1-A. The two were headed to Solid Gold, a high-end strip club in Fort Lauderdale.

If the boxing ring was Vinny's peace, then upon his entrance to Solid Gold strip club, he found his heaven. An eclectic mix of beautiful women danced on tables and hung on the poles on one of the club's many stages. Long-legged beauties in all shapes and colors danced throughout the room: redheads, blondes, brunettes, tall Texans, diminutive Brazilians, Southern belles, elegant Europeans, fitness wonders, busty models. They walked the club in packs, soliciting South Florida's finest for lap dances, massages, and drinks.

As Vinny signed autographs at his table, one dancer in particular took notice, a buxom blonde Mississippian by the name of Leigh Anderson. She sauntered over to Vinny with her 34 double Ds showing through her netted teddy. "So who are you?" she asked Vinny with an inquisitive Southern drawl. "Why are you getting so much attention with all the beautiful ladies in here?" Vinny sipped on his straw, and sucked up his Diet Coke.

"The real question is who are you and where have you been all of my life?" Vinny countered. Anderson pulled back her full-length teddy and straddled Vinny, opening her legs, revealing her red netted see-through G-string.

"Have you ever heard of Mike Tyson?" Vinny asked.

"Why, certainly. I met Iron Mike at the Olympic Gardens in Vegas. He's so sweet."

"Well, I ain't him. How about Sugar Ray Leonard?" Vinny asked again.

"I like that you don't know me. I'm Vinny Paz."

"Are you a boxer?" Anderson seductively asked as she started grinding on Vinny's lap and swung her sweet-smelling long blonde hair into Vinny's eyes.

"Tonight, I'm anything you want me to be, but yes, I'm a boxer. Like Joe Frazier."

The two spent the night and subsequent nights at Miami Beach's Fountainebleau Hotel. One week later, Leigh Anderson unpacked her clothes at Vinny's home at 4 Vatoli Circle in Warwick, while Vinny dressed for Tommy Mart's wedding. Tommy Mart was finally taking the plunge, marrying his high school sweetheart after ten years of dating. Leigh made her way around the house, figuring out where to put her dozens of pairs of shoes, her closet full of clothes, and the boxes of outfits and props she used as role-play for her job. Leigh relocated from Solid Gold in Fort Lauderdale to Providence's Foxy Lady, just like that, after a week of sex and solace with Vinny in Florida. The Ocean State was Leigh's new home address.

Forgetting or ignoring the fact that he weighed close to 170 pounds, Vinny wore a suit from his junior-welterweight days and did his best impression of 2 pounds of baloney in a 1-pound bag. Suits and formal dress weren't exactly Vinny's forte; neither was dealing with past relationships. Upon arrival at the wedding, Tommy Mart and I laughed in Vinny's face.

"What the fuck, did you paint that thing on? When's the flood?"

"Kid, this is a g-note suit. It's a Hugo Boss, my father got it for me," Vinny defended himself.

"When, for your confirmation?" We laughed harder the more Vinny attempted to defend himself.

"Ahh!! Fuck you guys," Vinny said as he walked away.

Nikki, Vinny's ex-girlfriend, had become good friends with Tommy Mart's bride, Liz. Awkwardly Vinny and Nikki were seated together at the wedding. When the seating arrangements were made and invitations mailed out, the two had still been romantically involved.

After a few glasses of wine, Vinny and Nikki loosened up a bit. They reminisced about the good times they had, and even danced to a couple of slow songs. Eventually the two snuck down to an empty, dark banquet hall. "Vinny, I miss you so much, baby." Nikki kissed Vinny's neck.

"Me too, Nikki." They continued. This time Dr. Cotter did not barge in and the two finished what they started. For Vinny it was just a moment of passion or a grudge fuck, because deep down he still resented Nikki. As for Nikki, Vinny looked healthy and normal. She did love him, but when the going got tough, Nikki got going.

I walked over to the head table and whispered in Tommy Mart's ear.

Tommy and I looked at the two empty seats and shook our heads as the rest of the table for twelve enjoyed the extravagant French wedding cake from Pastiche.

"He's writing checks somewhere in this fucking hotel he's not going to be able to cash," I said. "He's fucking around with Nikki, now he's got Leigh at home waiting for him. 'I got a bad feeling about this, sarge,'" I continued, mimicking the movie *Platoon*.

His bad feeling was more than warranted. Four hours later, Vinny heard a pounding on his front door. It was 4:30 a.m. "Who's that, baby?" Leigh asked, rolling over, burying her face in the mattress, and pulling the down pillows over her head.

Vinny jumped out of bed and ran down the stairs in boxer shorts and a beater. He peered through the peephole and saw a disheveled Nikki. Then he heard her slurring voice. "Vinny, I see you fucking looking at me. Let me in."

Vinny told Nikki to go away; he opened the door a crack and told her they could talk about it in the morning.

"It is morning!" She kicked her way through the door.

Vinny grabbed her by her waist, but she broke through his grasp and made her way through his foyer to his bedroom stairs. On the right of the stairway, Nikki noticed high-heeled shoes, clear heels no less. As her eyes followed the shoes upward to the next step, there was luggage and lots of it, lined against the stairway banister. Nikki turned back to Vinny. "You motherfucker! You just fucked me, now someone else is in your bed!" She started a sprint to the top of the stairs. Vinny again grabbed Nikki by the waist and this time picked her up in his arms and walked her down the stairs like he was carrying a baby. Nikki punched Vinny's chest and pulled his hair until they reached her car.

Vinny opened the door and put her inside, using his shoulder as leverage. "Vinny, how could you do this to me?" Nikki demanded. Vinny pushed Nikki inside the car and got in as she continued weeping.

"How could I do this to you?!" Vinny raised his voice. "Nikki, you left me for dead. You couldn't fucking look at me, remember? Well, fucking look at me now!" Vinny pulsated with anger, and a vein sprung from his forehead. "Go home, Nikki, you're drunk. You don't give a fuck about me."

Vinny made his way to his bedroom door and tried to get in. Leigh had locked the door.

"Leigh, let me in!" Vinny banged on the door.

"Is that psycho bitch gone?" Leigh shouted. When Leigh finally opened the door, Vinny found her sitting on the bed with a .22-caliber handgun, cocked and ready to shoot.

"What the fuck are you doing with a gun?" Vinny demanded. "Who's the psycho bitch, you or her? What were you gonna do, shoot her?"

"If I had to, Vinny. I'm from Mississippi. I learned how to shoot a gun before I graduated junior high school," Leigh gloated.

"Nobody's getting shot." Vinny grabbed the gun, emptied the rounds from the barrel, and locked the bullets in his tall cherrywood armoire, away from Leigh. Still in his boxers, Vinny made his way to the window and peeked through the vertical blinds. Nikki was gone, at least for now.

Vinny and Leigh backed out of the garage onto Tavoli Circle. It was roughly 10:00 a.m. and the two were on their way to Bickford's Restaurant for Leigh's favorite, the special grand-slam breakfast: two eggs, two pancakes, two sausages, two strips of bacon, and two pieces of toast. As Vinny put the car into drive, the vehicle rolled forward until he was about to step on the gas. Facing Vinny at roughly an eleven o'clock angle was Nikki, and she was revving the engine of her new red Nissan 300 ZX sportscar. The more she revved, the louder the engine roared. White smoke rose to the sky from her car's exhaust pipe. Vinny and Nikki stared each other down again like they had months earlier on Waterman Avenue. She floored her foot to the gas, and left 10-foot skid marks where she started her run. She smashed her car into Vinny's right front quarter and passenger door, squashing the hood and fender of his black BMW. Antifreeze leaked under Vinny's car and ran down the street. Nikki backed up, and again put her car into drive, ramming the BMW for a second time, leaving red paint trailing along the side of the car. This time Vinny's head jolted back as he covered Leigh from the shattering glass of the windshield. Nikki backed up again, but this time turned her car around, and sped away from Tavoli Circle. A shaken Leigh patted the glass off her sweatshirt and looked at Vinny in disbelief.

"Leigh, you might be from Mississippi," Vinny said, "but things can get pretty crazy up here in Rhode Island."

26　Stripped Again

It was now July 1992 and Vinny only had until October 1st to defend his title. If a tentative date wasn't in place soon to defend his belt against the No. 1 mandatory challenger, Julio Cesar Vasquez, Vinny would be stripped of his title by the World Boxing Association. Vinny had a decision to make: Should he take a title fight against a formidable foe like Cesar Vasquez, who was 39-1, and whose one loss in a professional fight was to Verno Phillips, a top contender? Or, should he take a tune-up fight to shake off the ring rust while at the same time testing his neck injury against a lesser-talented boxer? Either way, Vinny would have to seek medical clearance from the appropriate state athletic commission where his comeback fight would take place. Additionally, Main Events would need to find a network interested in televising the fight, and finally, if Vinny opted to fight Vasquez, he would have to agree to the terms proposed by Main Events. Needless to say, many hurdles needed to be cleared.

The Argentine-born Vasquez had suffered only one loss. He was disqualified in the sixth round for head-butting his opponent Verno Phillips, but according to the judges' scorecards Vasquez was well ahead on points. He was the WBA's No. 1 ranked contender, had 29 knockouts, and had already defeated perennial middleweight contenders Anthony Ivory and Tyrone Trice. Cesar Vasquez was a pro's pro. Although he had had many fights in his home country, particularly in the cities of Sante Fe and Buenos Aires, he also took on opponents in faraway places such as Croatia, Russia, France, the United States, and Spain. "El Zurdo," the sword, as he was known, was a road warrior who was unfazed by hostile crowds or the enormity of the event. The quality of opponent was something Vinny and Main Events had to take into consideration, with so many unanswered questions regarding his health and his readiness.

The Pazienza camp was split, but a decision had to be made. The Duvas felt Vinny should take a tune-up to test whether he could meet the demands of a live fight. They wanted to match Vinny against a fighter from San Francisco named Pat Lawlor. Lawlor was a mediocre fighter with little punching pop, but he had a solid chin and could take a good whupping. Because Lawlor had fought on USA's *Tuesday Night Fights* he did have a following. Main Events had told Vinny they would prepare an offer to HBO Sports and executive Lou DiBella, hoping the network would jump at the opportunity to showcase the first boxer ever to return to the ring after breaking his neck. But the fight scared HBO. If something were to happen to Vinny in the ring, in HBO's words, they did not want the blood, particularly Vinny's blood, on their hands.

Conversely, Vinny and Kevin's goals were grander: to defend Vinny's title against Vasquez. As usual, he viewed his comeback less from a business perspective and more as a personal challenge testing his bravado. Whether it was HBO, NBC, or the Home Shopping Network, it really didn't matter to him. Vinny believed his comeback would define his will, desire, and persona as a ring warrior. His legacy would be cemented in stone by defending his title against a real contender like Cesar Vasquez. Moreover, Vinny wanted to retain the title he had worked so hard for.

Kevin came to Rhode Island and moved into the Rooney Room. But this time Kevin was not alone: He brought along "Moutah" Pritchard, an up-and-coming middleweight who looked like a miniature Mike Tyson. Although Moutah was an amateur, he was 180 pounds of sculpted muscle and nastiness. He had just been released from the New York State Penitentiary. He needed a job and he needed money. Boxing-wise, Moutah wasn't as polished as Vinny's regular sparring partner Ray Oliveira, but he was a light-heavyweight who punched like a heavyweight. It was one thing taking punches from a 147-pound welterweight, still a dangerous proposition coming off a broken neck. But taking punches from a hungry light-heavyweight who was out to make a reputation for himself and an impression on his trainer was another. Kevin also brought along true heavyweight Tommy "The Tank" Murphy. The 235-pound Murphy was a big ol' country boy from the Florida panhandle, who in body stature and fighting style could pass for heavyweight title contender and *Rocky V* co-star Tommy Morrison. The two sparring partners stayed at the Warwick Holiday Inn. Angelo paid for all the fighters' expenses, meals included.

The gym sparring for the next six weeks at times proved to be both brutal and rigorous. But it completely erased any doubt from Kevin's mind whether Vinny physically could return to fight Cesar Vasquez.

Moutah approached each day in the gym as if it were his personal nirvana. The opportunity to spar with a two-time world champion and the possibility of getting noticed by Kevin and maybe by Main Events was his potential ticket to fame and fortune. Tommy "The Tank" was plodding and not as ornery as Moutah, but he chased Vinny around the ring with his heavy legs and ate more leather than he landed on Vinny. But when Tank's punches did land, they were thumping and immense, sometimes leaving Vinny seeing glittering flashes from the sheer heaviness of the blows. But Vinny's neck remained stable and the gym wars were testing his skills.

Kevin and Angelo contacted Main Events and with more medical reports and close observation from Dr. Cotter throughout the summer, Lou started to put together a deal to present to Julio Cesar Vasquez's managers for a middleweight championship fight. But the Vasquez management team may have been craftier than their fighter himself. As a result, when Main Events made their offer to Vasquez on behalf of Vinny for a title opportunity, Vasquez's manager Osvaldo Rivero expected the lion's share of the purse, not the norm in boxing where the champion would earn the higher percentage of the fight gate.

The Duvas miscalculated Vinny's ability to return to the ring. Main Events had previously offered Vasquez over $250,000 to fight Vinny in his mandatory defense, while Vinny would make only $40,000. In fact, they offered a $250,000 purse to Vasquez before Vinny ever went to see Dr. Calvo in Houston. In their wildest dreams, Main Events did not think Vinny would pass his physical in Houston.

With HBO not willing to negotiate the rights to the fight, only the USA Network made an offer, but it was for far less money than HBO would have offered if they had taken the fight. Osvaldo Rivero played his hand like a riverboat gambler. He still demanded $250,000, the same $250,000 Main Events had promised Vasquez before Vinny's visit to Houston. Knowing that time was running out on the champion and USA could not guarantee a purse that would go into the hundreds of thousands of dollars, Vasquez's management was squeezing Main Events and Vinny.

It was already late July and now Vinny had only three months to defend his title, or the WBA would take action. It was obvious the fight was never going to happen. There was also little chance of a major American television network paying a relatively obscure, albeit good, foreign fighter $250,000.

Things couldn't have worked out better for Rivero and Vasquez. In lieu of fighting Vinny, if he were in fact stripped of his title, the

No. 1 contender Cesar Vasquez would be paired against a much less formidable opponent, the WBA's No. 2 ranked middleweight Hitoshi Kamiyama.

It was time for Vinny to rethink his plans. With the Vasquez fight falling apart at the seams, Vinny received a certified letter from Panama City, Panama, and WBA president Gilberto Mendoza. The letter, in short, informed Vinny that if he did not defend his title against mandatory challenger Julio Cesar Vasquez, he would be stripped of his WBA Middleweight Championship. With such insurmountable political and economic circumstances stacked against him, it was time for Vinny to relent and recognize his WBA title was gone. Once again Vinny had to start from the bottom up.

27   Fight Night

Vinny expected that when he lost his title or when his career ended it would come at the pounding hands of another fighter. That was what he signed up for in 1976 when he told his father he wanted to be a boxer. That was the unwritten rule in the sport. Fighters fight until they can do so no more. The greatest of the greats left the ring betrayed by their aging, fading skills and their softening chins. Sugar Ray Robinson, Muhammad Ali, and Joe Louis, to name a few, were exiled from the ring, lying sprawled and battered against the ropes or facedown on the canvas with their eyes eclipsing into the darkest places. Rocky Marciano and Marvin Hagler were examples of a few who left the boxing game on their terms and on their feet, protecting their sensibilities and championship legacies from a cruel sport. Most fighters readily accepted that notion. When they lost, they wanted to do so on their terms. The WBA defeated Vinny on their terms, however, stripping him of his title and an accomplishment that only he and Roberto Duran could claim.

Main Events cheated Vinny of an opportunity to defend that title, offering a king's ransom to a fighter/opponent who never warranted such a payday while scaring away television networks with such a lofty price tag. If a network would have to pay Julio Cesar Vasquez a quarter of a million dollars, what would they have to pay Vinny Paz, a longtime drawing card and champion who was coming back from a broken neck?

But as always Vinny focused on the positive. Stay in the game; use your skills to win, not to lose; and if everything was even at that point, his will, determination, and desire would get him over the top. So Vinny kept on. His training camp with Kevin, Moutah, and The Tank went on, running, sparring, and training without a prospective fight. Ironically, Vinny's warrior mentality seemed to be working against him, as if he didn't know what was in his best interest. Vinny's greatest strength was also his greatest weakness, as his positivism blinded him from seeing the machinations of the jackals around him.

Finally, the call came from Main Events. Vinny, in the middle of another sparring session with Moutah, was interrupted. Angelo signaled Cipolla on the far end of the gym to turn off the blaring boom box and Angelo walked over to the electric ring clock and flipped the switch southward. Vinny stopped boxing in his tracks; nobody touches the Pazman's boom box while he's working out. "Tony, what the fuck are you doing?" Vinny's intensity spilled out of the ring.

Angelo grabbed the top rope in Vinny's corner and lifted himself up, rubbing his sportjacket against a sweaty Kevin. Vinny made his way to Angelo, spitting his mouthpiece in his glove. He knew it had to be something, because Angelo never interrupted Vinny's sparring. Angelo, Kevin, and Vinny huddled in the corner as Angelo spoke. Vinny's heart pounded as he sucked in air, his head down, staring at the blue canvas as his sweat dripped from the top of his headgear.

Kevin reached for a towel and wiped the sweat from Vinny's eyes. Tony took small steps along the ring apron, making his way closer to the corner. He squinted his eyes, trying to piece together what was being said. Tony was on Lake Erie.

Angelo spoke. "We've got a fight. Luis Santana on Tuesday night, December 15th, USA Network at Foxwoods." Santana was a true middleweight from the Dominican Republic who was an orthodox fighter with good, but not great skill. He wasn't flashy, but he was steady, throwing punches judiciously, keeping his opponents off-balance, changing up his looks and counter-punching them. He was 5'9" with long arms and a tight defense. He was the kind of fighter whose style could give Vinny problems, cut from the mold of Roger Mayweather, only without the punching power. He had a record of 38-16 and had been in the ring with the middleweight and welterweight iron, Simon Brown, Aaron Davis, Vincent Pettway, and Glenwood Brown. In the future, Santana would go on to win a world title after his fight with Vinny, defeating middleweight champion Terry Norris.

In terms of the venue for the fight, Foxwoods was an Indian casino that had recently opened in Ledyard, Connecticut. Vinny would provide them a great vehicle for entertainment, drawing in fans and gamblers alike from around New England and as far away as Philadelphia and Chicago. Moreover, the fight would be on national television, giving Foxwoods great exposure.

Finally, USA's *Tuesday Night Fights* had in the past taken chances with Vinny. The network was there when he was a fading junior-welterweight, giving him an opportunity to showcase himself as a middleweight. The network also had televised the fight with Gilbert Dele and prospered when they put Vinny on as their main attraction. Each time he fought on USA, they became the highest-rated boxing show on television, beating out their main competitor, ESPN. The only caveat for the network was that Vinny had to pass a series of stringent tests given by the Connecticut State Athletic Commission and by a commission put in place by Foxwoods Casino. Because Foxwoods was considered a sovereign state, an Indian reservation responsible for its own legal guidelines, they too put Vinny through rigorous medical tests before allowing him to fight there.

"What do you think?" Kevin looked to Vinny. Angelo awaited his response.

Vinny looked to Tony, his peace interrupted. "Start the clock." Vinny put his mouthpiece in and called over to Moutah, "Let's go." He got on his toes and started his dance around the ring.

28 Peace on Earth

On December 15, 1992, one day before his thirtieth birthday, Vinny was close to making his return to the ring. It was 9:45 p.m. and the crowd from Vinny's locker room had finally cleared. It was only fifteen minutes before fight time. Leigh Anderson, Tommy Mart, and I had come and gone, wishing her lover and our friend, respectively, good luck. The three of us took our places at ringside next to Vinny's friends from Kent County Hospital, Dr. Cotter and Dr. Kim, nurses Michelle and Robinson, and kids Butler and Jenny, along with many others.

Kevin, Tony, and Lou Duva made their way to the corner with buckets and towels in tow. Back in Cranston, Louise positioned herself in front of her homemade shrine with her sister and her daughter Doreen by her side.

In the dressing room, only Angelo and Vinny remained behind. Vinny retaped his hands more out of habit than need. Each time he ripped a piece from the white roll his mind flashed to another place. The ripping of the tape echoed in the almost empty room.

Rip. Vinny thought of the days when his father took him to CLCF. He taped the first piece around his right wrist, over his fist, and through his index finger. *Rip.* He envisioned his mother: He knew where she was, at that very moment. He taped the second piece around his left wrist, over his fist and through his index finger. *Rip.* He thought of that day on Post Road, in a careening car spinning through midair, not knowing where he would land. *Rip.* He thought of the pain of the screws going in and out of his skull from the insertion and removal of his halo. He continued to tape. *Rip.* He thought of his days of housewife hell, a bed in his mother's living room, and his trip to Houston. Again he just taped. *Rip.* He thought of his days in the gym throughout the hot summer waiting for this very moment.

"Vinny, make sure you keep your hands up. Make sure . . ." Angelo's instructions faded into the hollow room. Vinny, his thoughts his own, continued his reflection on the past year. He reached down and laced his boots and stretched his hamstrings. Standing back up, he bent backward, his hands on his hips, and then becoming erect, he rolled his neck from side to side.

"One minute, Vinny," the loud voice of a USA stagehand called from the entrance of the arena.

"All right, let's go, Vinny." Angelo reached for Vinny's white vest, trimmed in black and gold. Angelo held the vest up as Vinny walked into it and spun around. Angelo zipped the vest and dug his hand in a jar of Vaseline. Angelo wiped the thick jelly along Vinny's brow, disguising his scar tissue. He worked his way down to Vinny's cheekbones, then down to his neck where he began to rub.

"You're on, Vinny," the voice from behind the curtain again hollered out. Vinny could hear the chorus of boos that welcomed his opponent Luis Santana into the ring.

Angelo softly held Vinny's face. He kissed his cheek and looked into Vinny's assuring eyes and for that moment proudly saw his own life's accomplishments. Angelo then turned away without a word and walked toward the booming voice of the USA stagehand.

Vinny, alone in the dressing room, pounded the fists of his gloves together, threw a flurry of punches, and started his walk to the now opened curtain. With each step he took, the crowd's roar became louder and the arena's lights shone more brightly in the tunnel. Flashbulbs popped like shooting stars. The aisle cleared 3 feet wide as fans reached out to touch Vinny. He quickened his pace to a bouncing jog and raced by them, up the stairs, to the ring's apron. The arena's lights turned up. The crowd roared louder as the back of Vinny's jacket became visible. It read THE PAZMANIAN DEVIL IS BACK.

Epilogue

Vinny Paz would go on to defeat Luis Santana by a unanimous ten-round decision, resurrecting his boxing career, which was once assumed dead. In 1992, he was awarded Comeback Boxer of the Year by the World Boxing Association on the same night "The Greatest" Muhammad Ali was awarded Man of the Year. Together, the two shared the stage, and Vinny had to pinch himself to make sure this wasn't a dream. It was a long way from his 6 foot–by–4 foot room and his posters of Farrah Fawcett, Roberto Duran, and of course, the man he was sitting next to, Muhammad Ali.

Vinny would not lose another fight for more than three and a half years. He finally found his weight class, he found his style, and he found his trainer in Kevin Rooney. Of course, the one and most important constant in his life remained by his side—Angelo.

At middleweight, four months after defeating Luis Santana, Vinny beat Brett Lally in six rounds by way of knockout. Fourteen weeks later, on June 26, 1993, he was in the ring again, this time in a co-feature bout with stablemate Evander Holyfield.

The two of them filled the Atlantic City Convention Center as Vinny knocked out former British world champion Lloyd Honegan and Holyfield defeated up-and-comer Alex Stewart by unanimous decision.

Vinny remained active in 1993, fighting two more times, first in October against the greatest amateur he ever saw, Marvin Hagler's half-brother Robbie Sims. He defeated Sims in ten rounds, but was ever so cautious with the man he once so admired on the New England amateur circuit, gaining a unanimous decision and busting up Sims's body in the process. Sims said after the fight, "Vinny punches okay to the head, but he punches like a heavyweight to the body."

Vinny fought again three days after Christmas in an Aspen, Colorado, ski resort before retreating business tycoons, Hollywood moguls, and visiting L.A. ski bunnies against aspiring Canadian model Dan Sherry. After his eleventh-round knockout of Sherry, Vinny wiped the sweat from his eyes and looked into the cameras addressing his friends, doing his best impression of Robert De Niro in *Raging Bull*: "He wants to be a pretty boy, a model, but he ain't pretty no more." And Sherry wasn't pretty, on that night anyway, as he left Aspen beaten and bruised, convinced modeling was probably the best way to make a living.

The year 1994 was yet another turning point in Vinny's career. April 5th would be the last fight of his career with Main Events. Vinny and Angelo let their wounds heal after Lou, Danny, and the rest of Main Events never bothered to see Vinny after his car accident and his broken neck. From that point on Vinny and Angelo treated their relationship the same way Lou and Danny Duva always had, as solely a cold, calculating, self-serving business transaction. So after defeating Jacques LeBlanc in ten rounds in April of 1994, Vinny was promised a fight with boyhood idol Roberto Duran by former Mike Tyson manager and Kevin Rooney confidant Bill Cayton. Main Events was first given the opportunity to make the match, but Duran for some reason was out of their reach. But he was not out of Bill Cayton's reach, as the fight was made and would be fought at the brand new MGM Hotel Arena, capacity sixteen thousand plus, on June 25th. Vinny officially terminated his personal and professional relationships with Main Events and Lou and Danny Duva.

Duran was on the down side of his career for sure at 43 years of age, but he had won eight fights in a row and was working his way back to fighting the crème de la crème of the middleweight division. He was 93-9 and had more than 20 championship fights throughout his illustrious career. Duran fought the very best fighters who ever lived throughout the 1970s, 1980s, and 1990s, guys like Tommy Hearns, Carlos Palomino, Sugar Ray Leonard, Marvin Hagler, Kenny Buchanan, Davey Moore, and Iran Barkley. But now he was fighting short-enders on his comeback trail, guys who had blown up records and had been fighting guys with little ring credibility, fighters like Tony Menefee, Terry Thomas, and a local Boston kid who was undefeated after only 17 fights, Sean Fitzgerald. Vinny would be the toughest test of his career since he had lost a grueling middleweight championship fight to Iran "The Blade" Barkley in 1989.

Vinny was thrilled to be fighting the man whose picture he had hung on his bedroom wall. Duran loomed above him. The "Hands of Stone," as he was called, had awakened Vinny and put him to sleep every morning and night since 1974, until he finally bought his first home in the early 1990s. Duran was now looming above him again, this time in person, threatening to end Vinny's career again as his reputation would be forever damaged losing to a 43-year-old fighter, regardless of his legend.

Duran turned out to be the attraction in Las Vegas; he was the gate, and when Duran, Vinny's boyhood idol, held up a 3 by 5–foot picture of Vinny's bloodied face taken after his first championship win against Greg Haugen at the pre-fight press conference, the fight was on.

Unfortunately for Roberto Duran, Vinny was on too. He beat Duran from the outside, as expected—*"Manos de Piedra"* [hands of stone] always had a problem matching up with slick, speedy fighters—outjabbing and outhustling the 43-year-old legend. But Vinny, in a fight promoted as mano a mano, wasn't about to let Duran off the hook that easy. Not content to beat him sticking and jabbing, Vinny dug his feet in the trenches and did what he promised he was going to do, "out-Duran Duran," beating him on the inside with barreling hooks and slicing uppercuts. Roberto Duran was beat to the punch time and time again. Though he knocked down an aggressive Vinny with a flash right hand in the fifth round, he would ultimately succumb to the pressure of Vinny, losing a unanimous decision. The crowd couldn't have been entertained more, seeing a living legend Roberto Duran making his last stand against Vinny, the comeback kid.

A rematch was made for January 14, 1995. Vinny took a tune-up fight in the fall of 1994, defeating Rafael Williams, and before he knew it it was time to start the promotional whirlwind tour for Paz-Duran II. This time there were no pictures of Vinny's bloodied face or pre-fight insults. Instead, Vinny, Angelo, and Roberto Duran yucked it up on the airplane in first class, before press conferences, and at dinner. Angelo even gave Duran his private-stock homemade jug of wine and biscotti that Louise had made over the holidays as the tour rolled into Providence. Vinny had gained the respect of Roberto Duran through his fighting, but even more so by the wonderful relationship that Vinny had with his father. "He reminds me of my father," Duran told Vinny, meaning Angelo. The two shared personal stories as Vinny gave Duran a tour of his old neighborhood and the bedroom he grew up in, the bedroom in which the faded poster of Roberto Duran still hung. The mutual admiration continued regardless of the unfinished business they still had in the ring. The respect he earned on that tour over a month with Roberto Duran was as important to Vinny as any fight he'd ever won. After Vinny defeated Duran for the second time in less than a year, again by unanimous decision, the two embraced in the ring and Vinny raised Roberto Duran's arms up in victory. The two remain good friends to this day.

Six months later it was on to facing the best pound-for-pound fighter in the world and another crack at a world title. In June of 1995, Vinny was TKO'd by Roy Jones Jr. in the sixth round, losing out on an opportunity to capture the IBF Super-Middleweight Championship. Jones later went on to win a heavyweight championship. For the first time in Vinny's career, he had experienced a knockout at the hands of another fighter.

But Vinny did what boxing fans had come to expect. He picked himself up off the canvas and challenged an up-and-coming, undefeated, 33-0 fighter from Malden, Massachusetts named Dana Rosenblatt. It was seen as a possible changing of the guard on the New England boxing scene. A second straight loss might have had people once again calling for his retirement. The fight was billed as the "Neighborhood War." But Vinny's career had long ago surpassed regional success, and he introduced his challenger to big-time boxing, again deciding his own fate by emphatically knocking out Rosenblatt in the fourth round on August 23, 1996, in Atlantic City after a fourteen-month hiatus from the ring and boxing.

From 1996 to 2004 Vinny fought 13 more times, winning 10 and losing 3. Among those fights was a rematch with Rosenblatt, where the larceny of boxing proved to be still a very big part of the sport, as a judge who scored the fight fled Foxwoods Casino Hotel in the middle of the night to return safely to his Florida home and far away from Angelo, his plane ticket home bought by Rosenblatt's manager.

More important, in that span he lost both his father and his loving mother. Louise died of cancer in 2003 after a courageous battle, while Angelo lost his bout with Alzheimer's disease just six months after his wife passed. In the future, on his trunks he would wear the words, *Miss you Mom and Dad*.

On March 24, 2004, Vinny honored his father, earning his 50th win and final fight over Tucker Pudwill. Like always, Vinny was bleeding from his nose and from above his eyes. He had broken his right hand yet again in the second round, and it was all so apropos. He was losing badly to Pudwill throughout the first five rounds. As the ringside doctor inspected Vinny's cut on the apron of the ring at the end of round six, there was a chorus of boos from the crowd. "Let it go, doc, it's Vinny Paz who's fighting up there, ya know!" a voice called from the rafters. The doctor raised his hands to signify "fight on," and he made his way down the stairs this time to an ovation.

With Angelo always in his heart and Louise looking down on him, Vinny broke from the doctor and pounded on his chest as he took three giant steps, meeting Pudwill in the center of the ring. His rally was on. He banged Pudwill's body, and threw leading left hooks to his jaw. He bounced on his toes and spit his blood to the canvas when it dripped down the sides of his face and from his nose into his mouth. He went at Pudwill harder; he knew Angelo was with him all along, like he was after seeing *Rocky*, like he was at Lincoln Park and at Cranston Stadium. Vinny threw a right hand that rocked Pudwill and forced him to one knee and left him gasping for air. Vinny ran to his corner and waited for Pudwill to rise. He could hear the sound of his father's voice coming into the ring, always with him. "You got 'im, champ, you got 'im, champ!" As Pudwill got up, Vinny finished with a flurry, starting with a barrage of punches to the overwhelmed Pudwill's face, going down to his body and back up again to his head, until the bell rang and the fight ended. He ran to his corner and jumped on the turnbuckle, reaching for the sky, reaching for Angelo because Vinny knew, he just knew he was with him, like he was when he hoisted Vinny on his shoulders after winning his first world title back in 1987, and when he was with him at Sunrise Medical Hospital bringing him back to life from dehydration, like he was protecting him against the Duvas, this time helping bring Vinny back from defeat.

The fight ended with another victory filled with sweat, blood, and drama. The crowd rose together, appreciatively thanking Vinny, the honest fighter, for the past twenty-one years of entertainment. The standing-room-only crowd clapped on and Vinny just looked through the ropes in awe with tears filling his once-again swollen eyes and Angelo always in his heart.

Vinny's professional career spanned three decades and a total of twenty-one years. Within the time span from 1992 to 2004, after an almost fatal car accident and a broken neck, the Pazmanian Devil captured three more world championships, giving him a total of five world titles in three different weight classes: lightweight, junior-middleweight, and super-middleweight, making his story the greatest comeback in sports history.

Index

About the Author

Tommy Jon Caduto is a Rhode Island native and LaSalle Academy alumnus who has a bachelor of arts degree in the fields of history and political science from Rhode Island College. He attended the University of New England Graduate School with a focus in administrative education. After living and working in the surrounding Boston area for a number of years, he returned to Providence to work for the *Echo* as a freelance writer. He also took a job at Cranston East High School as drop-out prevention director and history teacher.

Caduto has drawn his inspiration from his childhood friend, Vinny Paz, who, after facing almost insurmountable odds, came back from a broken neck and resurrected his career and returned to boxing prominence. Caduto is inspired by many of his students who succeed in the classroom and in life through great adversity. He is moved by his loving parents who support him along every road he has ever traveled. He shares his most joyous moments with his loving wife, Jennifer, and their dog, Moochie. The three of them reside in Cranston, Rhode Island.